The Transformation of the U.S. Senate

The Transformation of the U.S. Senate

Barbara Sinclair

The Johns Hopkins University Press
Baltimore and London

©1989 The Johns Hopkins University Press
All rights reserved
Printed in the United States of America

The Johns Hopkins University Press
701 West 40th Street
Baltimore, Maryland 21211
The Johns Hopkins Press Ltd., London

Originally published, 1989
Johns Hopkins Paperbacks edition, 1991

Library of Congress Cataloging-in-Publication Data

Sinclair, Barbara, 1940–
    The transformation of the U.S. Senate.

    Bibliography: p.
    Includes index.
    1. United States.   Congress.   Senate—History.
    2. United States—Politics and government—1945–
I. Title.
JK1161.S56   1989   328.73'071'0904   88-46070
ISBN 0-8018-3766-9 (alk. paper). —ISBN 0-8018-4110-0 (pbk.)

Contents

Acknowledgments   vii

1 The Senate and Institutional Change: An Introduction   1

2 The Senate in the 1950s   8

3 The Impact of a Change in Membership:
The Democratic Classes of 1958–1964   30

4 The Transformation of the Washington
Policy Community   51

5 The Emergence of a New Senate Style   71

6 Institutional Consequences of Behavioral Change   102

7 Contemporary Senate Styles: The Choice of Issues   141

8 Committees and the Floor as Arenas for
Legislative Activism   155

9 Legislative Activism: A Quantitative Analysis and a
Case Study   174

10 The Use of Public Arenas and the Changing Bases of
Senate Influence   188

11 The Contemporary Senate: An Assessment   205

References   217

Index   223

Acknowledgments

My greatest debt is to the many knowledgeable people who shared their experience with and insights into the Senate with me. The senior staffers of the eighteen senators in my sample gave me a good deal of their most precious resource—time—and I am truly grateful. I promised all these people anonymity and thus cannot thank them by name. Their contributions will become obvious to the reader. All unattributed quotations are from interviews conducted by the author.

Senate Historians Richard Baker and Don Richie were very helpful in a variety of ways. Richard L. Hall read the entire manuscript and made extremely perceptive and constructive suggestions. Bob Peabody also reviewed the manuscript. I thank him and the many colleagues who read and commented on various convention papers and article manuscripts. Of course none of these people bear any responsibility for the final product.

I would also like to thank David Sturrock for his intelligent and conscientious work as my research assistant, Jenny Moe for getting my manuscripts typed, and Dottie Briggs and Aline Messer for the typing. The Research Committee of the Academic Senate of the University of California, Riverside, and the Everett McKinley Dirksen Congressional Leadership Research Center provided funding that greatly facilitated the research.

Some of the material appeared previously in "Senate Styles and Senate Decision-making, 1955–1980," *Journal of Politics* 46 (November 1986): 877–908, and "The Distribution of Committee Positions in the U.S. Senate: Explaining Institutional Change," *American Journal of Political Science* 32 (May 1988): 276–301.

The Transformation of the U.S. Senate

1 // The Senate and Institutional Change: An Introduction

The Senate has changed from an "encapsulated men's club" to a "publicity machine operated for the purpose of linking senators with national interest groups and factions," according to political scientist Nelson Polsby (1981, 22). The Senate used to be an institution "whose members knew each other well, worked and played together, and thought of politics as a team game," writes journalist Alan Ehrenhalt (1982, 2175). It has become the "individualist Senate," where "close personal relationships are rare, and individual rights not community feeling is the most precious commodity" (ibid.). "The Senate was a more structured and hierarchical place than it is today," says former Senator Edmund Muskie of the chamber he entered in the late 1950s, "but it was more comfortable too" (Broder 1986, 10).

Political scientists, journalists, and Senate insiders agree that between the 1950s and the 1980s the Senate changed immensely. Several political scientists have written insightfully about the early phase of that change (see Ripley 1969; Foley 1980; Ornstein, Peabody, and Rohde 1977; Rohde, Ornstein, and Peabody 1985), and numerous journalists have attempted to characterize the contemporary Senate (see especially Ehrenhalt 1982). Yet we still lack a comprehensive description and analysis of the transformation of the Senate. The purpose of this book is to describe how the Senate has changed, explain why it changed, and assess the impact of that change on the Senate's role in the political process.

In recent years, the Senate has been subjected to a barrage of criticism, from its own members as well as from outsiders (see, for example, Ehrenhalt 1982; Dewar 1984; Grabowski 1987; Hook 1988; Kassebaum 1988). Not only is the Senate no longer the world's greatest deliberative body; some senators say it is not much of a deliberative body at all. The Senate is long on activity and short on results, others contend. Senators Dan Evans and Lawton Chiles decided against seeking reelection in 1988, citing frustration with the policy process in the Senate. Is the Senate now less capable of playing the role we expect of it in the political process?

Although terminology and nuance may differ, there is wide agreement about the functions Congress is expected to perform within the political system. Congress is supposed to provide a forum in which the demands, interests, opinions, and needs of citizens find articulation. Congress is also supposed to be a reasonably efficient decision-making body, responding effectively to pressing national problems and translating majority sentiments into law (see Cooper 1977; Vogler 1983; Rieselbach 1986). Has change reduced the Senate's ability to perform either or both of these functions?

The Senate of the 1950s was characterized by a relatively unequal distribution of influence and constraining norms; it was a committee-centered, member expertise-dependent, inward-looking, and relatively closed institution. The typical senator of the 1950s was a specialist who concentrated upon the issues that came before his committees. His legislative activities were largely confined to the committee room; he was seldom active on the Senate floor, and he made little use of the media. He was deferential to his seniors, loyal to the institution, and highly restrained in the use of the powers Senate rules confer upon the individual.

In the Senate of the 1980s, influence is much more equally distributed and members are accorded very wide latitude; the Senate has become an open, staff-dependent, outward-looking institution in which significant decision making takes place in multiple arenas. The typical senator no longer specializes; he becomes involved in a broad range of issues, including ones that do not fall into the jurisdiction of his committees. Even though he serves on more committees than his predecessor of the 1950s did, he does not confine his activities to the committee room. He is also active on the Senate floor and often makes use of public arenas as well. He is less deferential to anyone and much less restrained in using the powers granted to him by the rules of the Senate.

What caused this change? An understanding of why the Senate changed is not only intrinsically interesting but also a prerequisite to an informed assessment of the Senate's current and its possible future performance of the functions we expect of it. Certainly judgments about the likelihood of various proposed reforms being instituted and of their having the effect intended by their proposers require an understanding of how and why the Senate changes.

An analysis of change in the Senate must be based upon theoretical propositions that take into account both the Senate's similarity to other institutions and its unique characteristics. Institutions, Cooper writes, are "planned social units that are created and structured to perform certain functions or tasks" (1977, 140). The U.S. Senate created by the Constitution clearly is a planned social unit. Although it was the product of compromise, and, consequently, expectations about its broader role in the political system were diverse, the tasks the Senate was assigned are reasonably clear: to legislate, to approve treaties by two-thirds vote, and to advise and consent on high presidential appointments.

Because an institution was set up to perform certain tasks does not necessarily mean it will do so and certainly does not mean that, after two hundred years, it will perform those tasks in the manner expected by the founding fathers. Nor does the existence of a modern consensus on the functions we expect the Congress to perform—a consensus to which most senators would subscribe—guarantee satisfactory performance. Much depends upon the incentives that the individuals who people the institution have for acting in a way that contributes to task performance. And that depends upon the interaction among those individuals' goals, the internal structure of the institution, and the external environment.

Institutions are characterized by fairly complex internal structures; in many instances, and certainly in the case of the Congress, the structure is specified in an elaborate set of rules. In most institutions, and again certainly in the Congress, formal rules are supplemented by norms or unwritten rules specifying appropriate behavior. These rules and norms produce considerable continuity and stability because they structure the behavior of the individuals within the institution.

How an institution functions is determined by the behavior of the individuals within it, but that behavior is molded by the institution's rules and norms. An institution like the U.S. Senate molds the behavior of its members because it is such a salient part of the environment in which those individuals pursue their goals. That is, behavior is a function of individuals' goals and of the salient characteristics of the environment in which they pursue those goals.

The goals of twentieth-century senators, I assume, consist of some mix of reelection, influence, participation in the making of good public policy, and, especially for the post–World War II period, a chance at the presidency (see Fenno 1973, 1978, 1982). The sort of behavioral strategies that are likely to facilitate the pursuit of senators' goals depends upon the environment, both within and beyond the institution. How the institution distributes resources via its rules, and how it conditions the use of resources through norms, are the most critical aspects of the internal environment.

For most senators most of the time, the best strategy for achieving their goals is to work within the existing structure, even if that structure is fairly far from optimal for the achievement of the senator's own goals. Because altering written rules and often less formal arrangements and procedures as well requires collective action, the senator who attempts to initiate such change is faced with the costs of organizing a winning coalition and the probability that he will fail. Not only must there be enough dissatisfied senators to make up a winning coalition, those senators must be willing to participate in the effort, rather than each hoping that others will bear the cost of bringing about change while they share in the benefit. Consequently, the Senate may be able to sustain a structure that hinders the advancement of the goals of an appreciable proportion of its members for some period of time. It cannot, I contend, do so indefinitely. Given the Senate's small size and the Constitutionally stipulated equality of its members, such a structure is unstable. After all, the Senate has no real control over who shall be a member; it can neither recruit nor expel. The members of the Senate are nominally equal; each represents one state, each has one vote. Current members can change almost all of the Senate's rules at will, albeit, in some cases, more than a simple majority is needed. These characteristics, I contend, place very real constraints on the types of rules and norms that can develop. In fact, one would expect members of such an institution to produce a structure reasonably conducive to the achievement of the goals of most of its members.

The Constitutionally determined characteristics of the Senate suggest that change will occur when old arrangements become a barrier to goal advancement for a significant number of members. In examining change in the Senate, we need to look for indications that an appreciable subgroup of members found obstructive the arrangements that for most members had been reasonably conducive to the achievement of their goals. This seems most likely to occur with a sizable influx of new members who differ from more senior members in goal-relevant ways. Their goals differ, or because they are differently situated politically, the behavioral strategies likely to be successful in goal advancement differ.

A major change in the institution's environment may disrupt the fit between current structure and the advancement of their goals for continuing members. Such change in the external environment may create new problems for or offer new opportunities to senators. Dealing adequately with the new problems or exploiting the new opportunities may necessitate structural change.

I argue that the transformation of the U.S. Senate was driven by two distinct processes. The new liberal northern Democrats who entered the chamber in large numbers between 1959 and 1965 found existing structures a barrier to the achievement of their goals, and pressure from them led to some change. But most of the change that occurred cannot be thus explained. Rather, it was the result of senators' reactions to later changes in the external environment. During the 1960s and 1970s the Washington policy system underwent a major transformation. A variety of factors, including the expanded role of government and the social movements of the 1960s, produced a rapid expansion in the number and diversity of groups active in Washington (see Walker 1983; Schlozman and Tierney 1983). At the same time, and clearly related to this phenomenon, there occurred a major change in the issue agenda. A variety of new and highly contentious issues ranging from environmental protection to abortion came to the fore; some older, previously noncontroversial issues became highly controversial—such as military procurement—and other older issues became even more salient and more controversial, for example, energy policy (Sinclair 1982). These changes, in interaction with factors such as the decline of political parties and the increased importance of the national media, especially television, disrupted a relatively stable, bounded, and predictable policymaking system that was characterized by a limited number of significant actors and relatively fixed lines of conflict. The new system that began to emerge during the late 1960s and came to fruition in the 1970s is much more open, less bounded, and less stable; it is characterized by a much larger number and greater diversity of significant actors, by more fluid and less predictable lines of conflict, and, consequently, by a much more intense struggle to gain space on the agenda (for similar arguments, see King 1978; Heclo 1978; Gais, Peterson, and Walker 1984).

As a result of this transformation, the Congress found itself subjected to a huge increase in the demands made upon it. Although this increase in demands presented problems for the institution, it offered individual senators opportunities to become involved in more issues and in a greater number of consequential decisions, opportunities useful in the pursuit of their goals. Moreover, the new Washington policy community offered senators the opportunity to advance their goals in

new ways and in a broader arena. Senators, more than any other class of
political actor except the president, possess resources that make them
extremely valuable allies in the new system. Senators have access to authoritative decision-making arenas and can command media attention.
As a result, they are well situated to take a prominent part in agenda
setting, which is a more important part of the policy process than formerly, and in the shaping of debate, which is increasingly done in public
arenas.

The opportunities offered to senators by the new environment can be
used to advance the full range of goals. Highly visible involvement in
national issues is clearly invaluable for the senator who aspires to the
presidency (see Peabody, Ornstein, and Rohde 1976). To the senator
who wants to participate in the making of good public policy, the new
environment offers more potential allies and more opportunities to
shape the policy agenda and public debate on issues. The emergence of
more issues and more groups has resulted in more views striving for
representation and ultimately in a larger number of potential leadership
slots. Thus, the influence-oriented senator as well as the policy-oriented
senator is provided with the opportunity, and has the incentive, to
become involved in a broad range of issues. Furthermore, since initial
agenda-setting and debate-shaping activities in public arenas can severely constrain the discretion of party and committee decision makers,
the influence-oriented senator has a strong incentive to participate in
those public activities. More groups and more issues are likely to mean
increased pressures on the reelection-oriented senator to get broadly
involved. Of course, the larger number of issues and decisions in which
a senator can become involved also gives the reelection-oriented senator
more opportunities to go to bat for his constituency. And the high
visibility made possible by the new environment can sometimes yield
reelection benefits; well-publicized advocacy of the popular side of a
major issue—opposition to Pentagon waste, for example—can significantly enhance a senator's reputation in his home state.

Taking full advantage of the opportunities offered by the new policy
system, and responding to the problems it created, required senators to
change not only their behavior but also institutional arrangements. I
argue that the result is the very different Senate of today—a highly
participatory and open body that accords its members very wide latitude,
but one that by virtue of those characteristics can encounter great
difficulty in making decisions.

How well or ill the Senate performs the functions we expect of it,
this study suggests, is largely a byproduct of senators' pursuit of their

individual goals. By molding the Senate to make it better suited for advancing their goals within the new environment, senators enhanced the institution's capacity to articulate interests and to participate in agenda setting and the shaping of debate but reduced the body's ability to make decisions with reasonable dispatch.

2 // The Senate in the 1950s

"Like a small town" is how old-timers describe the Senate of the 1950s. The frequently employed metaphor of the Senate as an exclusive men's club also conjures up images of an intimate but rather insulated and conservative place. Matthews (1960), Huitt (1965), and White (1956) pictured an inward-looking institution in which influence was unequally distributed and behavior was governed by constraining norms.

In this chapter I seek to provide a systematic description of the Senate of the 1950s to serve as a baseline against which change can be assessed. After briefly considering the character of the membership, I examine the distribution of resources and norms. How rules distribute resources and how norms condition the use of resources are critical determinants of the character of an institution. An analysis of their impact upon Senate decision making in the 1950s follows. The chapter ends with an analysis of the locus of influence: What sorts of members wielded influence in the Senate of the 1950s?

Although the Senate of the 1950s distributed resources unequally and limited its members' behavior through constrictive norms, I argue that it nevertheless did not seriously thwart the goal advancement of a majority of its members. For the typical senator of the 1950s, the institutional structure of the time allowed him to pursue his goals with a reasonable chance of success.

The Membership

During most of the 1950s, partisan majorities in the Senate were narrow. Republicans organized the chamber in the 83rd Congress(1953–54), in which they outnumbered Democrats 48 to 47; Wayne Morse, then an independent, held the remaining seat. The 84th and 85th Congresses saw Democrats with a narrow majority of 49 to 47.

During the 1950s, the ideological center of gravity of the Senate was conservative. Using conservative coalition scores as the measure of ideology,* one finds that the 83rd was distinctly the most conservative of these congresses; extreme conservatives—those who scored 80 or higher on the conservative coalition index—made up well over half the membership (see table 2.1). During the 84th and 85th Congresses, extreme conservatives numbered around 40 and, together with moderate conservatives (those with scores between 60 and 80), constituted well over a majority.

Table 2.1 Distribution of Conservative Coalition Scores in the Senate of the 1950s

	All Senators				
Congress	Liberal[a]		Moderate		Conservative
83rd	13[b]	10	5	16	59
84th	13	11	14	17	41
85th	17	7	12	22	40

	Northern Democrats				
Congress	Liberal		Moderate		Conservative
83rd	9	8	5	6	—
84th	12	8	3	5	1
85th	16	5	3	4	2

[a]See note below for definition of categories.
[b]Number of senators. All those who served long enough to be assigned a conservative coalition score are included.

---

* Conservative coalition scores for the 86th through the 98th Congresses were taken from *Congressional Quarterly Almanac*. Those for the 83rd through the 85th Congresses were computed by the author. In both cases, scores were adjusted so that they are not affected by absences. Extreme liberals are defined as those with scores below 20; extreme conservatives as those with scores above 80. Moderate liberals scored between 20 and 40; moderates between 40 and 60; moderate conservatives between 60 and 80.

The center of gravity of the Republican Senate membership was conservative; that of the Democrats, moderate (see table 2.2). Southern Democrats, who made up about 40 percent of the Democratic membership during these congresses, were conservative.[†] Northern Democrats, although tending toward liberalism, were heterogeneous in ideology. Although 42.3 percent of northern Democrats on the average fell into the extreme liberal category during these congresses, 33.6 percent were moderate or conservative (scoring over 40).

Table 2.2 Senate Conservative Coalition Scores by Party and Region

Congress	All Senators	Republicans	Democrats	Northern Democrats	Southern Democrats
83rd	72.0	88.5	54.6	35.3	79.0
84th	62.3	75.4	49.8	31.4	76.5
85th	63.6	78.6	47.9	28.9	76.3

During the 1950s, then, the Democratic party was not as sharply divided between liberal northern Democrats and conservative southern Democrats as it would later become. The northern contingent included a number of moderate and conservative senators, many from the western states. Over these congresses, the number of extremely liberal northern Democrats did increase from nine to sixteen, but even in the 85th they remained a distinct minority of their party and a small minority of the chamber membership. During the 1950s, the Senate was a clearly conservative body simply in terms of numbers.

The Distribution of Resources

The Senate is an institution with tasks to perform; it does so through organizational subunits and procedures specified by its rules. The rules and customs that structure Senate decision making simultaneously distribute resources across members. The committee system, for example, provides the primary division of labor in the Senate. Because a committee seat gives its holder privileged access to decision making in the committee's area of jurisdiction, committee positions are a key resource for senators in the pursuit of their goals. It can be argued that the distribution of valued committee positions is the single best observable indicator of the distribution of influence in the Senate that is available over time (but see Hall 1987b).

[†] The South is defined as the states of the old Confederacy except for Tennessee.

During the mid-1950s, the Senate had fifteen standing committees, the number set by the Legislative Reorganization Act of 1946. Most senators served on two.*

Although every committee position gives its possessor privileged access to the making of certain decisions and thus is potentially a resource of value, committees vary in the breadth and significance of their jurisdiction and, consequently, in their value to senators. To be sure, committee attractiveness is, in part, a function of senators' characteristics. Thus farm state senators find the Agriculture Committee valuable for reelection purposes; it holds little attraction for other members. Among the Senate's standing committees, Appropriations, Finance, Foreign Relations, and Armed Services have long been considered the most prestigious. Using data on transfers to and from committees, Matthews (1960, 149) found these four to be the most desirable. Their special status is recognized in the rules of the Senate and of the Senate parties (see Ripley 1969, 137; Schneider 1982, 9–10). In the 1950s a majority of senators held a position on one or more of these committees, but a large minority did not (see table 2.3). About one in ten members held positions on two of the top four.

During the 1950s the Democratic Appropriations Committee membership exhibited a high concentration of positions of influence. Given the Appropriations Committee's power of the purse and its role during this period as an appeals court from the decisions of the less generous House committee, membership yielded a high potential for influence, perhaps even more so than that on the other prestige committees (Fenno 1973, Chap. 5). During the 84th and 85th Congresses (1955–58), on the average, 6.5 chairmen of other committees served on Appropriations. Adding the chairman of Appropriations and the majority leader who served on the committee in the 85th Congress, this cadre of leaders held about two-thirds of the Democratic seats on the committee.

Other than possibly the top party leadership post, committee chairmanships are the most valued positions in the Senate. By informal practice, the Senate since the second half of the nineteenth century has limited a senator to chairing only one legislative committee (Schneider 1982, 1). No such bars to concentrating committee leadership positions developed for the minority. During the 1950s both parties allowed a

---

* Data on committee and subcommittee memberships and leadership positions are taken from *Congressional Quarterly Almanac* and from the *Congressional Directory*. All senators who served during a congress are included as long as they entered the chamber early enough to receive a full complement of committee assignments. Subcommittee membership data are not available for the 83rd Congress.

single senator to serve as ranking minority member on more than one standing committee. During the 83rd Congress, for example, three Democrats held two such positions each, with Senator Walter George serving as ranking minority member on both Finance and Foreign Relations. During the 84th Congress three Republicans and during the 85th four Republicans held such dual assignments.

Table 2.3 Distribution of Committee Positions in the Senate of the 1950s (Number of senators with given number of positions)

	Congress		
All Committees: No. of Assignments	83rd	84th	85th
2	85	75	76
3	18	21	22
4+	0	0	0
Top Four Committees: No. of Assignments			
0	43	39	40
1	51	46	48
2	9	11	10
Leadership Positions on Good Subcommittees: No.			
0	–	22	22
1	–	34	36
2	–	22	21
3+	–	18	19

Subcommittee leadership positions provide still another useful resource for the pursuit of senators' goals. The value of a subcommittee depends in part on the attractiveness of the parent committee. Post Office and Civil Service, District of Columbia, Rules and Administration, and Veterans Affairs have generally been deemed the Senate's least desirable committees (see Matthews 1960, 149; Smith and Deering 1984, 112). Leadership of a subcommittee on one of these committees is of limited value. Consequently, I examine here the distribution of subcommittee leadership positions (chairmanships and ranking minority member positions) on the remaining standing committees (referred to here as good committees and their subcommittees as good subcommittees).

Chairmanships and ranking minority member positions on subcommittees of attractive committees were quite widely distributed in the 1950s; a large majority of senators held at least one. Nevertheless, about a fifth of the Senate membership held no such subcommittee leadership position, while about a fifth held two such positions and another fifth held three or more (see table 2.3).

In the Senate of the 1950s, valued committee positions were far from maximally concentrated. More than half the senators served on a prestige committee; about three-fourths held a subcommittee leadership post on a desirable committee. Nevertheless, substantial numbers of senators lacked any of these valuable resources; at the same time, others held multiple positions.

Not all members were equally likely to hold valued committee positions. Seniority was a central determinant of the distribution of such positions. For the granting of committee chairmanships and ranking minority member positions, seniority on the committee was the only criterion. Committee chairmen and ranking minority members handed out subcommittee leadership positions largely on the basis of committee seniority. As a result, freshmen were disadvantaged. During the 84th and 85th Congresses, only two of twelve Republican freshmen held ranking minority member positions on subcommittees of good committees. Despite being slightly more numerous, the Democrats treated their freshmen somewhat better; six of fifteen freshmen chaired subcommittees of good committees during these congresses.

In making freshman committee assignments, the Democrats since 1953 had tempered the effects of seniority with the Johnson rule, which specified that every Democrat was to receive one major committee assignment before anyone received two. When the initial committee assignments of Democratic freshmen in the 1950s are examined, the impact of the Johnson rule is evident. Every Democrat was assigned at least one major committee. Assignments to the most prestigious committees, on the other hand, were extremely rare. Between 1953 and 1958, only three of twenty-four Democratic freshmen were assigned to the top committees, and one of these "freshmen" was Alben Barkley, former Senate majority leader and vice-president of the United States.

In the 1960s, Republican freshmen were less well off than Democrats. Without a Johnson rule, freshmen could and sometimes did end up with only minor committees. In the mid-1950s (84th and 85th Congresses), this fate befell four of eleven freshmen. In 1955, for example, Clifford Case was assigned to District of Columbia and Post Office; Carl Curtis received Post Office and Rules. Republican freshmen were even less likely than Democrats to be assigned to a prestige committee. Between 1953 and 1958, only two of twenty-six freshmen received such assignments; both of these exceptional assignments were made in the 83rd

Congress that the Republicans organized, and one of the two lucky freshmen had previous Senate experience.

In the Senate of the 1950s valued committee positions were relatively unequally distributed, with senior senators at a definite advantage. Committee chairmen's procedural powers were a valuable resource that only senior members possessed. The supply and distribution of still another critical resource, staff, further amplified seniority-linked differences in resources. Personal staffs were small, averaging only about eleven per senator in 1957. A senator's staff allotment depended upon state population, but a relatively high floor protected senators from small states. In any case, few senators had sufficient personal staff to assign more than a minimal number to legislative duties. Consequently, committee staff were a very important resource, and this resource was controlled by the committee chairman.

Norms

Institutions mold the behavior of individuals through norms as well as rules. Norms condition the use of institutional resources, often by limiting their use.

According to a standard sociological definition, "norms are rules for conduct," they are "the standards by reference to which behavior is judged and approved or disapproved" (Williams 1968, 204). As used in sociology and usually in political science, the concept of norms incorporates the notion of obligation; norms do not simply specify instrumental behavior of no particular interest to anyone else. In a modern institution, the existence of norms implies that the institution or its members collectively benefit from the behavior prescribed by those norms and therefore have an interest in promoting that behavior. That norms have this obligatory aspect also implies that abiding by norms involves some cost to the individual. If the payoff for norm-abiding behavior were intrinsically high—if it were the best way for a member to advance his or her goals—the development of a social rule obligating members to so behave would have been unnecessary. There is no norm obligating you to get your hand out of the fire.

Yet, given the Constitutionally-derived equal status of senators, the cost of norm abidance, I contend, cannot be too high. Because senators cannot be deprived of their seat or their vote, the sanctions available to enforce compliance will always be relatively limited.

These conclusions suggest that the prisoner's dilemma provides a good model for norm abidance in the Senate (see Axelrod 1984, 5). The story commonly used to illustrate this strategic situation (called a game in game theory) tells of two confederates in crime who are apprehended by the police and separated. The police do not have enough evidence to convict them of the crime of which they are in fact guilty, unless they confess, but the police do have evidence to convict them of a lesser crime. The payoff matrix reflects this in that the reward R for mutual cooperation (neither confessing) is greater than the punishment P for mutual defection (both confessing). Obviously, if the prisoners could make a binding agreement they would cooperate. The police have, however, separated them to prevent communication and offer each a deal: If you will defect—inform on your confederate—you will be set free and the book will be thrown at your partner in crime. Each prisoner now has to choose whether to cooperate or defect. If he cooperates, he might get R but he also might get S, the sucker's payoff, which is the worst outcome for him. On the other hand, if he defects—informs on his confederate— he can do no worse than P, which he will receive if his confederate also confesses and he protects himself from S. If his confederate does not confess, he gets the temptation payoff, T, the highest in the matrix.

The defining characteristic of the prisoner's dilemma is that each player is better off defecting no matter what the other player does, but the result of mutual defection is an outcome not as good as that obtainable through mutual cooperation. Clearly, if such a game is played once, mutual defection is the most likely outcome. Players involved in repeated play of such a game just as obviously have an interest in finding some way of reaching the outcome of mutual cooperation.

The lurid story used to illustrate this strategic situation not withstanding, consider how it is similar to the problem of norm abidance in the Senate. Abiding by norms involves some cost; not conforming results in a higher payoff whatever other senators do (that is, $T > R$ and $P > S$). On the other hand, the cost of conforming is not too high (that is, $R > P$), and, in fact, everyone is better off if everyone conforms. Note that the model requires that the benefit of mutual cooperation accrues to the players as individuals. The prisoner's dilemma is a good model for norm abidance only as long as senators as individuals receive a benefit when all abide by the norms. Any contribution to institutional functioning would simply be a byproduct.

Axelrod shows how such norms could develop. The frequent interactions needed for cooperation to emerge became a reality in the Senate in the second half of the nineteenth century, when the membership became fairly stable. Although our information is scanty, it seems likely that a number of the norms that Matthews identified in the 1950s developed in the wake of that stabilization of membership.

Within Axelrod's theory, norms such as these develop when interacting individuals use what he labels TIT FOR TAT type strategies (1984). Such strategies have the following characteristics: the user never defects first, he is relatively forgiving of others' defections, *but* he does retaliate against a defector. This retaliation, meeting noncooperation with noncooperation, is in essence the application of a sanction on the nonconformist. Thus the application of sanctions on nonconformists by conforming members acting individually is an integral part of the development of norms. The application of social pressure requires no collusion.

In addition, once norms have developed, the resources that the rules give the leaders can be and are expected to be employed against the nonconformist. The existence of these sanctions changes the payoff matrix, increasing the costs of nonconformity. However, in the Senate, the stock of such sanctions is distinctly limited. Used against the stray maverick, they may produce conformity (depending upon the maverick's payoff matrix) and are likely to be quite effective at discouraging senators from attempting to get the temptation payoff. However, if for a group of considerable size the cost of norm abidance is sufficiently large that their payoff matrix is not of the prisoner's dilemma type (that is, if $P > R$), the sanctions available are unlikely to be sufficient to produce conformity in the long run. To summarize, in an institution like the Senate, the payoff matrix for norm abidance must actually fit the prisoner's dilemma for a substantial proportion of the membership. By the definition of norms, norm abidance always costs something. If it costs too much, the situation is unstable and likely to lead to change.

An analysis of the norms Matthews identified in the 1950s within this framework should help us understand why senators conformed to restrictive norms and lay the groundwork for explaining later change. According to Matthews, the senator of the 1950s was expected "to specialize, to focus his energy and attention on the relatively few matters that c[a]me before his committees or that directly and immediately affect[ed] his state" (1960, 95). He was also admonished to be a work horse rather than a show horse, to do the "highly detailed, dull and politically unrewarding" tasks that make up "the great bulk of the Senate's work" (94).

That most senators of the 1950s did, in fact, specialize is indicated by a study of floor behavior. The offering of floor amendments by senators is one of the few quantitative indicators of norm abidance available over time. If senators specialize in the matters that come before their committees, relatively few should offer amendments to bills from committees on which they do not serve. In the mid-1950s (84th Congress), only thirty-three senators did offer and push to a roll call at least one such amendment. Most of the senators who engaged in such behavior did so in a highly restrained fashion; the mean number of amendments they offered was 1.7 and only six senators offered more than two. Specialization should certainly entail senators offering amendments to bills from only a few committees. If we define as a specialist any senator who offered amendments to bills from three or fewer committees, then in the mid-1950s almost all senators were specialists. The four generalists made up a tiny deviant minority.

The specialization and legislative work norms contributed to the institution's ability to carry out its legislative functions, as Matthews pointed out. The specialization norm reinforced the division of labor provided by the committee system; in combination with the legislative work norm, it enabled senators to develop expertise and thus enabled a small membership with little staff to handle a considerable workload. Within our framework, these institutional benefits cannot, however, explain the existence of the norms. In fact, nearly universal conformity to these norms did provide direct benefits to senators in terms of their individual goals. As long as all senators specialized, each gained considerable autonomy in the area of his specialization; in other areas, these norms enabled each senator to rely upon cues from specialists confident that they rested upon expertise.

Clearly, however, specialization and legislative work also entailed costs for the individual senator; opportunities for involvement in issues that might pay off in terms of goal advancement had to be forgone if they fell outside the purview of his or her committees. Since most senators served on only two committees, the specialization norm was quite restrictive in effect.

For the typical senator of the mid-1950s and before, these costs were not exorbitant. Given the greater economic and social homogeneity of many states thirty years ago, the narrower purview of federal government involvement, and the smaller number and lesser diversity of organized interests, matters that "directly and immediately" affected a senator's state and thus his reelection did tend to be "relatively few." And the committee assignment process tended to place senators on the committees that dealt with those issues. The decision-making autonomy that the specialization norm gave committee members, who in the case of constituency-oriented committees like Agriculture and Interior shared similar constituency interests, greatly facilitated the servicing of major state economic interests so vital to reelection.

A political agenda that was relatively narrow in scope, highly stable, and seemingly impervious to conscious manipulation in content, combined with the narrow and stable interest group structure, offered the policy-oriented senator few opportunities to become involved in a range of issues. Promising issues and effective interest-group allies were not legion. As long as a policy-oriented senator had attractive committee assignments and his policy preferences were reasonably consonant with those of more senior members, the costs of specialization were not great. Such a senator knew that if he abided by the norms he would eventually become one of a fairly small number of important decision makers on policy questions within the jurisdiction of his committees. Furthermore, as the conservative cast of the membership suggests, a substantial majority of senators in this period appear to have been oriented toward the status quo in terms of policy.

Since Senate decision making was committee centered, a senator's primary arena for developing influence was his committees. Thus the best strategy for an influence-oriented senator involved specialization and the development of expertise. A few senators seem to have developed influence of wider scope (Richard Russell, for example), but that influence was built upon a base of specialization and expertise.

The costs of conforming to the specialization and legislative work norms and to most of the other norms as well were highest to the senator whose primary goal was a shot at the presidency. With the spread of television during the 1950s, it became possible for a senator to become a household name. Television coverage of his organized crime hearings made Estes Kefauver something of a national hero and a viable presidential candidate for the rest of the decade (Polsby 1984, 50). For a senator who was not a Senate leader, the sort of behavior likely to garner national publicity was behavior at odds with the norms. Given the costs of such behavior in terms of the accomplishment of the other goals, it made sense only for the senator for whom a shot at the presidency dominated all other goals and for whom this seemed the only possible route to the presidency—for example, a Kefauver, not a Lyndon Johnson or even a John Kennedy. Such senators seem to have been relatively few.

In the 1950s, the freshman senator was expected to serve an apprenticeship. "The new senator is expected to keep his mouth shut, not to take the lead in floor fights, to listen and learn" (Matthews 1960, 93). Data on floor behavior indicate that most freshmen conformed to the apprenticeship norm. In the mid-1950s few freshmen offered floor amendments that got to a roll call vote; during the 84th Congress, only about one in four freshmen offered even a single floor amendment, and the average number of amendments per freshmen was .3, well below the modest mean figure of 1.2 for all members.

For the institution and for more senior members, the apprenticeship norm assured that senators without at least a modicum of expertise would not participate significantly in decision making. Furthermore, apprenticeship bolstered the other norms by limiting the participation of the nonsocialized. For the junior senator, apprenticeship involved costs. However, in the 1950s for senators with relatively safe seats—who therefore could count on long tenure—the costs were not very high. In a complex legislative body dealing with often complex subject matter, during a period when junior members had access to very little staff, a period of learning was necessary before a member could hope to take an effective part in decision making. Serving an apprenticeship gave the new member time not only to develop some expertise but also to learn the Senate norms. Thus the new senator was less likely to do something that would cost him the respect of his colleagues. And, in the intimate Senate social system, the respect of one's colleagues was a prerequisite to influence. For the senator who could afford to think in terms of the long or at least the medium run, serving an apprenticeship was not all that costly.

The reciprocity norm specified that senators should be willing to do favors for one another and, once a bargain had been struck, a senator should keep his word. A second element admonished senators to be highly restrained in the use of the great powers the Senate rules confer upon each individual (specifically, the right to extended debate). "The spirit of reciprocity results in much, if not most, of the senators' actual power not being exercised," Matthews wrote (1960, 101).

During the 1950s, senators were in fact quite restrained about prolonging floor consideration by offering amendments and pushing them to a roll call vote. During the 84th Congress, only about half the membership (forty-seven) offered even one floor amendment, and those who did averaged only 2.4 amendments each. Only fifteen senators offered more than two amendments that got to a roll call vote. The filibuster, the ultimate in unrestrained use of senators' individual powers, was rare in the 1950s. Only two occurred between 1953 and 1958.

By encouraging bargaining and discouraging obstructive behavior, the reciprocity norm clearly contributed to the Senate's ability to make decisions. Again, however, individual rather than institutional benefits explain the norm's persistence. If all senators abided by the norm, individual senators benefited from being able to make favorable bargains and by not being inconvenienced, or worse, by others senators' obstructive behavior. Since for most senators goal advancement depends to some extent upon the passage of legislation, obstructionism can be a major threat. The restraint element of the reciprocity norm also reinforced committee autonomy by discouraging noncommittee members from offering floor amendments, thus protecting committee members' decision-making powers.

Conformity, however, involved some cost. The bargaining situation in which binding agreements are not possible is the archetypical prisoner's dilemma. Keeping one's end of the bargain costs something, so reneging is the best strategy. But that leads to everyone reneging and consequently a loss to everyone. As Matthews explained, "this mode of procedure requires that a senator live up to his end of the bargain, no matter how implicit the bargain may have been" (1960, 101). The norm benefited everyone by making productive bargaining possible. The high rate of interaction among senators in the 1950s served as a force for conformity with the norm. In such an intimate setting, a reputation for not keeping one's word spread quickly and cost one dearly.

The cost-benefit calculus with respect to the other aspect of the reciprocity norm is a good deal more complex. The Senate rules do give each senator immense power; restraint in its use involves real costs. Restraint was never total. Southern Democrats used the filibuster on civil rights legislation which, they believed, affected severely their reelection and perhaps also their policy goals. But barring a large minority perceiving a core goal to be at stake, the payoffs of extended debate were somewhat muted in the 1950s and before, and so the costs of restraint were less than they were to become. As Oppenheimer (1985) argues, the larger the chamber's workload and consequently the greater the time pressure under which it works, the more effective extended debate is as a strategy for stopping legislation, exacting concession, or even forcing action on something else. In the 1950s, the Senate's workload was still not so great as to make the mere threat of extended debate by an individual or small group a powerful bargaining tool.

The relatively bounded, stable, predictable policy system of the 1950s, with its limited number of significant actors and relatively predictable lines of conflict, did not encourage extensive or widespread use of the floor for agenda setting or for generating outside pressure on the Senate. Doing so successfully requires that there be an audience outside the chamber that can be aroused and when aroused can influence other senators. A few senators did attempt to employ this strategy. However, a relatively quiescent public and a relatively insulated Senate worked against the success of that strategy and thus discouraged its use.

Explaining the Senate norm of courtesy, Matthews wrote, "A cardinal rule of Senate behavior is that political disagreements should not influence personal feelings" (1960, 97). The courtesy norm prevented conflicts over policy from escalating into bitter irreconcilable personal conflicts. It thus facilitated productive bargaining among senators and, consequently, Senate decision making. But even this norm involves some, though relatively minor, costs. In addition to whatever emotional costs are entailed in a senator's reining himself in during the heat of battle, abidance with the norm may require a senator to pull his punches in debate, which may cost the senator something in his relations with allied interest groups.

According to Matthews, "A senator whose emotional commitment to Senate ways appears less than total is suspect. . . . One who seems to be using the Senate for the purposes of self-advertising and advancement obviously does not belong" (1960, 102). The norm of institutional patriotism required senators to refrain from criticizing the Senate or from doing anything to bring the institution into public disrepute. The norm of institutional patriotism contributed to maintaining the prestige of the Senate, a benefit to the members collectively. It also reinforced the other norms. Conformity did, however, entail some costs for senators individually, especially in that it barred excessive self-advertisement and directed senators to focus their attention and energy inward on the Senate. Yet, during the 1950s, for most members, the best strategy for goal advancement entailed being inward looking and focusing upon their work and their colleagues within the institution. Consequently, the costs of conforming to the norm of institutional patriotism were not excessive.

Adherence to the norms of the Senate of the 1950s can be characterized by the prisoner's dilemma. Conformity involved some cost to the individual, but by and large, if everyone conformed, everyone was better off. Widespread conformity with the norms provided direct benefits to senators in terms of their individual goals. The norms may also have contributed to the institution's ability to perform its functions, but in no case did mutual cooperation have only an institutional payoff.

There were mavericks during the 1950s who did not conform. For the small group of action-oriented liberals in the Senate prior to 1959, conforming with the norms was much more expensive than for most members. These senators had broad interests in policy, and their views on policy were sharply different from those of the Senate majority, especially from those of committee leaders. Adherence to the norms of specialization, reciprocity, and institutional patriotism would have barred these senators from pursuing the only strategy with some probability of paying off in terms of their policy goal. As a minority, and a relatively junior one in a chamber that distributed influence on the basis of seniority, these liberals had no real chance of decisively influencing the policy process through traditional legislative activities within the chamber. Therefore, they addressed an audience outside the chamber and used public forums, particularly the Senate floor, to do so. Thus liberals more frequently offered floor amendments than the average senator; in the 84th Congress, extreme liberals offered 2 amendments per capita, considerably more than the mean of 1.2 for all senators. Wayne Morse and Hubert Humphrey were among the five senators most active in offering floor amendments. Morse was the senator most active in offering amendments to bills from committees on which he did not serve, and Paul Douglas was among a group of five senators tied for second most active. In the mid-1950s, liberals were much more likely than other senators to speak frequently on the floor. During the 83rd and 84th Congresses, 12 percent of liberals ranked high in the frequency of floor speaking and 23 percent ranked medium. In contrast, no other senators ranked high and only 5 percent ranked medium.* Liberals were also more likely to introduce bills in a wide range of areas (Matthews 1960, 114).

Such activism on the floor did not pay off immediately in terms of policy results, but as an agenda-setting activity, it at least offered the prospect of future payoffs related to achieving policy goals. The substantial publicity that these senators' activities received undoubtedly reinforced the liberals' belief that this strategy would eventually pay off (see Hess 1986, 118). The strategy did, of course, involve deliberate violation of the norms, and, almost certainly as a result, at least some of these senators were subject to sanctions. William Proxmire, for example, was repeatedly denied assignments on prestige committees (Bullock 1985, 799; see also Clark 1963). Probably the greatest cost was exclusion from the mutually beneficial exchange of favors among conforming senators. These sanctions may well have served as a warning to other senators, but they did not change the behavior of the action-oriented liberals. For them, norm abidance was simply too expensive (Huitt 1961).

Our framework and this case suggest that norms will lose their hold when the costs of conformity increase in a major way. Of course, this increase must occur for more than a small subset of members. During the 1950s, the action-oriented liberals were a small minority; as such, their nonconformity did not threaten the norms. Most senators adhered to the norms because the structure that resulted when all or most members conformed was conducive to the advancement of their goals.

---

* Matthews bases his ideological categorization on *New Republic* scores (see pp. 276–78).

The Character of Senate Decision Making in the 1950s

Senate decision making in the 1950s was committee centered. The committee system specified by the Senate rules, combined with a workload large enough to make such a division of labor necessary, guarantees that Senate committees will be important arenas of legislative decision making. In the 1950s, Senate committees were not simply important, they were highly autonomous. The norms of specialization and reciprocity reinforced committees' advantaged position in decision making by defining as illegitimate most behavior by nonmembers aimed at influencing a committee's legislation. Senators were admonished to confine their time and attention to matters coming before their committees, to defer to the expertise of senior committee members on other legislation, to be highly restrained in using floor time for any purpose, and certainly to refrain from offering amendments to legislation from committees on which they did not serve.

Most committee decisions were accepted by the Senate without even a roll call vote. In the mid-1950s (84th Congress), 97.8 percent of the bills that passed the Senate did so without being subject to a recorded vote. Of the measures that were contested to the extent that they elicited at least one roll call, substantial proportions received only one; 60 percent of all contested measures and 40 percent of all contested bills were thus minimally contested. Many of the recorded votes were overwhelming votes on final passage. Most bills were not subject to major attempts to alter them on the floor through amendments. No floor amendment that got to a roll call vote was offered to about a quarter (27.3 percent) of contested bills, and 78 percent of contested bills were subject to two or fewer amending roll calls.

During the 84th Congress, only thirty-three floor amendments were adopted by roll call vote. Less than a quarter (23.6 percent) of all contested bills were amended at the floor stage, and contested bills were only a tiny fraction of all bills passed. To a large extent, the Senate accepted the decisions of its committees without change.

If Senate decision making was committee centered, within committees it was dominated by leaders chosen on the basis of seniority. Rules and customs gave committee chairmen extensive procedural powers. The committee chairman set the committee agenda, called committee meetings, appointed subcommittee chairmen, and largely determined the choice of conferees (Huitt 1965, 89). The norms of apprenticeship and the concomitant expected deference to senior members reinforced the dominance of these senior leaders. So too did the distribution of staff.

The chairman controlled the committee staff; in some cases, some staff members answered to the ranking minority member. Junior members had to rely upon usually overburdened personal staffs for help. Furthermore, mark-up sessions in which legislation is actually written were closed, in many cases to all staff other than that of the committee. Not even committee members' personal staff were allowed to attend. By virtue of the expertise they derived from many years on the committee, and of their command of procedural and staff resources, seniority-determined leaders dominated their committees.

The typical policy-making structure of the 1950s has often been labeled the iron triangle. That is, the congressional committee with jurisdiction, the executive branch bureau that administered the policy, and the small number of nonconflicting interest groups with a stake in the policy allied to make policy decisions with little to no interference from so-called outsiders. To a large extent, this small and stable group of participants was autonomous in making decisions.

The iron triangle model, when applied to any and all policy areas indiscriminately, is undoubtedly an exaggeration. Nevertheless, both the political environment of the 1950s and the structure of congressional decision making were conducive to the development and maintenance of iron triangles. The number of organized interests active in Washington was small by later standards. Established affluent interest groups were primarily economically based; neither the disadvantaged nor diffuse broad-based interests were much represented. With the interest group universe being relatively small and nondiverse, there was little or no conflict among organized groups in a number of policy areas.

Because Senate decision making was committee centered, interest group representatives established relationships with the members of the committee that handled the area of interest to them. The long tenure of committee members and the stability and often the narrowness of groups' interests, which led many to concentrate their attention on a single committee in each chamber, produced long-term, stable relationships. Furthermore, because of the way the committee assignment process worked, the interest groups lobbying committee members often represented a major state economic interest.

Much committee decision making took place in a non-conflictual environment. The groups interested in the committee's decisions agreed among themselves, and their "demands" were ones that committee members were inclined, for reelection reasons, to be attentive to.

Senate rules and norms served to block other participants from having much influence on committee decision making and outputs. Participation by senators outside the committee violated Senate norms.

Furthermore, most senators lacked the resources to do so with much hope of success. A shortage of staff was a major barrier, but so too was the committees' practice of holding closed mark-ups. Writing a bill in closed session deprived those senators not on the committee, and non-privileged interest groups as well, of timely information. It made it more difficult for outsiders to attempt to influence committee decisions or to challenge those decisions on the floor.

Direct public pressure was also not likely to have much effect upon the character of committee policy outputs. First, public pressure for a change in policy outputs was rare. In many cases, decision making took place in a nonconflictive environment, so media coverage was sparse. With no information, public pressure for change was unlikely to build. Second, because committee members perceived themselves to be safe electorally as long as they satisfied the major interests in their states that had long-standing relationships with the committee and perceived any other course as being risky, public pressure for change was easy to ignore. Unless public opinion was extremely intense and likely to be long lasting, rare circumstances at any time, acceding to public opinion was riskier than ignoring it.

Legislative decision making in the 1950s took place in relatively non-permeable and highly autonomous committees. As a result, the Senate policy-making process was highly segmented and much of it was relatively insulated from public pressure.

The Locus of Influence

Influence on policy decisions in the Senate of the 1950s resided primarily in the committees and especially in their leaders. An assessment of the likely impact on policy of this distribution of influence requires a close look at the ideological complexion of committee leaders and of the membership of committees.

Chairmen and ranking minority members were predominantly conservative in the 1950s. Republican committee leaders were overwhelmingly either moderate or extreme conservatives; on the average, 84 percent scored above 60 on the conservative coalition index over the 83rd through 85th Congresses. Among Democratic committee leaders, conservatives outnumbered liberals in each of the three congresses; on the average, almost half (48.3 percent) were moderate or extreme conservatives; less than a third (30.6 percent) were moderate or extreme liberals, and the rest were moderates.

Committee leaders were reasonably representative of their party contingents in the Senate. Using the mean conservative coalition score as the criterion, we find that Republican chairs as a group were somewhat more liberal than the typical Republican senator in the 83rd Congress; in the 84th and 85th, Republican ranking minority members were highly representative. Democratic committee leaders were consistently more conservative than the typical Democratic senator, but the differences were not large, averaging five percentage points over the 83rd through 85th Congresses. This mildly unrepresentative conservative cast of committee leaders stemmed from southerners being somewhat overrepresented. In the 83rd Congress, southerners held seven of fifteen ranking minority member positions; in the 84th and 85th Congresses, they held eight of fifteen chairs. Thus, southern senators occupied about half the committee leadership positions during a period in which they constituted about 40 percent of the Democratic membership.

Committee leaders from the South were overwhelmingly conservative; on the average, 83 percent were either moderate or extreme conservatives during the 83rd through 85th Congresses. Only once, in the 84th Congress, did a southern committee leader fall into the liberal range; Lister Hill's conservative coalition score of 33.3 in that congress put him in the moderate liberal category. Democratic committee leaders from the North were most frequently liberals; over the three congresses, 60 percent were on the average. The remaining committee leaders from the North were primarily but not exclusively moderates. Carl Hayden, chair of Appropriations, scored in the conservative range in the 85th and fell just on the moderate side of the borderline in the 84th. In their conservative cast, southern committee leaders were representative of the southern Democratic membership as a whole; so too were northern Democratic committee leaders representative of an ideologically heterogeneous group of northern Democratic senators.

Although less consequential than committee leadership positions, subcommittee leadership posts also confer some influence. To assess the ideological complexion of subcommittee leaders and, therefore, their likely impact upon policy decisions, mean conservatives coalition scores are used. The mean for any group of subcommittee leaders is a weighted mean, a senator's score being weighted by the number of positions that he held on subcommittees of good committees.

In the mid-1950s (84th and 85th Congresses), the typical Republican ranking minority member on a subcommittee was a moderate conservative, a little but not much less conservative than the Republican membership as a whole. Whereas the mean conservative coalition score for all Republicans in the two congresses was 77, that for subcommittee leaders was 73.

Because of the differences between northerners and southerners,

talking about the typical Democrat chair of a subcommittee makes little
sense. As groups, southern chairs and northern chairs faithfully reflected their membership. Thus the average southern chair was a moderate conservative with a mean conservative coalition score 75.9; the
average northern chair, a moderate liberal with a mean score of 26.3

There was little difference in the proportion of senators from the two
regions who chaired a subcommittee of a good committee; it was over 80
percent for both groups. The group of subcommittee chairs as a whole
was representative of the Democratic membership.

In the 1950s committee chairmen were highly influential. Nevertheless, the thrust of committee policy outputs depended upon the character of the committee's total membership, not just upon the preferences of its leadership. To assess the ideological center of gravity of each
committee, the median conservative coalition score of its membership
is used. The median is that score that divides the membership into two
equal parts, half of which have higher scores and half lower, thus reflecting the likely position of a majority.

In the 83rd Congress, the ideological center of gravity of thirteen of
the fifteen committees fell into the extreme conservative range. With a
median score of 78, the Labor and Public Welfare Committee was just
shy of the cutoff for the extreme conservative category. Foreign Relations, with a median of 46.9, was unrepresentatively liberal. The 83rd
was an extremely conservative congress; the median conservative coalition score of the full membership was 89.5.

From the 83rd to the 84th Congress, the center of gravity of the full
Senate moved left and so did the membership of every committee. Although all committees exhibited some responsiveness to the shift, the
magnitude of change varied considerably from committee to committee.
In the 84th and 85th Congresses, the committees were less ideologically
homogeneous than they had been in the 83rd. The center of gravity of the
Senate membership as a whole was moderate conservative in these two
congresses; the median score was 71. The modal committee was also
moderately conservative; in the 84th Congress, seven of fifteen fell into
that category and in the 85th, six of fifteen did.

In the 84th Congress, Appropriations, Finance, and Agriculture remained, as they had been in the 83rd, extremely conservative. In the 85th,
these three committees were joined by Armed Services and Judiciary in
the extreme conservative category. Thus some of the Senate's most
prestigious committees were least responsive to the change in the overall ideological center of gravity and consequently became unrepresentatively conservative. In contrast, the Senate's least prestigious committees tended to be atypically liberal. In the 84th Congress, the center of

gravity of the Labor Committee was moderately liberal; four committees fell into the moderate range—the prestigious Foreign Relations Committee and the relatively undesirable Rules, District of Columbia, and Post Office and Civil Service committees. During the 85th Congress, the Foreign Relations, Labor, District of Columbia, and Post Office and Civil Service committees had centers of gravity in the moderate range. With the notable exception of Foreign Relations, the atypically conservative committees tended to be more prestigious than the atypically liberal committees, but the former were not as far to the right of the chamber median (a mean of 11.8 points) as the latter were to the left of the chamber median (a mean of 21.6 points).

In the 1950s, conservatives dominated most of the committees, especially the most important ones, but conservatives also dominated the Senate membership in terms of sheer numbers. In terms of its leadership and its rank and file, the Senate committee system of the 1950s was both conservative and representative.

The Senate of the 1950s as an Environment for the Advancement of Senators' Goals

In the Senate of the 1950s, valuable resources were distributed unequally. Senior members were advantaged and junior members disadvantaged in the distribution of desirable committee positions, of subcommittee leadership slots and staff, and, consequently, of the influence that derived from commanding these resources. Norms constrained senators' behavior and reinforced the power of senior leaders and of committees.

Nevertheless, most senators of the 1950s did not find this structure a major barrier to the achievement of their goals. Committee autonomy and seniority assured the senator that, as long as he achieved reelection, he would eventually become one of a small group of often like-minded decision makers on the issues within the jurisdiction of his committees. The committee assignment process tended to ensure that those matters would be the ones that the senator was most interested in influencing, especially for reelection reasons. Meanwhile, the trading of favors that the recriprocity norm dictated appears to have assured even the most junior senator of help if he really needed it for reelection purposes—at least as long as he abided by the norms.

Further, the policy decisions reached by the committees tended to be broadly acceptable to the Senate membership. During the 1950s, the ideological spread of the Senate was relatively narrow by later standards; the membership was predominantly conservative and moderate. The committees, which were representative of that membership, found it fairly easy to produce broadly acceptable legislation. In the Senate of the 1950s, committee autonomy certainly did not entail large numbers of senators being forced to accept policy decisions they considered abhorrent.

In sum, for the typical senator of the 1950s, the payoffs for going along, although deferred, were substantial, and the costs were not exorbitant.

3 // The Impact of a Change in Membership: The Democratic Classes of 1958–1964

An influx of new members, it was hypothesized, is a likely source of pressure for institutional change. High turnover should not, however, be sufficient. Only if new members find current Senate structures a significant barrier to the achievement of their goals are they likely to try to bring about change. For most of its members, the Senate of the 1950s was reasonably conducive to the advancement of their goals. It follows that if a change in membership led to institutional change, the new members must have differed from more senior senators in ways related to their goals. Either their goals differed or, because they were differently situated politically, the behavioral strategies likely to lead to the achievement of their goals differed. The large group of northern Democrats that first entered the Senate between 1959 and 1965 did find Senate structures a barrier to the advancement of their goals. The impact of these members on the Senate, and the Senate's on them, is the subject of this chapter (see also Foley 1980; Rohde, Ornstein, and Peabody 1985; on the 89th Congress particularly, see Price 1972).

Membership Change

The 1958 elections disrupted the very close party balance that had characterized the congresses of the 1950s and established a Democratic preponderance that lasted through the 1970s (see Figure 1).

In the 1958 elections, Democrats gained twelve Senate seats. The fifteen-member Democratic class, which included Edmund Muskie,

Figure 3.1   Party Strength in the Senate 1953-1986

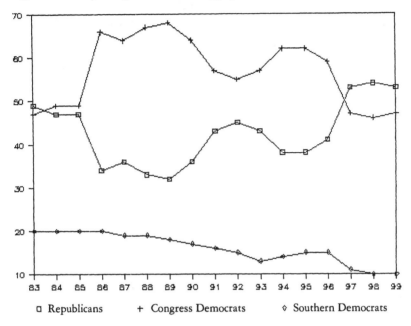

□ Republicans   + Congress Democrats   ◇ Southern Democrats

Phillip Hart, and Eugene McCarthy, was by far the largest Democratic class of the thirty-year period under study; the only larger party class was the sixteen-member freshman Republican contingent elected in 1980. These new Democratic senators differed from their senior party colleagues in region of origin, ideological proclivities, and electoral security. They were all northerners, whereas four in ten of their party colleagues were from the South. They were a markedly liberal group. In contrast, most southern Democrats were conservatives while senior northern Democrats were ideologically quite heterogeneous. Thus, the mean conservative coalition score for freshmen was a low 17.9; that for all more senior Democrats was 46.5; for more senior northern Democrats, the mean was 25.1. Over two-thirds of the freshmen were extreme liberals (their score was below 20) compared to half of their more senior regional party colleagues. In contrast especially to their southern colleagues, most of the class of 1958 had won by narrow margins and could not feel electorally secure. Only two had received as much as 60 percent of the vote; the other thirteen averaged 55 percent of the vote.

The class of 1958 was just the beginning of a wave of change in membership. Between 1959 and 1965, another twenty-three northern Dem-

Table 3.1 Ideological Polarization of the Democratic Party After the 1958 Elections (Mean conservative coalition scores)

Years	Northern Democrats	Southern Democrats	Difference
1953–58	31.9	77.3	45.4
1959–66	21.2	81.4	60.2

ocrats entered the Senate. Abraham Ribicoff, Birch Bayh, Edward Kennedy, Robert Kennedy, George McGovern, Gaylord Nelson, and Walter Mondale entered the chamber during this period. This group tended to be even more liberal and even less electorally secure than the class of 1958. Of the twenty-three, nineteen were elected (the others were appointed), and of those only four had won with 60 percent or more of the vote; the other fifteen averaged 52 percent of the vote. In each of the three succeeding congresses (87th, 88th, and 89th), northern Democratic freshmen were more liberal than senior northern Democrats even though the senior group itself became increasingly liberal. During the 89th Congress, northern Democrats first elected before 1958 averaged 25.2 on the conservative coalition index, the fourteen remaining members of the class of 1958 averaged 19.0, and the nine more junior northern Democrats averaged 12.8. Of the most senior group, 52.9 percent were extreme liberals; of the 1958 class, 78.6 were; and 84.2 percent of the most junior group were.

These members changed the composition of the Democratic membership and of the Senate. They, of course, made the Senate much more heavily Democratic and the Senate Democratic party much more northern. During the 1950s, southerners had made up about 40 percent of the Democratic membership. With the 1958 election, southerners dropped to about 30 percent, where they remained during the 1960s. The new northern Democrats also made the Senate and the Democratic party considerably less conservative. Not only were they a great deal more liberal than southern Democrats, they were also considerably more liberal than more senior northern Democrats. As a result, the Democratic membership became much more deeply ideologically polarized along regional lines during this period (see table 3.1). The regional and ideological divisions coincided with large seniority differences. By 1965, two-thirds of northern Democrats had first entered the Senate in 1959 or later; only 10.5 percent of southern Democrats had entered the chamber since 1958. The dwindling southern component of the Democratic membership, thus, was much more senior than the growing northern component.

The kind of change in membership that occurred between 1958 and 1964 might well lead to pressure for structural change. Certainly these new senators differed from more senior members in goal-related ways. As liberals, the new members' notions of what constituted good public policy differed, often radically, from those of more conservative senior members (see Foley 1980). The electoral insecurity of many of the new northern Democrats might also give them a very different perspective than that of more secure senators. Their time horizon, for example, might well be shorter and their tolerance for deferred payoffs less.

Whether such differences are likely to actually lead to pressures for structural change depends upon whether the current structure facilitates or obstructs the new members' goal advancement. We need to know the impact of Senate norms and of Senate structures for the distribution of resources on these senators' pursuit of their goals.

The Senate's Response to the Liberals

For most senators of the 1950s, conforming to the Senate norms was not exorbitantly expensive. The costs of a particular form of behavior depend, however, upon a senator's political situation. Members of the class of 1958 were differently situated politically and thus faced different problems in the pursuit of their goals than the typical more senior senator. Most of these new Democrats had won by narrow margins, and few could feel electorally secure. Most had run on a platform of progressive policy change, and, according to all contemporary accounts, many were deeply committed to that goal. For these members, serving an apprenticeship was not a minor inconvenience, as it was for a senator who could afford a longer time perspective. The goal of reelection dictated legislative activity, whether effective or not, right from the beginning. These senators needed to show their constituents that they were working toward fulfilling their campaign promises, and doing so required visible activity. The unusual amount of media coverage that the class of 1958 received increased its members' incentives to ignore the apprenticeship norm and play an active role immediately (Foley 1980, 122–26). It ensured that a senator's activities would be highly visible to his constituents, while a lack of activity would also be obvious.

By all accounts, senior senators made no real attempt to get the class of 1958 to serve an apprenticeship (Foley 1980, 126; Rohde, Ornstein, and Peabody 1985, 176). Given the unusually large size of the class, the imposition of uncongenial modes of behavior on the members of that class through the use of sanctions would have been extremely disruptive and probably unsuccessful. Senior senators may have expected the suspension of apprenticeship to be temporary. However, the continued influx of electorally insecure liberal northern Democrats between 1960 and 1965 doomed the norm. For these members, as for the class of 1958, serving an apprenticeship would have been much too costly in terms of the advancement of their goals. Furthermore, they had the precedent of the class of 1958, which had not been held to the apprenticeship norm. Thus, as an expectation and largely also as a pattern of behavior, apprenticeship died a quick death in the period following 1958. In this area, the Senate accommodated itself to the class of 1958 rather than the class accommodating itself to Senate ways.

The size of the class was clearly the key factor. Small groups of newcomers who find the norms a barrier will have little effect on the Senate as an institution; the influx of a large group, in contrast, will lead to change. The stock of sanctions is not sufficient to enforce compliance when the group is large, yet tolerance of widespread nonconformity quickly leads to the demise of the norm.

As a whole, the Democratic class of 1958 was extraordinarily well treated in the committee assignment process. Eight of the fifteen members were assigned to the prestige committees—two to Finance and three each to Appropriations and Armed Services. Eugene McCarthy, for example, was assigned to Finance; Gale McGee received an Appropriations seat, and Clair Engle a position on Armed Services. The class fared much better than any other during the 1950s and 1960s. Clearly Majority Leader Lyndon Johnson and the Democratic Steering Committee altered the usual decision rules in order to accommodate this unusually large class. Just as clearly this was a one-time deviation; there was no permanent change in the decision rules. The freshmen who entered the chamber in the 1960s were no more likely to get one of these choice assignments than those elected before 1958. Between 1961 and 1970, only three of thirty-three Democratic freshmen won positions on prestige committees.

In the 1950s, Republican freshmen were less well off than Democrats. Without a Johnson rule, freshmen could and sometimes did end up on only minor committees. The 1958 election debacle gave junior Republicans the lever they needed to impose something like the Johnson rule (see Ripley 1969, 137). Everett Dirksen, who was then running for minority leader, and other senior leaders shocked by the party's poor showing at the polls were receptive to junior members' insistent pleas for better committee positions (MacNeil 1970, 152, 164–65). Never again was a freshman Republican given only minor committee assignments. Assignments to the prestige committees, on the other hand, remained extremely rare. Between 1961 and 1970, only two freshmen were placed on the top four committees, and one of the those was Barry Goldwater, who was returning to the Senate after his unsuccessful run for the presidency.

To some extent, then, the Senate accommodated itself to the needs of the new members. The northern Democratic liberals that entered the chamber between 1959 and 1965 were not held to the apprenticeship norm, which, for them, might have spelled political suicide. The class of 1958 received special treatment in the committee assignment process. Ironically, the events of this period led to a permanent change in committee assignment distribution rules among Republicans but not Democrats. The Democratic classes of 1960, 1962, and 1964 fared much less well in the committee assignment process than the class of 1958.

The Distribution of Valued Committee Positions

Whether an influx of new members leads to pressures for structural change depends upon whether current structure facilitates or hinders new members in their goal pursuit. That, in turn, is dependent upon how Senate structures distribute resources. In this period of rapid change in the composition of the Senate membership, what happened to the distribution of valued committee positions?

During the 1950s (83rd through 85th Congresses), southern Democrats were more likely to hold a position on a prestige committee than were northern Democrats (see table 3.2.). The proportion of northerners who served on one of these committees increased in the 86th Congress, reflecting, in part, the excellent assignments received by the freshmen of 1958. Southerners also did better in the 86th Congress, and the difference in success rates for the two regional groupings was similar to what it had been in the mid-1950s. During the 87th through 89th Congresses, as the Democratic party increasingly became heavily northern and the regional groupings were becoming increasingly distinct ideological groupings, northerners' success at getting assignments to the top four committees slipped, and the gap in success rates beween northerners and southerners increased appreciably. Furthermore, during the 1950s and through the mid-1960s, southern Democrats were much more likely than their northern colleagues to hold two such prize assignments; over the 84th through 89th Congresses, 26.3 percent of southerners held two prestige committee positions, while only 4.1 percent of northerners did.

Table 3.2 Distribution of Valued Committee Positions Across Regional Party Groups, 1953–1970 (Percent of group holding one or more)

Congress	Top Four Committee Assignments			Subcommittee Leadership Positions		
	North Dem.	South Dem.	Republicans	North Dem.	South Dem.	Republicans
83rd	53.6	63.6	58.5	—	—	—
84th	51.7	75.0	57.4	89.7	80.0	68.1
85th	56.7	70.0	55.4	83.3	85.0	70.8
86th	64.4	80.0	63.9	62.2	85.0	80.6
87th	57.8	75.0	60.5	64.4	75.0	78.9
88th	55.1	78.9	57.6	59.2	84.2	84.8
89th	58.0	84.2	62.5	64.0	73.7	96.9
90th	65.2	77.8	62.2	76.1	66.7	86.5
91st	57.5	70.6	61.4	85.0	70.6	84.1

In the mid-1950s, both northern and southern Democrats were highly likely to chair a subcommittee of a good committee, but northerners were actually slightly more successful at obtaining one of these valued positions than their southern colleagues. During the 86th through 89th Congresses, however, the success rate of northern Democrats slipped significantly from its level in the mid-1950s and fell far behind that of southern Democrats. The large increase in the Democratic membership during this period put a considerable strain on the supply of subcommittee chairmanships. In the distribution of these now scarcer resources, northerners lost out disproportionately. This was not, however, simply a problem of supply. During the same congresses that saw a number of northerners without a single good subcommittee chairmanship, over half (51.4 percent) of southerners chaired two or more good subcommittees. (So, too, did 28 percent of northern Democrats.)

Seniority, we know, was a key distribution criterion. Was the advantage of southern Democrats in gaining valued committee positions simply a function of their greater seniority? In the 1950s and the 1960s, senior senators were more likely than junior senators to hold a position on one of the top four committees. The mean correlation of prestige committee assignments and years of seniority was .46 for the 84th through 89th Congresses. The relationship between seniority and subcommittee chairmanships, in contrast, developed only after the 1958 election; the correlations in the 84th and 85th Congresses were not significant (a mean of .09); the mean for the 86th through 89th Congress was .42.

Seniority, thus, was related to the possession of valued committee positions. But do seniority differences completely account for the advantage southern Democrats held over northern Democrats in the possession of these resources? The unequal distribution of subcommittee chairmanships on desirable committees after 1958 was simply a function of differential seniority. Once seniority is controlled for, the number of such positions held is not related to ideology or region. The awarding of prestige committee positions, in contrast, appears to have been ideologically biased (see also Swanson 1969). Probit analyses indicate that, in the 1950s and 1960s, conservatives were more likely than liberals to hold one or more prestige committee assignments even after seniority differences are taken into account.*

Seniority was a more important determinant than ideology; among senators of middle seniority, however, the most liberal senators were less successful than their more conservative colleagues in getting prestige committee assignments. In the 88th and 89th Congresses, for example, few freshmen held such assignments, while most senators who had served more than two terms did. At these extremes of seniority, ideology had no influence on the likelihood of holding a prestige committee asignment. Among nonfreshmen first termers and second termers, however, extreme liberals were less likely to hold one of these prized positions than were more conservative members (see table 3.3).

The largely northern and liberal Democratic classes of 1958 through 1964 were, of course, disadvantaged by the Senate's heavy reliance on seniority as a major criterion for the distribution of valued committee

Table 3.3 Impact of Ideology on Committee Assignment Success for Senators of Moderate Seniority (Percent of group holding top four committee assignments)

	88th Congress		89th Congress	
Seniority	Extreme liberals	All others	Extreme liberals	All others
First Term	38.5	50.0	33.3	100.0
	(13)[a]	(8)	(12)	(1)
Second Term	0	83.0	60.0	77.8
	(2)	(12)	(15)	(9)

[a]Number in group.

---

* The independent variables used were the log of years of seniority and log of conservative coalition score. The coefficient of the seniority variable is at least twice its standard error in every congress from 1955 through 1970. Conservative coalition score is marginally significant (coefficient is greater than its standard error but not twice as great) in every congress from 1955 through 1970 except for the 85th.

positions. In the awarding of prestige committee assignments, they were further disadvantaged by a bias against more liberal members.

The Locus of Influence

The differences in seniority between southern conservatives and northern liberals supplemented by some bias in the assignment process resulted in conservatives wielding disproportionate influence in the committee system.

In the mid-1950s, it will be recalled, committee chairs were only slightly more conservative than the average Democrat; but in the late 1950s and the 1960s, as the Democratic Senate membership became more liberal, Democratic committee chairs actually became more conservative. The result was massive unrepresentativeness; the mean difference between the chairs' average conservative coalition score and that for all Democrats for the 86th through 91st Congresses was 24 (see table 3.4). Over half the chairmanships (54.2 percent) were held by conservatives (those who scored 60 or above on the conservative coalition index) during these congresses, even though less than 30 percent (28.7) of the Democratic membership was conservative.

Table 3.4 Ideological Representativeness of Committee Leaders (Leaders' conservative coalition score minus that for group as a whole)

	Republicans	Democrats		
Congress		All	North	South
83rd	-7.7	3.3	-1.2	2.7
84th	1.8	4.4	-2.2	.4
85th	1.3	7.7	-.6	3.3
86th	8.1	23.8	14.0	1.1
87th	9.4	25.5	18.0	3.0
88th	2.7	24.6	7.2	2.2
89th	-3.8	24.6	6.7	6.1
90th	3.3	24.0	17.5	.6
91st	3.7	21.2	11.7	-3.0
92nd	6.4	20.0	12.4	2.7
93rd	6.6	31.5	8.0	3.6

The overrepresentation of southerners among Democratic committee leaders accounts for a part but not all of the leaders' unrepresentativeness. From the late 1950s through the mid-1960s, while southerners were decreasing as a proportion of all Democrats, their share of committee chairmanships actually increased. From 1959 through 1970, southerners held nine or ten of sixteen chairmanships.

Also contributing to the unrepresentativeness of Democratic committee leaders was the atypical conservatism of those northern Democrats who became leaders. From the 86th through the 91st Congresses, northern committee chairs were consistently and significantly more conservative than the average northern Democrat; they scored, on the average, 12.5 points higher on the conservative coalition index. During that period the northern Democratic membership changed, but the chairs who attained their positions by virtue of seniority did not. In effect, they were representative of the Democratic Senate membership of the early 1950s, not that of the period following 1958. Thus, during the 1950s and 1960s, most of the northern Democratic committee leaders came from the mountain and border states (approximately 70 percent on the average for the 83rd through 91st Congresses). The Northeast and industrial Midwest averaged less than one chairmanship per congress during the 1950s and 1960s.

After 1958, the distribution of subcommittee chairmanships among ideological groupings no longer accurately mirrored the Democratic membership (see table 3.5). In the 85th Congress, the proportion of subcommittee chairs held by extreme liberals and by extreme conservatives almost exactly equaled these groups' proportions of the total membership. In the 86th and 87th Congresses, extreme liberals did somewhat less well than they deserved on the basis of their numbers and extreme conservatives did somewhat better. As the influx of liberals continued in the early and mid-1960s, the inequality became greater. In the 88th and 89th Congresses, extreme liberals were severely disadvantaged and extreme conservatives substantially advantaged. In the 88th Congress, for example, extreme liberals constituted 42 percent of all Democrats but held only 26 percent of subcommittee chairs of good committees. In contrast, extreme conservatives who made up 18 percent of the membership held 31 percent of the subcommittee chairmanships.

The substantial ideological shift in the Senate membership in the wake of the 1958 election was reflected in the membership of most committees. The median conservative coalition score of the total membership dropped from 71.4 in the 85th Congress to 54.7 in the 86th Congress; a modest monotonic decline over the succeeding congresses brought it to a low of 43.6 in the 89th Congress. The ideological center of gravity of twelve of fifteen committees moved left from the 85th to 86th Congress. The extent of that move varied considerably across committees, and, as

Table 3.5 Distribution of Subcommittee Chairmanships Among Liberal and
Conservative Democrats

Congress	Extreme liberals as % of		Extreme conservatives as % of	
	All Dem.	Subcommittee Chairs	All Dem.	Subcommittee Chairs
85th	32.0	32.4	26.0	25.7
86th	40.0	35.0	21.5	23.8
87th	42.2	41.0	20.3	25.6
88th	41.8	26.4	17.9	30.6
89th	53.6	44.6	23.2	38.6
90th	29.7	23.3	18.8	29.3
91st	40.4	34.9	22.8	31.4

a result, the committees became much more diverse ideologically in the
period following 1958.*

The ideological skew of some committees was the result of their differential attractiveness to liberals and conservatives. From 1959 through
1970, the Agriculture Committee was consistently much more conservative than the Senate membership as a whole. The much greater attractiveness of this committee to senators from the more rural states and
the tendency of these senators to be conservative produced the committee's unrepresentative membership. For similar reasons, the Labor
and Public Welfare Committee and the Banking Committee became
liberal strongholds in this period. Banking was atypically liberal
throughout the 1960s (1961–70). Labor had been well to the left of the
Senate membership before the 1958 election and became even more so
thereafter; its median varied between a high of 25.6 and a low of 14.4 in
the period from 1959 to 1970.

The unrepresentativeness of the prestige committees cannot be so
easily attributed to their differential attractiveness to liberals and conservatives. To be sure, conservatives may have valued a position on
Armed Services more highly than liberals (see Bullock 1985, 798); such
differences in preferences may account at least in part for Armed Services being unrepresentatively conservative in all but one of the con-

---

* A committee is categorized as unrepresentatively conservative or liberal if its median
conservative coalition score is at least 10 points higher or lower than the chamber
median. Between 1959 and 1970, a mean of 10.5 committees per congress were unrepresentative, while only 5.7 committees on the average were unrepresentative in the 83rd
through 85th Congresses.

gresses between 1959 and 1970. Appropriations and Finance, both of which had been to the right of the Senate membership in the mid-1950s (84th and 85th Congresses), were even more so in the period following 1958. Between 1959 and 1970, both had centers of gravity far to the right of the Senate membership as a whole. These two committees are broadly attractive to senators; liberals' underrepresentation was not the result of their own preferences. Conservatives' greater seniority and some bias in the assignment process account for conservative domination of these committees. The only prestige committee not dominated by conservatives was Foreign Relations; atypically liberal in the 1950s, it was representative of the more liberal Senate membership between 1959 and 1968.

The Senate of the 1950s had been dominated by conservatives, but conservatives' prominence in positions of influence had largely reflected the conservative cast of the membership as a whole. After 1958 the center of gravity of the Senate membership moved sharply left, but because of their seniority, conservatives continued to hold what now became a highly disproportionate share of the positions of influence.

Liberal Discontent, Policy Change, and Institutional Change

The cohort of northern liberals elected to the Senate between 1958 and 1964 entered an institution in which seniority was a central criterion for the distribution of valued resources. It was not a totally inflexible institution; in a modest fashion it accommodated itself to the career needs of these new members. The apprenticeship norm was suspended and the large class of 1958 was given exceptionally good committee assignments. Nevertheless, the seniority system remained basically intact; and, as a result, northern liberals, despite their increasing numerical strength, held a disproportionately small share of positions of influence in the committee system.

For many members entering the Senate between 1959 and 1965, progressive policy change was a primary goal. According to contemporary accounts and interview-based studies, they were deeply committed personally; certainly their supportive coalitions had been built upon promises of such policy change (see Foley 1980). An inability to make any sort of progress could cost them dearly, especially among their activist supporters.

Consequently, the newcomers' disadvantaged position in the committee system produced more frustration than that usually experienced by junior members in a seniority-bound institution. Dominance of committee leadership positions and of the membership of prestige committees by senior senators meant conservative dominance. The result was frustration of the liberals' policy goals.

A speech by Senator Joseph Clark, one of the liberals who entered the Senate before 1958, attests to the liberals' discontent. On February 19, 1963, he took the floor of the U.S. Senate to inveigh against the "Senate establishment" that, he said, was blocking President Kennedy's program. According to Clark, a bipartisan, senior, and conservative group of members controlled the Senate (Clark 1963). The establishment's power derived from its control of committee leadership positions— chairmanships and ranking member positions—which, in turn, derived from the seniority system. In addition, on the Democratic side the establishment dominated the Steering Committee that makes committee assignments, and it used that control to discriminate against liberals in the assignment process, thus perpetuating the establishment's dominance of the key committees beyond what its numbers or seniority would justify. The result was an insulated Senate, oriented toward maintaining the status quo. "We now stand at the beginning of the third session of what might be called a Kennedy Congress, but actually it is not a Kennedy Congress, and it seems to me that it is not going to be a Kennedy Congress," Clark said. "The principal reason why it is not going to be a Kennedy Congress, so far as the Senate is concerned, is, in my opinion, that we are operating under archaic, obsolete rules, customs, manners, procedures, and traditions—and because the operation under those obsolete and archaic setups is controlled by this oligarchical Senate establishment, a majority of the Members of which by and large are opposed to the program of the President" (ibid., 25).

Senators who find advancement of their goals stymied in the committee process have the option of taking the battle to the Senate floor. The permissiveness of Senate floor rules always makes that a possibility. To be sure, attempting to overturn committee decisions on the floor may be a violation of Senate norms. If, however, floor activism offers a senator his only chance of furthering his goals, no available sanctions are likely to be sufficient to produce conformity.

Disadvantaged by the distribution of positions of influence in the committee system, northern liberals did, to some extent, turn to the Senate floor as an alternative arena. Floor amendments that were pushed to a recorded vote became much more frequent after 1958. In the 86th Congress 204 such amendments were offered, up from 115 in the 84th Congress; the number rose to 392 in the 88th Congress.

In the 86th Congress, extreme liberals were more active on the floor than the average senator; however, extreme conservatives were marginally more active still. And, in the 88th Congress, extreme conservatives were by far the most active group, while extreme liberals were less active than moderates. The very junior character of the extreme liberal group depressed its mean activity level below what we might otherwise expect. During this period, the floor participation rate of junior members was increasing, but freshmen still participated at levels significantly below those of more senior senators.

Senators did use the floor more during this period, but it was not only the northern liberals who did so. The increase in floor activity was widespread; in both the 86th and the 88th Congresses, sixty-three senators offered at least one amendment that got to a roll call, up from forty-seven in the period before 1958 (84th Congress). The mean number of amendments offered by the floor activists also increased, from 2.4 in the 84th to 3.3 in the 86th to 6.2 in the 88th Congresses.

Although the liberal newcomers were by no means solely responsible for the increase in floor amendments, the increased floor activism was indirectly linked to the presence of the liberals and to the political forces of which they were a product. The 1958 elections signaled an end to the quiescent 1950s. The civil rights movement had been growing increasingly visible for several years and was evoking a sympathetic response among northern whites. Its demands consequently had to be taken increasingly seriously. Liberals inside and outside of the Congress interpreted the 1958 elections as a mandate for progressive policy change. In 1960, John Kennedy, running on a progressive platform, won the presidency, albeit by a narrow margin.

The change in political climate as well as the increasing numbers of liberals in the Senate affected the Senate's agenda. The contested workload grew. Only fifty-five bills were subjected to even a single roll call vote in the 84th Congress; in the 86th and 88th Congresses almost twice as many were (106 on average). In the period following 1958, more highly controversial measures reached the floor; in the 88th Congress, 10.3 percent of contested bills elicited ten or more roll call votes, up from 3.6 percent in the 84th and 4.3 percent in the 86th.

The titanic struggle over the 1964 Civil Rights Bill illustrates, in exaggerated form, the changed situation. Despite their dominant position in the committee system, conservative southern Democrats could not prevent the bill from being considered on the floor. Proponents bypassed the unsympathetic Judiciary Committee. Undeterred by norms dictating restraint, southern Democrats used every power available to senators to delay and obstruct. Over one hundred amendments were offered and forced to a roll call vote; debate stretched out over several months. Eventually the more numerous proponents, with the sizable liberal bloc at their core and backed by a determined president, prevailed. The fifty-seven day filibuster was broken and the landmark civil rights bill passed the Senate.

In that case and frequently in the mid-1960s, increased activism on the floor by conservatives was a defensive reaction to liberal policy proposals. The result of liberal policy action and conservative reaction was a more contentious Senate that made more important decisions on the floor.

Liberals' frustrations on policy matters in the late 1950s and early 1960s, so well exemplified by Clark's speech, were replaced by a sense of accomplishment in the mid-1960s, the peak years of the Great Society (see Price 1972). Structural barriers to policy change—conservatives' dominance of the key committees and of committee chairmanships, the filibuster—were overcome without being altered. Sheer numbers, a sense of mandate, and a skillful and activist president overwhelmed what had appeared to be insurmountable obstacles to progressive policy.

Liberals' great policy successes lessened the pressure for comprehensive structural change. So, almost certainly, did a piecemeal accommodation of these senators' career needs that took place during the 1960s. Certainly in part in response to pressures from the cohort of liberal Democrats that entered the Senate between 1959 and 1965, the supply of valued committee positions expanded during this period. To be sure, the number of positions on the prestige committees increased very little after the initial expansion to accommodate the class of 1958. Positions on other attractive committees, however, increased significantly from 133 in the 86th Congress to 143 in the 90th.

Probably more important to the junior liberals was the expansion in the number of subcommittees. The usefulness of subcommittee chairmanships for publicizing problems and policy proposals and for increasing a senator's visibility made them especially attractive to policy-oriented senators. The number of subcommittees grew by five from the 85th to the 86th Congresses. After decreasing in the early 1960s to the same level as in the 85th Congress, the number jumped from 91 in the 88th to 99 in the 89th and then rose to 101 in the 90th Congress. This growth all occurred on attractive committees. The service committees experienced no subcommittee expansion.

By the 90th Congress, northern Democrats were actually more likely to chair a subcommittee of a good committee than southern Democrats. In the late 1960s (1967–70), 80.6 percent of northern Democrats and 68.7 percent of southern Democrats chaired at least one good subcommittee. During the 89th Congress, only 43.7 percent of the northern Democratic cohort that entered the Senate between 1959 and 1965 had chaired good subcommittees. During the 90th Congress, 63.3 percent did, and during the 91st, 84 percent did. The increase in the supply of good subcommittees and these members' growing seniority together erased the regional disparity that had been so evident in the early and mid-1960s.

Staff, so necessary for maximizing the value of committee positions, increased during this period. From 1955 to 1965, Senate personal staff grew from 1044 to 2029; it then increased to 2428 in 1970 (U.S. Congress, House 1980, 540). In 1967, the Senate increased senators' clerk hire allowance specifically to allow senators to hire legislative assistants (*Congressional Quarterly Almanac* 1967, 511).

The piecemeal accommodation of the liberals' career needs was facilitated by Majority Leader Mike Mansfield's permissive and accommodating leadership (see Rohde, Ornstein, and Peabody 1985, 162–65). Although nominally a decision of the Senate as a whole, the size of committees is actually set by the party leaders after negotiation with their members and with each other. Mansfield's belief in the equality of all senators may also have influenced Democratic committee assignment practices (see Peabody 1981). The Democratic leader chairs the Steering Committee and appoints its members. Mansfield did use that appointive power to liberalize the Steering Committee's membership and thus make it more representative of Senate Democrats (Rohde, Ornstein, and Peabody 1985, 163–64). It was, however, senior committee leaders who determined the subcommittee structures of their committees; a significant number of them were also willing, albeit sometimes only under pressure, to accommodate their junior colleagues' career needs by creating new subcommittees.

The liberals did attempt to bring about institutional change by changing Senate rules. During the 1950s, the filibuster had come to symbolize to liberals the antidemocratic character and the status quo orientation of the Senate. In 1953 and in 1957, liberal attempts to alter Rule 22, the cloture rule, were easily defeated. The results of the 1958 elections gave the advocates of change new hope. To forestall a major revision, Majority Leader Lyndon Johnson sponsored a successful proposal altering the absolute two-thirds needed for cloture to a requirement of two-thirds of those present and voting. The liberals' proposals for significant change were defeated. During the 1960s, liberals' efforts to change Senate rules to make invoking cloture easier became a biennial ritual; each of these attempts ended in defeat.

The 1970 Legislative Reorganization Act represents a somewhat more successful effort to bring about structural change through formal rules changes. Since the 1950s, liberal reformers had been arguing for a variety of reforms aimed at reducing the power of minorities to block progressive legislation. The biennial battle over Rule 22 was only the most visible such effort. Joseph Clark, a leading reformer, repeatedly brought up a package of proposals aimed at facilitating a majority's ability to work its will (*Congressional Quarterly Almanac* 1965, 596). In his famous 1963 speech, he proposed expanding the size and changing the party ratio on the top committees to make them more representative of the increasingly liberal Democratic membership.

In 1963 Senator Clark and twenty-nine cosponsors introduced a resolution establishing a joint committee to study congressional reform (*Congressional Quarterly Almanac* 1965, 594). After amending it to prohibit the committee from proposing changes in Senate or House rules, the Senate Rules Committee favorably reported the resolution. However, Senator Richard Russell objected to considering the resolution as long as Clark proposed to delete the prohibition on rule changes on the floor. Russell's opposition was sufficient to kill the resolution and no action was taken in 1963 or 1964. The big liberal victory in the 1964 elections revived the drive for reform. The Senate and the House passed resolutions establishing the Joint Committee on the Organization of Congress. The Senate resolution stipulated that the committee could not make any recommendations about "rules, parliamentary procedure, practice and/or precedents" or "the consideration of any matter on the floor" of the Senate or House (*Congressional Quarterly Almanac* 1965, 594). Clark's attempt to delete the provision on the floor failed on a 58–29 roll call vote.

The Joint Committee, to which Clark was not appointed, held extensive hearings in 1965 and issued a comprehensive report in 1966. In 1967, the Senate passed a bill incorporating many of the committee's recommendations, but the House refused to act. Finally, in 1970, both houses passed the reform measure that became the Legislative Reorganization Act.

Clark's goal, and presumably that of an appreciable number of northern liberals, was a redistribution of influence in the chamber, one that would make the passage of progressive legislation easier. Senators for whom that was the overriding priority were, however, in the minority; only twenty-nine voted to delete the restrictions on what the Joint Committee could recommend. As Clark pointed out, by upholding these restrictions, senators were voting against the possibility of recommendations "which might conceivably overthrow the balance of power in the Senate, which is now exercised by the minority bipartisan group which I have chosen to call the Senate establishment" (*Congressional Quarterly Almanac* 1965, 595). Senator A. S. Mike Monroney, to be cochair of the Joint Committee, stated that the choice was between "Congressional reorganization within the authorization of this [resolution] or no reorganization at all" (ibid.). Then and later, Monroney justified reforms in terms of making Congress better able to handle its growing workload and to maintain its position in the political system vis-á-vis the executive branch.

The motives that led senators to support the reform effort were varied (*Congressional Quarterly Almanac* 1966, 542). The Legislative Reorganization Act that passed in 1970 was a product of compromise, both in committee and on the floor.

Given this history, it is not surprising that the act contained only modest provisions for the redistribution of influence. Although the committee did not and could not deal with the seniority system directly, the bill did place some restraints on the powers of committee chairmen. In its 1966 report, the committee had argued that "the power of the chairman is a more fundamental issue in sound committee operations than is his method of selection" (*Congressional Quarterly Almanac* 1965, 545). The act allowed a committee majority to call a meeting once the chairman had refused a request to do so, authorized the ranking majority member to preside in the chairman's absence, required committees to adopt and publish rules of committee procedure, and provided that committee reports on bills be filed within seven calendar days after a majority of the committee requested that the report be filed (*Congress and the Nation* 1973, 387–88). Various other provisions protected the rights of minority and rank-and-file committee members. Minority party members were, for example, guaranteed the right to call witnesses, and debate time on a conference report was to be divided equally between the minority and the majority. Committee members were guaranteed three days to file supplementary, minority, and additional views to be included with the committee report. A provision requiring that the committee report be available for three days before a committee could bring a measure to the floor increased the information potentially available to noncommittee members and therefore their capacity to mount a challenge on the floor.

By and large, Senate committee chairmen were not arbitrary dictators, and, by 1970, most committees provided their rank-and-file members considerable opportunities to participate (see Ripley 1969, 109–22; Fenno 1973, Chap. 5). These rules, thus, codified and strengthened existing informal practice rather than drastically altering committee procedures.

The Legislative Reorganization Act limited each member to service on no more than one of the four most prestigious committees (*Congressional Quarterly Almanac* 1970, 450). Republican conference rules had contained such a limit since 1965 (Ripley 1969, 137), but the Democrats had no such rule. In the years between the 1958 election and the passage of the act, Democrats had been assigning members to a second prestige committee with decreasing frequency. The practice, however, was not defunct; ten members were given such assignments during the six congresses, five in the 86th and 87th Congresses and five in the four succeeding congresses. The act contained a grandfather clause and thus did not actually redistribute current assignments. Still, both parties complied with this rule, and, over time, it would affect the distribution of assignments on prestige committees.

The 1970 Legislative Reorganization Act further specified that a senator could chair no more than one subcommittee of each of his major committees. This rule had little if any impact, partly because it contained a grandfather clause but also because it seems often to have been ignored.* In the two congresses immediately before the act went into effect, seven Democrats on the average chaired two or more subcommittees of a committee on which at least one majority party member chaired no subcommittee. In the three congresses after the rule went into effect, the mean was ten, of whom 5.7 appear not to have been covered by the grandfather clause.

The greatest beneficiaries of the lack of enforcement of the rule were northern Democrats who entered the Senate after 1958. In the three congresses after the rule went into effect, they made up half of the members with two subcommittee chairmanships on committees on which some majority member chaired no subcommittee, and constituted 70 percent of those not covered by the grandfather clause. These northern Democrats therefore had no incentive as a group to push for enforcement.

In sum, the provisions for the redistribution of influence of the Legislative Reorganization Act can reasonably be attributed to pressure from liberal northern Democrats. Those provisions were, however, modest in design and even more modest in impact. The liberal Democratic group that entered the Senate between 1959 and 1965 may even have contributed to limiting the impact of the rule on subcommittee chairmanships; certainly they benefited from lack of enforcement of the rule. In 1965 when the Joint Committee was established, many in that cohort still saw themselves as outsiders, disadvantaged by the system; by

---

* No distinction is made here between regular and special subcommittees because often a subcommittee will appear in one guise in one congress and, in the next congress, in the other. Thus, some of the rules violations found may technically not have been violations. It seems likely, however, that some subcommittees were designated as special so as to circumvent the rule.

1971, when the act went into effect, junior senators were still disadvantaged, but the members of the cohort entering between 1959 and 1965 were no longer junior and no longer poor in resources. Thus, during the 89th Congress, 60 percent of these senators did not hold a position on a prestige committee, and almost 60 percent lacked a good subcommittee chairmanship. By 1969–70, over half (52 percent) served on a prestige committee, and 84 percent chaired a good subcommittee.

An Assessment of the Impact of the Democratic Classes of 1958–1964 on the Senate

The liberal northern Democrats who were elected to the Senate between 1958 and 1964 produced no institutional revolution in the Senate. Rules changes during this period were modest. The transition of this large group of senators from outsiders to participants with considerable institutional resources occurred without major direct redistribution of resources.

Still, these senators did change the Senate. Their most obvious and dramatic impact was on the institution's ideological center of gravity. The influx of northern Democrats between 1959 and 1965 altered the membership from predominantly conservative to highly polarized with a large liberal contingent. That membership change made possible the burst of progressive policy change that occurred in the mid-1960s. Despite their disproportionately large share of positions of influence in the committee system, conservatives could not halt most of the civil rights and social welfare legislation of the Great Society.

Furthermore, as they accumulated seniority the northern liberals increasingly gained valued committee positions, and the distribution of such positions across ideological groups began to change. By the end of the 1960s, committee chairmen as a group were still much more conservative than the average Democratic senator, but the distribution of subcommittee chairmanships across ideological groups was much less disproportionate than in the mid-1960s.

A second, more subtle change also occurred during these years. By the end of the 1960s, the Senate was a more participatory and less committee-centered institution than it had been in the 1950s (see Ripley 1969; Rohde, Ornstein, and Peabody 1985). The demise of the apprenticeship norm, the increase in staff, and committee chairmen's more restrained use of their powers made it easier for less senior senators to participate meaningfully in the legislative process. So too did the expansion in the supply of valued committee positions and their somewhat broader distribution. These changes were the result of membership change. Because of their electoral insecurity and their commitment to policy change, the liberals could not afford politically, nor were they willing, to wait before participating. Pressure from this large group produced a number of small changes that culminated in institutional change.

The Senate of the late 1960s was also less committee centered than the Senate of the period before 1958. During the 1960s, the intense, ideologically charged battles over Great Society legislation frequently spilled over on to the floor. These were not the sort of issues that committees could settle to the satisfaction of the full membership, especially since so many committees were ideologically unrepresentative. Both liberals and conservatives used the floor to alter the work of or circumvent altogether unsympathetic committees. As a result, norms of specialization and restraint were somewhat weakened. The extreme committee autonomy of the 1950s no longer characterized Senate decision making by the end of the 1960s.

4 // The Transformation of the Washington Policy Community

During the 1960s and 1970s the Washington policy community underwent a transformation that resulted in a major change in the U.S. Senate. The combination of an expanded issue agenda, the explosive growth of interest groups, and the increased role of the media in the policy process produced a new Washington policy community, one that rewards senators for different forms of behavior than did the old policy system. This chapter documents that transformation and shows how it provided incentives for senators to change their behavior.

The Expansion of the Issue Agenda

The political agenda can be defined as the set of problems and policy proposals being seriously debated by the attentive public and by policy makers.* The number of people concerned and the intensity of their concern varies across issues on the agenda. Some issues engage the attention only of a relatively small set of specialists in and out of government; others are of intense concern to millions of ordinary citizens. Consequently, the political agenda is best conceptualized as roughly pyramidal, with a limited number of highly salient issues at the top and an increasing number of progressively less and less salient issues toward the base.

---

* This section is heavily based on Sinclair, *Congressional Realignment*. See also Kingdon 1984.

Over time, the identity of the issues toward the top of the agenda will, of course, vary. In addition, the number of such issues may also vary. A major expansion of the issue agenda, I contend, contributed critically to the transformation of the Washington policy community.

The political agenda of the 1950s showed strong continuity with the agenda of the early postwar years; it also displayed considerable stability over the course of the decade. The agenda of the 1950s included few issues highly salient to the general public, and, even in terms of issues of concern to broad attentive publics, it was fairly narrow by later standards.

In the area of foreign and defense policy, here called international involvement (see Clausen 1973), the agenda narrowed and became less contentious from the 1940s to the 1950s. During the early part of the presidency of Harry Truman, the shape of American postwar foreign policy was at issue. During the latter part, the conduct of the Korean War was a matter of controversy. Among policy makers and the small portion of the public attentive to foreign policy issues, the cold war consensus had a firm hold by the early 1950s; the containment policy developed under Truman and its underlying premises regarding the necessity of an active U.S. role to counter an expansionist Soviet Union were widely accepted. When President Dwight Eisenhower settled the Korean War early in his first term, foreign policy questions receded in saliency among the general public. The range of opinion among political elites was sufficiently narrow that much of foreign and defense policy moved beyond debate. The issues on which there were differences of opinion—the details of the foreign aid program, for example—were ones that engaged the attention primarily of policy specialists.

In the broad area of government management of the economy, the issue agenda of the Eisenhower years shows strong continuity with that of the Truman period. The basic shape of that debate, the question of how much responsibility the federal government should assume for the management of the economy, dates back to the New Deal, as did many of the more specific programs and policy proposals at issue in the 1950s. Controversy centered on the tax code, specifically its progressivity, on the use of public works for pump priming, and on the issue of public versus private power.

The only new issue to attain a place on the agenda was the matter of special aid to depressed areas. During the postwar years, it became increasingly clear that, even when the overall employment level was high, concentrated pockets of severe unemployment remained. In 1955 the Democratic majority of the Joint Economic Committee proposed a program to aid such chronically depressed areas. The major elements were long-term credit and technical assistance for new industry, a public works program, and subsidized retraining of jobless workers (Sundquist 1968, 63). Although new in the narrow sense, the proposal for aid to depressed areas clearly grew out of the policy thrust of the New Deal. It, like other issues in the government management area, evoked considerable, primarily partisan conflict among policy makers and interested political elites but did not engage the attention of broader publics.

Debate on agricultural policy throughout the 1950s followed the familiar lines drawn during the New Deal. The Eisenhower administration's determined attempt to reorient farm policy imparted a higher level of intensity to the old conflict over high rigid price supports versus lower flexible supports (Sinclair 1982, 67–69, 81–82). This was, however, a conflict that engaged the attention of only a small group of participants with a direct material interest in the outcome.

The social welfare agenda during the Eisenhower years also shows strong continuity with that of the Truman administration. The basic debate over how much responsibility the federal government should assume for helping individuals directly stems from the New Deal, and most of the more specific issues at controversy during the 1950s are also traceable to the 1930s. Public housing, the regulation of labor unions, and the raising of the minimum wage were the most contentious of the continuing issues. The only relatively new element added to the social welfare agenda during this period was general aid to education. Broadly debated in the immediate postwar years, it moved to the center of conflict during the 1950s (*Congress and the Nation* 1965, 1195–1215).

The stability, continuity with the past, and low saliency that generally characterized the issue agenda of the 1950s are least descriptive of the domain of issues involving civil liberties. Early in the decade, concern over subversive activities and over McCarthyism were the dominant issues, at least among political elites; although the issue continued on the agenda through the 1950s, Senate censure of Joseph McCarthy in late 1954 greatly reduced its saliency. Civil rights for blacks, which had regained agenda status in the late 1930s, was a continuing issue but one with little saliency beyond the participants and those directly affected. For decades, a small group of civil rights proponents consisting primarily of the National Association for the Advancement of Colored People and its congressional allies had waged a lonely and losing struggle against powerful southerners in the Congress. The hopelessness of breaking a Senate filibuster had, in fact, led proponents to shift their efforts away from the Congress. However, the 1954 Supreme Court decision declaring school segregation unconstitutional and, later in the decade, the growing civil rights movement thrust the issue to the center of controversy. In the late 1950s civil rights became a highly salient issue and the movement's struggles elicited sympathetic concern in the North. Thus, in 1957, segregation headed the list of most important issues in the Gallup Poll (Gallup October 1971, 57).

In the early 1960s, the civil rights movement became increasingly active and visible. The spring and summer of 1963 saw a series of massive demonstrations, culminating in the August march on Washington. Southern reprisals against black protests, made vivid to millions by extensive television coverage, shocked the nation. As a result, the civil rights issue, which had waned somewhat, again became highly salient among the general public and remained so through mid-decade (Nie, Verba, and Petrocik 1976, 100–103).

Broad public support provided an impetus to action. The weak but symbolically important civil rights acts of 1957 and 1960 were followed by strong and comprehensive legislation in 1964 and 1965. With the passage of these bills—which prohibited discrimination in public accommodations, in employment, and in federally funded programs, and enacted meaningful voting rights guarantees—the character of civil rights issues began to change. Civil rights advocates' demands for further progress involved much more intrusive federal action; open housing legislation and strengthened equal employment enforcement powers, for example, would potentially directly affect northern middle-class whites. In the mid-1960s, with the issuance and enforcement of school desegregation guidelines by the Department of Health, Education, and Welfare, busing became a major issue.

Ghetto riots, antiwar protests, crime, and changing lifestyles among youth added still another set of salient issues to the civil liberties agenda in the late 1960s. These manifested themselves in a diversity of conflicts—battles over the appropriate response to civil disobedience, controversy over whether crime should be treated as a social problem or whether tougher criminal penalties and less attention to procedural rights were the answer, and campaigns to legalize marijuana.

For most of modern American history and through the mid-1960s, civil rights meant civil rights for blacks. In the late 1960s and throughout the 1970s, rights for an increasing number of other groups attained a place on the agenda. The rights of women, of various racial and ethnic groups, especially Latinos and Native Americans, of the young, the old, the poor, and the physically disabled became issues. Of the many specific issues stemming from these broad new concerns, the Equal Rights Amendment and the Legal Services Corporation occasioned an especially high intensity of conflict.

By the early 1970s, then, the civil liberties agenda was broader and included more highly salient and contentious issues than it had in the

1950s. To the issue of civil rights for blacks in the South were added the issues of busing and affirmative action, of how to combat crime and social unrest, and of the rights of a seemingly ever-expanding list of groups. Nor did most of these issues fade during the 1970s. With the end of ghetto riots and antiwar protests, urban unrest and public disorder receded as issues but crime remained a continuing matter of concern. More groups, including such unpopular claimants as homosexuals, demanded rights. The Supreme Court's legalizing of abortion added another highly divisive issue to the agenda.

Major change in the agenda of social welfare issues can be dated to the mid-1960s. With the introduction and passage of the Economic Opportunity Act of 1964, that agenda was permanently altered. President Lyndon Johnson's antipoverty program, of which the 1964 act was an important but not the only component, was a true departure from past social welfare policy because its intent was specifically to aid the poor minority in a comprehensive fashion. The thrust of previous major social welfare legislation had been to help the nonrich majority. The new thrust was never fully accepted, and antipoverty programs and proposals remained highly controversial throughout the 1970s and into the 1980s.

Other Great Society legislation significantly expanded the federal role in a number of areas. General aid to education, as well as a myriad of special education programs, Medicare/Medicaid legislation, aid to the arts and humanities, and urban mass transit subsidies were among the new programs. Some of these extensions of the federal role were highly controversial and others provoked much less disagreement; some continued to be contentious, while others became broadly accepted. However, the reach of these programs is so broad and so many people— clients, service providers, state and local elected officials and administrators—are affected that the existence of the programs permanently expanded the agenda. Those affected by the programs have a major continuing interest in not only the broad shape but also the details of the programs.

During the 1970s several other issues were added to the agenda of social welfare issues. Welfare reform was a periodically salient issue that was never resolved. After a considerable period of time on the agenda, Congress passed a public service employment program. The Comprehensive Employment and Training Act (CETA) was controversial at its inception and continued to provoke controversy until it was killed early in the Reagan administration. Even that did not settle the issue of job training and job creation, which remains on the agenda.

While the social welfare agenda expanded to include new issues, old controversies did not fade away. The minimum wage and the regulation of labor unions and of collective bargaining continued to provoke controversy.

In the mid- and late 1960s, the government management of the economy agenda underwent a change as environmental issues and consumer protection made their way onto the agenda. By 1970, environmental issues had become highly salient to the public at large. Thus a 1970 Harris Poll found that 41 percent mentioned air and water pollution as one of the problems Congress should do something about. In 1971, 72 percent chose pollution in response to a similar question. Over 80 percent of the respondents in both years favored increased government spending on pollution control (Harris 1970, 46, 48; 1971, 55, 58). This issue remained among the most frequently mentioned in 1972 and 1973.

Between the mid-1960s and mid-1970s, the Congress passed a spate of legislation that greatly expanded the federal government's role in protecting the consumer and the environment, frequently through regulating business. The Traffic Safety Act of 1966, which mandated performance standards for autos and tires; the Clean Air Act of 1970, which forced the development and use of new technologies; and the 1972 Consumer Product Safety Act, which made the Consumer Product Safety Commission a permanent regulatory agency, are only the most prominent examples. The passage of this legislation permanently altered and expanded the agenda. As was the case in the area of social welfare, the broad reach of the legislation assured these issues a continuing place on the agenda.

The 1970s saw an expansion of the government management agenda in other directions as well. The state of the economy is a cyclical issue, becoming salient to the general public when the economy is not performing well. During the 1970s and early 1980s, recurrent bouts of high inflation, frequently in combination with weak economic growth and high unemployment, assured that the economy would often be the most salient of issues. The 1973 Arab oil embargo thrust energy to the center of the agenda, and high energy prices and the fear of supply disruptions kept it on the agenda.

Even in the relatively narrow area of agricultural policy, the agenda began to change in the late 1960s. The size of subsidy payments to individual farmers became an issue, with conflict revolving around setting ceilings. In the 1970s environmental concerns increasingly intruded into the agricultural policy area; pesticide control, for example, became a major issue. High inflation, including soaring food prices, and the growing federal deficit made agricultural policy per se more broadly contentious. The expensive subsidy program was no longer perceived as a purely distributive policy that helped farmers without cost to anyone else.

In the area of international involvement, the Vietnam War led to a fundamental transformation of the agenda. The war that two presidents could neither win nor end shattered the postwar foreign policy consensus. In the late 1960s and early 1970s, the war itself was a highly salient issue to the general public as well as among political elites. Among the politically attentive, opposition to the war led many to reappraise the direction of United States foreign and defense policy more generally. Assumptions that had been widely accepted were questioned, and previously uncontroversial matters provoked heated debate. The size of the military budget, the need for a variety of expensive and deadly new weapons systems, aid to repressive regimes, and the United States role in the Third World were brought into question. These issues did not fade with the end of the Vietnam War; no new consensus emerged, and foreign and defense policy questions continued to excite controversy, usually among attentive publics but sometimes in the general public as well, throughout the 1970s and into the 1980s. Thus, by the early 1970s, the agenda of issues concerning international involvement had become not only highly conflictual but also much broader than it had been in the 1950s and early 1960s.

Growth and Change in Interest Groups

Between the 1950s and the 1980s, the number and diversity of interest groups involved in the Washington policy process grew explosively. The 1981 edition of *Washington Representatives* lists almost 7,000 organizations as having an ongoing presence in Washington (Schlozman and Tierney 1986, 66–67). These are organizations that maintain a Washington office or hire counsel or consultants on retainer. Many groups and organizations occasionally active in Washington but without a continuous presence are not listed. By the late 1970s, *Time* magazine estimated that the number of Washington lobbyists stood at 15,000. More than 4,000 individual corporations keep representatives in Washington; the District of Columbia Bar has over 37,000 members; and 247 out-of-town law firms have branch offices in Washington (U.S. Congress, Senate 1986, 25).

Reliable data on the earlier universe of Washington interest groups do not exist. One count estimated the number of organizations at 1,180 in 1947–48 (Salisbury 1984, 72–73). If that figure is taken at face value, the increase has been almost sevenfold. Several recent studies of group representation in Washington provide some evidence to substantiate the widespread impression of an explosion in numbers. Schlozman and Tierney report that, of the groups listed in *Washington Representatives 1981* as having their own Washington offices, 40 percent had been founded since 1960 and 25 percent since 1970 (1986, 75). Jack Walker's study of membership associations concerned with some aspect of national public policy produced quite similar findings: the 1960s and 1970s were years of rapid growth in the number of groups. Approximately 30 percent of the groups in his sample originated between 1960 and 1980 (1983, 395). Schlozman and Tierney's study also shows that the 1960s and 1970s saw increasing numbers of organizations establishing Washington offices.* Of the organizations included in their sample, 61 percent had opened a Washington office since 1960 and 38 percent since 1970. Over a third (36 percent) consisted of organizations that had existed in 1960 but had established a Washington office since that time (1986, 81). The available evidence points to the 1960s and 1970s as a period in which a great number of new groups were formed, while many existing organizations perceived it to be in their interest to establish offices in the nation's capital for the first time.

As the universe of interest groups was expanding, it was also becoming a great deal more diverse. Organizations representing economic interest—corporations, trade associations, farm groups, and unions—were joined by more groups speaking for the disadvantaged and by groups representing diffuse and often noneconomic interests, such as environmental preservation. Between 1960 and 1980, Walker found, citizens' groups multiplied at twice the rate of all types of occupationally based groups (1983, 394–95). According to Schlozman and Tierney's data,

> seventy-six percent of the citizens' groups, 56 percent of the civil rights groups, and 79 percent of the social welfare and poor people's organizations but only 38 percent of the trade associations and 14 percent of the corporations were founded since 1960. In addition, 57 percent of the citizen's groups and 51 percent of the social welfare and poor people's organizations but only 23 percent of the trade and other business associations and 6 percent of the corporations were founded since 1970. These figures confirm the observation that there has been an explosion in the number of groups representing the interests of broad publics and the disadvantaged (1986, 75).

The growth of the intergovernmental lobby and the rise in the number of lobbyists hired by foreign governments have further expanded the range of interests directly represented in the Washington

---

* Their sampling of organizations with a Washington office overrepresented organizations that were especially active in the policy process.

policy process. Although cities, counties, and states enjoy a presence in Washington by virtue of membership in organizations such as the National League of Cities, many of the larger entities have also established an individual presence, often with a permanent office. For example, over two-thirds of the states were individually represented in Washington as of the early 1980s (Schlozman and Tierney 1986, 56). Organizations representing the interests of functional specialists such as highway engineers or county welfare directors are a growing part of the intergovernmental lobby (ibid.). Increasingly, individual government agencies, for example, the Kansas City Board of Public Utilities, also have a presence in Washington. As of 1982, foreign governments were represented by approximately 1,000 registered agents (ibid., 54; see also U.S. Congress, Senate 1986, 27–28).

This transformation of the interest group universe and the expansion of the issue agenda discussed earlier are obviously related, but in a highly complex fashion. The civil rights movement was instrumental in thrusting black civil rights to the center of the agenda in the late 1950s and early 1960s. It also served as an exemplar for the other social movements of the 1960s. The Chicano movement, the women's movement, the handicapped rights movement, and the homosexual rights movement probably owe their very existence to the civil rights movement. Although it developed in response to the Vietnam War, the antiwar movement also owed much to the civil rights movement. The environmental and consumer movements of the late 1960s developed within and probably were dependent upon the climate of political mobilization that the civil rights movement did much to create. These two movements especially but a number of the others as well depended also upon the post–World War II growth of a large affluent middle class receptive to quality of life issues and other noneconomic appeals.

These movements were instrumental in projecting a large number of new issues onto the political agenda. Furthermore, the social movements of the 1960s spawned new groups and reinvigorated existing ones. The presence of such formally organized groups then made it less likely that the concern at issue would slip from the agenda once the initial enthusiasm of the movement was spent. These organized groups, usually headquartered in Washington, worked to maintain their issue's position on the agenda. That many groups found sources of financing other than membership dues made the groups' existence less vulnerable to variations in the saliency of their issue (see Walker 1983, 397–401).

From the mid-1960s through the early 1970s a body of legislation that immensely expanded the role of the federal government was passed. Some of the new programs, such as general aid to education and medical care for the elderly, represented the culmination of the New Deal policy thrust; others, including civil rights and environmental legislation, were a response to the social movements of the 1960s. But whatever its origins, the consequence of this legislation was that far more people were now more directly affected by the actions of the federal government. In response, a myriad of groups of the affected formed or, if already in existence, became more active in lobbying in Washington. This process of group formation and activation produced various organizations of direct recipients of government programs. Of the forty-six groups representing the elderly in Walker's study, for example, over half were formed after 1965, the year Medicare and the Older Americans Act were passed (1983, 403). Service deliverers both private and public frequently organized or became more active. For example, the Medicare/Medicaid program increased hospitals' stake in federal government decision making, giving the American Hospital Association, a trade association of both public and private hospitals, strong reasons to increase its activity in Washington. The name of the National Association of Student Financial Aid Administrators suggests that the group was formed as a response to new federal programs. Many of the social and economic programs passed in the 1960s and early 1970s are administered by state and local governments, strengthening the incentives for those entities to maintain an organized presence in Washington.

The success of consumer and environmental groups in winning passage of regulatory legislation in the late 1960s and early 1970s led to a counter-mobilization by business. This legislation brought federal government intrusion into what had been private business decisions. Consequently, more corporations had a larger stake in federal government decisions. Furthermore, business felt under attack and on the defensive during this period. In the 1950s, due at least in part to the sparsity of serious competitors, business occupied a privileged position; businessmen frequently did not have to play an active part in Washington policy making because their interests were so seldom threatened (Wilson 1981, 58). The rise of consumer and environmental groups, their domination of the agenda, and their very considerable legislative success led many in the business community to decide that a stronger and more skillful presence was needed.

The mobilization of business took several forms. Increasing numbers of individual corporations set up Washington offices. As late as 1961, the giant multinational International Telephone and Telegraph (ITT) did not maintain a Washington office (Wilson 1981, 56). Between 1968 and 1978, the number of corporations with Washington public affairs offices rose from 100 to over 500 (Berry 1984, 20). Other firms upgraded existing offices; for example, General Motors increased its Washington office staff from three to twenty-eight between 1968 and 1978 (ibid., 22). Meanwhile, new trade associations formed, and existing ones moved to Washington and increased their activity.

Another thrust of the mobilization of business involved the creation of an important new peak association and the revitalization of the major existing peak associations. The Business Roundtable, a lobbying group consisting of approximately 200 chief executive officers of Fortune 500 firms, was founded in 1972 (see Wilson 1981, 78–79). The National Association of Manufacturers and the Chamber of Commerce, the older associations that claimed to represent the interests of business generally, were perceived as rigidly ideological and not very influential in the 1950s and 1960s (ibid., 58–59). Both increased their staffs and became more aggressive in lobbying during the 1970s (Berry 1984, 40). The Chamber of Commerce, through skillful use of sophisticated new technologies, has become a much more formidable participant in the Washington policy process (ibid., 154–55; Wilson 1981, 76–77).

The 1970s saw a second countermobilization. In response to liberal advances in the 1960s and early 1970s, a variety of opposing groups organized or revitalized. The New Right includes many opposed to the sort of government intrusion into the economy that much of the new regulatory legislation entailed and those who hold to older cold war notions of American foreign policy. The newer element of the New Right, however, is the often religious-based opposition to social change that manifests itself in controversy over the so-called social issues—busing, prayer in the schools, family issues generally, the Equal Rights Amendment, and gay rights. Of the many new groups expressing this point of view the Moral Majority, founded in 1979 by television preacher Jerry Falwell, is probably the best known. A number of anti-abortion groups sprang up in response to the 1973 Supreme Court decision legalizing abortion, and opposition to abortion is a central tenet of all New Christian Right groups.

Thus, between the 1950s and the 1980s, the universe of interest groups expanded in both size and diversity. Clearly not all of the participants are groups in the traditional sense. Many are corporations, subnational government entities, and institutions such as universities (Salisbury 1984). Nor do all of the citizens' groups, in fact, have members.

Even using the term broadly, there are other new participants in the Washington policy process that cannot be labeled interest groups. Think tanks, for example, usually do not lobby directly, but, by providing expertise and intellectual legitimacy, they may significantly influence the policy process. Both the number of think tanks and their ideological diversity have increased. The Brookings Institution has been joined by the Institute for Policy Studies on the left, the American Enterprise Institute on the center right, and the Heritage Foundation on the far right. In addition to such broad-gauge think tanks, ones that focus on a narrower set of concerns have also proliferated. For example, a compilation in the early 1980s identified twenty women-oriented research centers that study a wide range of issues affecting women (Deckard 1983, 380–81). By 1987, there were fifty-one think tanks based in the Washington area (*Washington Post National Weekly Edition,* May 4, 1987, 35).

Political action committees (PACs) are still another new and important, if indirect, participant in the Washington policy process. The growth in the number of PACs is too well known to belabor; between 1974 and 1982, the number in existence increased from about 600 to almost 3,400 (Berry 1984, 23–24). Many PACs are arms of organizations that also do lobbying. Thus, 101 of 175 organizations in Schlozman and Tierney's sample of groups active in lobbying in Washington had PACs (1986, 226). Having a PAC provides these organizations with another tactic for attempting to influence the policy process. There are also independent PACs not associated with any other organization, the National Conservative Political Action Committee (NCPAC) being the most notorious.

In addition to the regular participants in the Washington policy process, there are very large numbers of groups and individuals sporadically involved. All sorts of organizations without a continuous Washington presence—corporations, governmental and quasi-governmental entities, professional associations, and the myriad and rapidly increasing number of local citizens' groups—also sometimes become involved in the process (see Berry 1984, 22; Schlozman and Tierney 1986, 66). The great reach of federal government policy increases the likelihood that such groups will at some point perceive a vital interest to be at stake.

The growth of a large, educated, affluent middle class and technological developments in communications and computers have combined to greatly increase the number of individuals sporadically involved in the Washington policy process. The post–World War II development of a large, educated, and affluent middle class has often been posited as a necessary condition for the development of public interest groups that occurred in the late 1960s and early 1970s. Education provides both skills and a sense of political efficacy; affluence, the luxury to be concerned with issues not directly economic, and sufficient personal wealth to make membership dues inconsequential. Common Cause founder John Gardner built up a membership of 230,000 in little more than a year (Berry 1984, 29). Of course, most middle-class people, however defined, are not members of public interest groups, and most members of such groups do no more than pay their dues. Nevertheless groups like Common Cause and the Sierra Club have significant numbers of active members and much larger numbers that can be activated occasionally (see Wilson 1981, 117-19).

A number of technological developments—WATS lines, faster and cheaper computers—have made it easier for groups to activate their members. The use of grass-roots techniques is by no means confined to citizens' groups. Business interests have made extensive use of the full range of grass-roots tactics from bringing local businessmen to Washington to lobby to massive letter writing campaigns (see Schlozman and Tierney 1986, 184-97). The Chamber of Commerce, with its own private, closed-circuit television network, BIZNET, is pioneering new techniques for grass-roots mobilization. The new technologies that make it easier for groups to mobilize their members in a timely fashion can also be used to mobilize the unorganized around some issue. Banks, savings and loans, and their trade associations, through a highly sophisticated public relations campaign, generated an avalanche of mail to Capitol Hill in 1983 urging repeal of the newly passed withholding tax on interest and dividend income (ibid., 190). The technology of direct mail makes it possible to identify and reach those likely to hold a particular position on any given issue. The emotional appeals typically used are aimed at activating the recipients and are particularly likely to be successful if tied to highly salient current events (see Berry 1984, 86).

The media, through their coverage of an issue, may stimulate a segment of the public to engage in political acts. As the affluent, educated middle class grew, so did the attentive public, that segment of the population that regularly attends to public affairs. Between 1952 and 1972, the proportion of adult Americans with some college education effectively doubled from 15 to 29 percent (Miller et al. 1981, 2); the proportion reporting that they had written a letter expressing an opinion to a public official rose from 17 percent in 1964 to 27 percent in 1972 (ibid., 305). It is attentive publics—those people who regularly follow public affairs in general or those who pay close attention on certain issues—that are most likely to be politically activated by media coverage or by group appeals. And these are primarily, though not exclusively, well-educated and affluent members of the middle class. Occasionally, however, media coverage—especially television—of an issue will result in very widespread concern and in a broader mobilization.

In sum, the number and the diversity of actors engaged in the Washington policy process has increased immensely since the 1950s. As a result, there are now few policy areas in which all the organized interests are in agreement; conflict rather than consensus is the norm (see

Schlozman and Tierney 1986, 284–86). The set of significant actors in a given policy dispute is not only likely to be larger and more diverse than it used to be, it is also less predictable, and consequently the lines of conflict are less stable. When, for example, consumer or environmental groups become involved in agricultural policy, they not only increase the level of conflict but change the terms of the debate. The existence of a broad range of sporadically participating actors further decreases predictability, as does the existence of an ill-defined but large number of groups and individuals that can potentially be mobilized. The result is a much less bounded system.

This change in the universe of interest groups has greatly increased the demands on Congress. In attempting to influence the policy process, some groups use the courts and many lobby the executive branch. The primary target, however, is Congress (see Schlozman and Tierney 1986, 272–73). Groups, of course, want favorable policy decisions but, given the multitude of demands on the time and attention of congressmen, groups must also concern themselves with just what gets on the agenda. The change in the universe of interest groups has resulted in a fierce struggle for space on an increasingly crowded congressional agenda. As the next section will discuss, this struggle for space on the agenda is one factor contributing to the enhanced role of the media in the policy process.

The Role of the Media

In the 1970s and 1980s, the media play a greater role in the political process than they did in the 1950s. There is much more media coverage of political Washington, especially of Congress, and that coverage reaches a much bigger audience. Between 1960 and 1976, the number of radio and television journalists accredited to the congressional press galleries grew by 175 percent to about 600; the number of print journalists increased by 37 percent to approximately 1,100 (Robinson 1981, 83). Approximately 10,000 news journalists representing more than 3,000 news organizations were operating in Washington as of the mid-1980s (Linsky 1986, 3).

Until 1963, the television networks broadcast one fifteen-minute news show per day. These were "essentially radio newscasts read in front of cameras" (Ranney 1983, 66). Film and graphics were seldom used; the shows consisted primarily of reporters reading news items culled from the wire services or from newspapers. In 1963, the networks expanded their evening news shows to 30 minutes, and budgets were increased, thus immediately doubling the amount of coverage and beginning the process of making the newscasts visually compelling. The 1960s and early 1970s provided the dramatic events that brought out television's potential for presenting the news with a vividness, immediacy, and impact the print media could not match. The Kennedy assassinations, civil rights marches, urban rioting, the Vietnam War, and the Watergate hearings were extensively covered on television, and, as a result, their impact was probably heightened (Rubin 1981, 150). The amount of news coverage by the networks has also expanded with the addition of the morning news shows and of regular late night newscasts.

The audience, potential and actual, for television news has grown explosively since the early 1950s. In 1950, only 9 percent of American homes had a television set. By 1955, this had shot up to 65 percent; by 1960, to 87 percent. By the 1970s, almost all households—95 percent—had at least one television (Ranney 1983, 8).

Television has become the major source of news for most Americans. The nightly network news shows have an audience of approximately 50 million viewers (Rubin 1981, 152). According to Roper polls, Americans' reliance on television as their principal source of news has increased. In 1959, 29 percent reported getting most of their news from television alone; by 1982, this increased to 46 percent. Those who relied upon newspapers alone decreased from 31 to 24 percent during this period (Ladd 1985, 486). By margins of about two to one, people trusted television news above that reported in newspapers (ibid., 490).

To be sure, the news content of the nightly network news shows is often meager and the presentation fragmented, while the morning shows contain more entertainment than news. Nevertheless, more people are now exposed to national news than in the past. Those who now rely primarily upon television probably did not closely follow newspaper coverage of national affairs in the past.

Because of their organizational structure, the networks' news shows are, of course, national in focus. In fact, network television news is much more national in outlook than newspaper news and also much more political. Comparing lead stories in newspapers and on television, Richard Rubin found that in 1963 about 60 percent of the top stories on television were political and that the proportion increased to about 80 percent by 1975. In contrast, only a little over 25 percent of the top stories in newspapers were political, and there was no trend over time (Rubin 1981, 152–54). Rubin concludes, "Network television focuses its audiences' interest not only on national stories but on stories that are linked to either national political figures or institutions" (ibid., 152).

More narrowly focused media that reach attentive or specialized publics have also grown. By 1960, all three networks had established a

Sunday interview show. Although their current audience of two to four million households each is small by television standards, the elite character of the audience and the frequency with which the interviews are quoted in other news outlets magnifies their impact (*Los Angeles Times,* October 21, 1985). The "MacNeil/Lehrer Report," which focused upon one story each night and thus could treat it in some depth, began broadcasting five nights per week on the Public Broadcasting System in the mid-1970s. In the early 1980s, it became an hour-long news show. Its viewership averaged 1.5 to two million viewers per show by 1986; eleven million people viewed the "MacNeil/Lehrer News Hour" at least once a week (*Los Angeles Times,* September 9, 1986). C-SPAN, a cable network that broadcasts the House of Representatives' floor sessions as well as committee hearings, press conferences, and other political events in Washington, came into existence in the late 1970s.

Highly specialized print media also have burgeoned. A response to the growth of governmental activities, they provide specialized information to affected constituencies (see Hess 1981, 33–34). A 1977 survey found that almost one-fourth of Washington reporters worked for such publications (ibid.), an indication of their proliferation.

Most people, then, are regularly exposed to national news via television and will quickly become aware of highly dramatic or dramaticized events and issues. The growing attentive public has available to it a great deal of information conveyed by both print and electronic media.

Because of the increase in media coverage, political decision makers and other key actors in the Washington political community operate in a very different environment than did their counterparts in the 1950s. It is a more open environment, one in which their activities are more likely to be subject to public scrutiny. The explosion in the number of groups makes more policy decisions conflictual and therefore newsworthy. The change in journalistic norms that has made the national media tougher has also contributed to creating this more open environment (see Robinson 1981).

When combined with congressional rules changes that opened up committee mark-up sessions and conference committees, the greater media attention has made congressional decision making a more public enterprise and has made it more difficult for established actors to exclude new entrants completely. Openness aids less advantaged actors because it makes it easier for them to get the timely information necessary for effective action. In fact, citizens' groups (and the media) were important allies of congressional reformers in their successful effort to open congressional mark-ups and conference committees to the public (McFarland 1984, 111, 171). Media attention may also alert previously uninvolved groups and individuals that their interests are at stake and result in their becoming participants. The openness that more media coverage has helped to create thus enhances the unbounded and fluid character of the Washington policy community.

Changes in the political environment, even more than changes in the media themselves, have enhanced the role of the media in agenda setting broadly defined. The media can be an extremely useful tool for publicizing a previously unrecognized problem, for shaping debate on an issue, and for moving an issue up on the agenda and forcing it to a decision. The interrelated explosion in the number of groups and the number of issues during the 1960s and early 1970s immensely increased competition for space on the agenda. To convince decision makers that they should attend to a given issue requires convincing them there is a cost (perhaps electoral) to not attending or a benefit from doing so. And that requires convincing them that a large number of people, or at least people particularly important to the advancement of their goals, are concerned with the issue. Media can help create that concern or the appearance of it.

Civil rights provides the most spectacular early example of television's impact upon the political agenda. Because civil rights forces needed northern public support, their tactics were intentionally dramatic. "The civil rights movement would have been like a bird without wings if it hadn't been for the news media," said John Lewis, a leader of the 1965 march on Selma. Heavy television coverage brought sit-ins and marches as well as southern reprisals into living rooms across the country and raised civil rights to the center of the political agenda. In a poll taken in late 1960, 46 percent said that the new president and the new Congress should "do more to end segregation" (Gallup October 1972, 170). By mid-1963, after the massive and heavily covered march on Washington, over half the respondents to a Gallup Poll named civil rights as the most important problem facing the American people, and race remained among the most frequently mentioned problems throughout 1964 and 1965 (Nie, Verba, and Petrocik 1976, 102–103). The high saliency of civil rights pressured decision makers to act. Almost certainly, it was a necessary condition for overcoming the structural barriers, especially the Senate filibuster, that had prevented real policy change.

The lessons inherent in the civil rights movement's successful use of the media to influence the political agenda were widely learned. The movements of the 1960s played to the television cameras. Adeptness at staging media events became an important strategic skill for those attempting to focus attention on an issue. The citizens and consumer groups that formed in the late 1960s and early 1970s were highly dependent upon the media, print as well as television, to spread their message and thereby generate pressure for action (see Pertschuk 1982, 32–36). Reporters found these groups' issues intrinsically newsworthy, and many group leaders—Ralph Nader and John Gardner, for example—proved to be extremely skillful at presenting their case in a fashion attractive to the media (ibid., 32–33; McFarland 1984, 82–83, 126–127).

Because of its reach and impact, television coverage can make an issue into a highly salient national concern almost overnight, the burgeoning of the drug issue in 1986 after the cocaine-related deaths of two young star athletes being a recent example. When an issue becomes hot, both incentives and pressures to action are created.

Much agenda-setting activity is aimed at narrower audiences—the attentive public, specialized issue publics, and segments of the Washington policy community. Stories and Op-Ed pieces in the prestige press—the *Washington Post,* the *New York Times* and the *Wall Street Journal*—and appearances on the Sunday interview shows or the Mac-Neil/Lehrer show can serve to focus the attention of these narrower audiences on an issue or shape the character of debate on a policy controversey. Because the Washington policy community is so much larger than it used to be, and because there is so much competition for its members' attention, the media are an increasingly important communications channel and focusing device. Furthermore, the attentive public is now so large that the mobilization of a relatively modest segment—to write their congressman, for example—represents a significant expansion of the conflict and exerts considerable pressure on decision makers.

Most if not all the participants in the policy process have strong incentives to attempt to use the media to focus attention, to shape debate, and to build pressure towards action. Even actors that formerly preferred insider strategies because of privileged access to decision makers (that is, well-connected, establishment groups) or to congressional agendas (that is, committee leaders) are pushed into using outsider strategies. Since the debate in public arenas may so define the alternatives that the congressional committee's choices are narrowly constrained, committee leaders have an incentive to participate in that public debate.

The Washington policy process, in sum, is a much more open and public process than it used to be.

The Impact on Senators' Goal-Directed Calculus

Between the 1950s and the 1980s, a new Washington policy system emerged. The new system is much more open, less bounded, and less stable. It is characterized by a much larger number and greater diversity of significant actors, by more fluid and less predictable lines of conflict, and, consequently, by a much more intense struggle over space on the agenda.

By the early 1970s, the environment in which senators pursued their goals had changed sufficiently to alter their goal-directed calculus. The explosive growth in groups and in issues has greatly increased the demands made of senators, and, as long as they can be met, more demands translate into opportunities useful to senators in the advancement of their goals. The demands that groups make of senators are not just for support but increasingly for active leadership. The intense struggle over space on the agenda that characterizes the new system makes senators ideal allies within it. They have direct access to authoritative decision-making arenas, and they can command media attention. As a result, senators are better situated than any other class of political actor except the president to take a prominent part in the agenda-setting process.

Senate rules and customs make it possible for a rank-and-file senator to affect the congressional agenda in a way no ordinary House member can. A senator can use his committee positions, especially any subcommittee chairmanships, and the Senate floor to focus the attention of relevant members of the Washington policy community and of specialized publics on an issue. In addition, such activities may result in media coverage, and if they do, concern may spread beyond narrow publics. This may increase the pressure for action. Conversely, media attention to an issue may stimulate hearings and floor activity, which may then lead to further media coverage.

Television producers' need for spokesmen on issues and their preference for senators over representatives in that role means that a senator visibly involved with an issue that becomes salient will almost certainly get requests to appear on television. If the issue is really hot, that senator may appear on the evening network news or on the morning shows, as well as on a Sunday interview program. A lesser issue may rate an appearance on MacNeil/Lehrer. Such invitations offer the senator the opportunity to further publicize the issue, to attempt to shape the debate on it, and to stimulate pressure toward action.

The print media also need spokesmen and are only a little less partial to senators. Association with a salient issue will bring the senator attention from the prestige press as well; he will be mentioned, quoted, and may even have an Op-Ed piece published.

The senator who is frequently involved in hot issues becomes nationally prominent. For most senators, becoming well known among the general public is not a realistic goal; it may happen, as with Sam Ervin, but depends not just on skills and effort but also on luck. However, given the number of issues on the agenda, the velocity with which issue saliency changes, and the media's need for spokesmen, becoming prominent among the attentive public or certainly among some specialized issue publics is a realistic possibility for a large proportion of the Senate membership. Such prominence makes a senator a more valuable ally and, other things being equal, a more formidable participant in the policy process.

The new environment rewards senators for a behavioral style that entails high activity across a variety of issues and in multiple arenas; both the style and the resultant national prominence yield handsome payoffs across the full range of senators' posited goals. For the senator who aspires to the presidency, highly visible involvement in national issues is a prerequisite. More issues and more groups result in more interests and more views striving for representation and consequently more leadership slots. These present both the policy-oriented senator and the influence-oriented senator with more opportunities to advance their goals. Such senators have an incentive to become broadly involved, both for the direct payoff in terms of policy or influence and for the indirect payoff in terms of national prominence. The prominent senator is perceived to be a major player, and he is sought out as an ally. More groups and more issues increase the pressure on the reelection-oriented senator to get broadly involved and, at the same time, give him more opportunities to go to bat for his constituency. And the high visibility that the new environment makes feasible can sometimes be used to yield reelection benefits; highly publicized advocacy of a popular position—opposition to Pentagon waste, for example—can significantly enhance a senator's reputation with his constituents.

The new environment, thus, offered senators new opportunities, opportunities useful in the pursuit of the full range of goals. But taking advantage of these opportunities required senators to change their behavior, to become more broadly active across a variety of issues and in multiple arenas. The next two chapters will show that senators have in fact changed their behavior and have, in the process, changed the institution—specifically, how it distributes influence and how it makes decisions.

5 // The Emergence of a New Senate Style

When asked why he almost never spoke on the floor, Carl Hayden—one of the powerful senior senators of the 1950s—explained that doing so meant committing oneself to a position publicly thereby severely reducing the flexibility so necessary for effective bargaining within the chamber. If the archetypical senator of the 1950s was a Carl Hayden, exercising his influence behind closed doors and little known to the public at large, his counterpart of the 1980s acts very differently. Sam Nunn, Bill Bradley, and Richard Lugar, all among the most admired of current senators, are highly knowledgeable in complex policy areas. They are not specialists; instead, they involve themselves in a broad array of issues. Their committees are important but by no means their only arenas for participation; they make use of the floor and of external public arenas as well. Aware of the contemporary Senate's openness and sensitivity to external stimuli, they often use the media and other public arenas to influence both their colleagues and other key actors in the Washington policy community.

An institution like the Senate will change when an appreciable number of its members find that its structure hinders rather than facilitates the pursuit of their goals. We have seen that the large liberal Democratic cohort that entered the Senate between 1959 and 1965 did find the structures of the 1950s Senate ill suited to their special political needs and that by the late 1960s they had managed to bring about signficant change. During the 1970s, the Senate underwent a greater transformation. That change was the result of senators' responses to the transformation of the Washington policy community; senators changed their behavior and the institution to take advantage of the opportunities the new environment offered them.

The previous chapter argued that the new environment rewards senators for broad involvement across issues and arenas. That is, such involvement pays off in terms of the full range of possible goals. Broad involvement, however, requires certain resources. This chapter shows that, during the 1970s, senators greatly expanded the supply of staff and of committee positions—resources particularly useful for broadening senators' involvement across a number of issues. The chapter then examines the change in senators' behavior. Because it yields quantitative and thus comparable data over time, floor behavior is analyzed. Senators' floor behavior did change, and in just the way expected. Senators became much more active on the floor and involved themselves in a greater range of issues. Finally, the Senate norms of the 1950s will be reexamined. The transformed Washington policy community sharply increased the opportunity costs to senators of abiding by some of the norms, and those norms have lost their hold. In sum, a new Senate style took shape in the 1970s; senators developed a new set of behavioral strategies through which they pursue their goals. The typical contemporary senator, well endowed with resources and little constrained by norms in their use, is highly active across a number of issues and in a variety of arenas.

The Expansion of the Supply of Resources

During the 1970s the supply of valued committee positions and of staff increased and the distribution became more equal. Senators made those changes, I argue, in order to equip themselves to take advantage of the opportunities the new environment offered.

Valued committee positions became more broadly and more equally distributed during the 1970s (see table 5.1). In the 1950s, most senators held assignments on two standing committees; in the 1960s and through the mid-1970s, a substantial minority served on three. By the mid- to late 1970s, a majority of senators held assignments on three or more standing committees. Since committee membership greatly facilitates involvement in decision making on the issues within the committee's jurisdiction, the typical senator of the mid-1970s and later was considerably better situated for broad involvement across a number of issues than his predecessor.

Table 5.1　The Distribution of Committee Positions by Time Period (Mean number of senators with a given number of positions)

All Committees: No. of Assignments	1953–58	1959–74	1975–86
2	79	57	48
3+	20	44	53

Top Four Committees: No. of Assignments	1953–72	1973–78	1979–86
0	38	30	19
1	50	66	80
2	12	5	2

Leadership Positions on Good Subcommittees: No.	1955–70	1971–78	1979–86
0	24	8	4
1	32	22	29
2+	45	71	68

The most desirable committee assignments also became more broadly distributed during the 1970s. Through the early 1970s, a large minority of senators did not hold an assignment on one of the four most prestigious committees, while at the same time a significant number of their colleagues held two. In the 1970s, this changed rapidly. By late in the decade, eight out of ten senators held an assignment on a prestige committee. Both parties had adhered to the provision in the Legislative Reorganization Act of 1970 that limited senators to one such assignment each; by the late 1970s, only John Stennis of Mississippi and Harry Byrd, Jr., of Virginia had dual assignments protected by the grandfather clause.

The concentration of Appropriations Committee positions in the hands of senior senators who also held other leadership positions, so characteristic of the majority Democrats in the 1950s and 1960s, broke up during the 1970s. From the 84th through the 91st Congress (1955–70), an average of 7.3 chairmen of other committees served on Appropriations. Adding the chairman of Appropriations and the majority leader, who almost always served on the committee, this cadre of leaders on the average held almost 60 percent of the Democratic seats on the committee. This concentration decreased markedly in the 1970s. During the remainder of the period of Democratic control (1971–80), an average of 3.2 chairs of other committees served on Appropriations, and the leadership cadre as defined above held a third of the Democratic seats on the committee.

Subcommittee leadership positions are an extremely useful resource for the advancement of senators' goals within the new Washington policy community. Increasingly serving as personal vehicles for their chairmen, subcommittees provide an excellent forum for engaging in agenda-setting activities and bring with them badly needed legislative staff resources. During the 1970s, the distribution of leadership positions on subcommittees of attractive committees became distinctly broader. In the 1950s and 1960s, a quarter of the Senate membership held no good subcommittee leadership position; during the 1970s, that number decreased almost to the vanishing point. The typical senator of the 1970s and 1980s holds two or more such leadership positions.

The change in the distribution of valued committee positions in the 1970s, like the more modest change that occurred in the 1960s, was made possible primarily by an expansion in the supply, not by redistribution. The total number of positions on standing committees, the number of positions on the four most prestigious committees and the number of positions on the other attractive committees all grew, albeit erratically, during the 1970s and 1980s (see table 5.2).* The Senate made sporadic attempts to rein in this proliferation, but with only temporary success; pressures for expansion always built up again quickly. Immediately after one such reform attempt in the 99th Congress, the total number of committee positions and the number of positions on prestige and on other attractive committees were all substantially higher than they had been in any Congress prior to the 1970s. Only the number of slots on the not very desirable service committees was lower.

The number of subcommittees shot up during the early 1970s, with the increase coming primarily on prestige and on other attractive committees. Between the 90th Congress (1966–67) and the 93rd (1973–74), the number of subcommittees of such panels rose from 86 to 113. Senate rules changes in the mid-1970s reduced the total number of subcommittees, but the service committees contributed disproportionately to the decrease. During the mid-1970s, two of the service committees were abolished and the other two disbanded their subcommittees. Senators were willing to sacrifice these less valuable subcommittees in the name of efficiency reforms. Subcommittees of prestige and of other attractive

---

* The Small Business Committee became a standing committee during the 97th Congress. Because this did not involve any expansion in the committee's meager legislative jurisdiction nor apparently any other consequential change, it was treated as a special committee, not a standing committee, in the 97th, 98th, and 99th Congresses. If Small Business had been counted as a standing committee in the 98th and 99th, the expansion in the number of committee positions and in the number of subcommittees in the 1980s would have appeared considerably greater, but these would not, in fact, have been new.

Table 5.2 Increase in the Supply of Committee Positions and Subcommittees[a]

Congress	No. of Committee Positions				No. of Subcommittees			
	Total	Top Four	Other Good	Service	Total	Top Four	Other Good	Service
83rd	211	68	114	29	—	—	—	—
84th	213	68	114	31	86	26	45	15
85th	213	68	114	31	91	26	48	17
86th	236	78	133	25	96	29	52	15
87th	240	78	137	25	95	28	51	16
88th	246	78	143	25	91	27	49	15
89th	250	80	142	28	99	27	57	15
90th	252	80	143	29	101	28	58	15
91st	245	74	143	28	99	29	55	15
92nd	247	72	141	34	118	33	68	17
93rd	244	75	135	34	130	41	72	17
94th	253	77	143	33	126	42	70	14
95th	244	77	149	18	100	40	57	3
96th	251	80	151	20	91	37	54	0
97th	265	83	158	24	93	35	58	0
98th	273	84	165	24	94	35	59	0
99th	263	85	151	27	83	33	50	0

[a]Numbers as of the begining of each congress.

committees, on the other hand, are more valuable and less easily curtailed. Even after the 1977 committee reforms, the number of such subcommittees was higher than in any Congress prior to the 1970s. (The Quayle reforms of 1985 cut the number of subcommittees on attractive—but not top—committees back to their level of the mid-1960s. Whether that will last remains to be seen.)

The increase in the supply and the broad distribution of valued committee positions in the 1970s erased the regional disparities among Democrats characteristic of the 1960s. After 1974, northern Democrats were usually about as likely as southern Democrats to serve on a prestige committee (see table 5.3). By the late 1960s, northern Democrats had overtaken and surpassed their southern colleagues in their frequency of holding at least one subcommittee leadership position. After 1972, differences between the two groups disappeared; members of both were highly likely to hold such a position. A major source of friction within the Democratic party was thus eliminated.

Table 5.3 Distribution of Valued Committee Positions Across Regional Party Groups (Percent of group holding one or more)

Congress	Top Four Committee Assignments			Subcommittee Leadership Positions		
	North Dem.	South Dem.	Republicans	North Dem.	South Dem.	Republicans
83rd	53.6	63.6	58.5	—	—	—
84th	51.7	75.0	57.4	87.7	80.0	68.1
85th	56.7	70.0	55.4	83.3	85.0	70.8
86th	64.4	80.0	63.9	62.2	85.0	80.6
87th	57.8	75.0	60.5	64.4	75.0	78.9
88th	55.1	78.9	57.6	59.2	84.2	84.8
89th	58.0	84.2	62.5	64.0	73.7	96.9
90th	65.2	77.8	62.2	76.1	66.7	86.5
91st	57.5	70.6	61.4	85.0	70.6	84.1
92nd	57.9	70.4	63.0	89.5	70.6	95.7
93rd	60.5	80.0	69.7	95.3	93.3	95.7
94th	67.4	68.7	76.3	87.0	87.5	95.3
95th	70.8	82.4	73.7	87.5	88.2	100.0
96th	77.3	80.0	77.0	97.7	100.0	100.0
97th	77.8	81.8	83.3	100.0	100.0	94.4
98th	80.0	90.0	83.6	97.2	100.0	92.7
99th	81.1	90.0	84.9	97.3	100.0	92.5

As the supply of valued committee positions increased, seniority became a less important criterion of distribution in both parties. In the
1950s and 1960s, junior members were disadvantaged and senior members advantaged. For Democrats, the mean correlation between the
number of prestige committee assignments held and seniority was .45
over the period from 1953 to 1974. For the remainder of the period under
study, however, the mean correlation dropped to .21. Clearly, in the
1970s, seniority became a considerably less important basis for distribution of the most desirable committee assignments among Democrats.

From 1959 through 1976, the relationship between seniority and the
number of subcommittees chaired among Democrats was substantial,
with a mean correlation of .41. The correlation dropped to .25 in the 95th
Congress, and was negative in the remaining congresses under study
(-.28). By the 1980s, then, junior members were actually marginally advantaged.

During the 1950s, 1960s, and well into the 1970s, seniority was a very
important basis for the distribution of prestige committee assignments
among Republicans. The correlation between seniority and the number
of such positions held averaged .70 from 1955 through 1972. It fell to a
mean of .56 during the period from 1973–1978, then to .35 in 1979–80. In the
Republican controlled 97th, 98th, and 99th Congresses, the correlation

averaged .19 (which was not significant at the .05 level). Thus, by the 1980s seniority no longer appeared to be a significant determinant of prestige committee membership among Republicans.

The pattern is quite similar for subcommittee leadership positions. The correlation between seniority and the number of ranking minority memberships held averaged .58 for the period from 1955 to 1970; it fell monotonically to a nonsignificant .12 in 1977–78 and stood at a nonsignificant .19 in the last Democratic-controlled congress. In the 97th, 98th, and 99th Congresses the correlations were actually negative, though only that for the 97th was even marginally significant.

During the 1970s, both parties changed their implicit rules for the distribution of valued committee positions to decrease the disadvantage of freshman status. In the early 1970s, it was still relatively rare for a Democratic freshman to get assigned to a prestige committee; one did in the 92nd and one in the 93rd Congress. In the 94th Congress, three of nine freshmen got such assignments. In each of the remaining congresses between 1977 and 1984, half or more of the freshmen received assignment to one of the four top committees; two of the five 99th Congress freshmen did. Overall, almost 60 percent of the Democratic freshmen who entered the Senate between 1977 and 1984 got such assignments. Thus, beginning in the mid-1970s, Democratic freshmen began to fare much better in the committee assignment process.

In the 1950s and 1960s, Republican freshmen were even less likely than Democrats to be assigned to a prestige committee. Between 1953 and 1970, only four freshmen got such assignments, and two of those had previous Senate service. Such assignments remained quite rare until the late 1970s; between 1971 and 1978, only two freshmen received such assignments. Then abruptly, the Republicans altered their decision rule: five of the eleven-member freshman class in the 96th Congress received prestige assignments; twelve of the seventeen 97th Congress freshmen got such assignments, and three of the six freshmen in the 98th and 99th Congresses did. Therefore about 60 percent of the freshmen who entered those four congresses were placed on one of the top four committees. The extremely favorable assignments the 1980 freshmen received might be explained purely as a response to the group's extraordinary size and to increases in positions made available by the change in partisan control of the Senate. Size might also explain the treatment of the freshman class of the 96th Congress. That the pattern has persisted for four consecutive congresses almost certainly means a permanent shift in the decision rule.

Freshmen's success at obtaining subcommittee leadership positions on good committees improved considerably earlier. Here the Republicans changed first. In the 1950s and early 1960s, most Republican freshmen did not hold a ranking minority member slot; from the 84th through the 87th Congresses, only 23.6 did. Thereafter, at least half the freshmen in each congress but one held such a position, and the mean for the 88th through the 99th Congresses was 74 percent. Since the Republicans were a minority—and usually a fairly small minority—during most of this period, the supply of ranking positions relative to number of members was quite large, making broad distribution easier. That every freshman held a ranking minority position in the 94th, 95th, and 96th Congresses suggests that a sense of entitlement may have developed. When Republicans took control of the Senate, supply relative to numbers became less favorable; nevertheless seventeen of twenty-three freshmen in the 97th, 98th, and 99th Congresses chaired subcommittees of good committees.

In the period after the 1958 election, freshmen Democrats very seldom chaired a good subcommittee. This was a period of large Democratic majorities, which put considerable strain on the supply of subcommittee chairmanships. In the late 1960s, freshmen fortunes began to improve, though erratically; between 1969 and 1976, an average of 38 percent of freshmen chaired subcommittees. The late 1970s and early 1980s saw a major further improvement, with 75 percent of the freshmen Democrats holding subcommittee leadership positions.

Junior members, especially freshmen, benefited from changes in the supply and distribution of valued committee positions that occurred during the 1970s. They had been most disadvantaged when the supply was tight. However, not only junior members benefited. The increase in supply meant more for everyone. The typical senator of the 1980s serves on three or more standing committees, one of which is a prestige committee, and chairs or is ranking minority member on two or more good subcommittees. These multiple positions enhance a senator's potential for involvement in a broad range of issues.

The extent to which a senator can actualize that potential depends heavily upon his possession of other resources, especially staff. Senate staff grew rapidly during the 1970s. Between 1970 and 1975 the total staffs of Senate standing committees doubled, rising from 635 to 1,277 (Ornstein, et al. 1984, 124). Personal staffs more than doubled between 1967 and 1977, growing from 1,749 to 3,554. Believing themselves to be at a disadvantage vis-à-vis senior members who had authority over some committee staff, junior senators in the mid-1970s combined across party lines to increase staff resources available to less senior senators. Over the opposition of their senior colleagues, especially committee chairmen, they passed Senate Resolution 60, which authorized each senator to hire a personal legislative assistant for each committee assignment (see *Congressional Record* June 9, 1975, 17836–63).

The 1970s, then, was a period of institutional change. Partly through formal rules changes but primarily through informal accommodation, senators very significantly increased the supply and moved toward a more equal distribution of those resources—valuable committee positions and staff—particularly useful for extending their involvement across a broad range of issues.

The Emergence of a New Senate Style

The new Washington policy community rewards senators for broad involvement across multiple issues and arenas. By expanding the supply of facilitative resources, senators have equipped themselves for such involvement. But did senators alter their behavior? This section will show that senators' behavior did, in fact, change in the manner expected.

It is possible and often necessary to base our assessments of changes in the behavior of political actors on interview data. Thus we can compare what senators and other political actors told Matthews in the 1950s with what similarly situated actors tell us today. It is still possible to find and interview people who were active in the Washington political community during the 1950s. Although these data can be valuable and are used throughout this study, problems of reliability and comparability over time are obvious. Quantitative data on senators' behavior over time would provide a more reliable basis for inferences about change, and senators' floor behavior yields such data. For that reason, senators' floor behavior, specifically the offering of amendments to measures on the floor of the Senate, is analyzed here.[*]

If senators expanded the arenas of their involvement beyond their committees, the Senate floor is the most likely arena to have been

---

[*] One might argue that the increase in floor amending activity represents simply a shift in arena, from committee and behind the scenes to the floor, rather than an expansion in arenas of involvement. The literature (see, for example, Price 1972, 1985; Smith and Deering 1984; Evans 1986), interview data, and committee workload data presented below argue strongly against this possibility. In addition, if committees became relatively inactive and insignificant as decision-making arenas, senators' accumulation of increasing numbers of committee assignments would be difficult to explain. Similarly, the available information does not support the argument that senators have always been generalists involved in a broad array of issues but that the main forum for this involvement has merely shifted from locations behind the scenes to the Senate floor. To be sure, in the more accommodating Senate of the 1950s committee nonmembers

Table 5.4 Increase in Senators' Participation on the Floor

Congress	No. of senators who offered one or more amendments	Mean amendments per sponsor	No. of senators who offered given no. of amendments					Maximum no. offered
			1-2	3-4	5-9	10-19	20+	
84th	47	2.4	31	9	6	0	0	8
86th	63	3.3	33	17	9	4	0	17
88th	63	6.2	23	15	12	8	5	37
	(59)[a]	(4.8)						(23)
90th	74	5.3	34	16	11	11	2	50
92nd	90	6.7	17	27	28	13	5	30
94th	94	7.4	28	13	31	15	7	69
96th	89	6.2	18	26	31	12	2	51
97th	91	6.4	14	31	29	14	3	27
98th	86	4.8	26	29	23	6	2	26
99th	92	5.0	32	23	26	10	1	27

[a]Figures in parentheses are for the 88th excluding the battle over the 1964 Civil Rights Bill.

affected. Activity on the Senate floor, specifically the offering of amendments, gives senators the opportunity to become involved in an array of issues broader than those under their committees' jurisdiction and to do so in an arena that combines easy access and high visibility.

If floor participation is defined as offering at least one amendment on which the Senate takes a recorded vote, moderate to high participation is the norm throughout the period under study. Even in the mid-1950s, almost half the senators participated in this fashion (see table 5.4). Nevertheless, notwithstanding this high initial base, the breadth of participation increased steeply over time. By the early 1970s almost all senators offered at least one amendment on the floor.

As the breadth of participation has increased, so too has the frequency. More senators are offering amendments on the floor, and they

---

and committee leaders may have been more inclined to work out their differences privately before the bill reached the floor. Yet, if many senators had acted as behind-the-scenes generalists, surely some evidence thereof would exist. Very likely, then as now, much of the behind-the-scenes accommodation occurred on fairly narrow matters related to concerns of the consituency. Of course, a shift from committee to floor in legislative activity would itself be important. The argument here, however, is that more than simply a shift is involved. At the same time, the limitations of floor data need to be recognized. Because they do not reveal what happened before the floor, other data as well as the literature are used to bolster the arguments based on amending data. (For an excellent discussion of some of these methodological issues, see Hall 1987b.)

are each offering more. The mean number of amendments per active senator climbed from 2.4 in the mid-1950s to a high of 7.4 in the mid-1970s; it dropped thereafter but remained substantial.

During the 1970s, a corps of hyperactive senators developed. In the 84th Congress, no senator offered ten or more amendments; the three most active senators offered eight amendments each. In the 86th Congress, four senators offered ten or more amendments. The number of senators to do so increased steadily until it hit a high of twenty-two in the 94th. The mean for the congresses of the 1970s and 1980s is fifteen.

In the 1950s and early 1960s, northern liberals who developed reputations as mavericks were prominent among those senators who offered ten or more amendments in at least two congresses. By the late 1960s and 1970s, both parties and all regions contribute hyperactives. Republicans as a whole were somewhat overrepresented, as were senators from the ideological extremes of their party. Among Republican hyperactives during the 1970s were extreme conservatives Jesse Helms of North Carolina and James Buckley of New York (who was actually elected as a Conservative) but also Robert Packwood of Oregon and Jacob Javits of New York, both liberals by Republican standards. Edward Kennedy of Massachusetts and James Allen of Alabama are among the Democratic hyperactives of the 1970s. With the switch to Republican control in 1981, Democrats came to make up a disproportionate share of the hyperactives—about 70 percent in each of the three congresses from 1981 through 1986. Kennedy and Howard Metzenbaum, both on the left of their party, offered ten or more amendments in each of these congresses. More centrist Democrats such as John Melcher, Bill Bradley, and Daniel Patrick Moynihan did in two of the three. Even with his party in the majority, Jesse Helms remained hyperactive on the floor, offering on the average a little more than twenty-two amendments per congress.

The development of the hyperactive senator, while dramatic, should not obscure the across-the-board increase in activity. The typical senator of the 1970s and 1980s is much less likely than his earlier counterpart to engage in restrained activism on the floor (that is, to offer only one or two amendments). In the 84th Congress, most senators were highly restrained in their floor behavior, with only fifteen offering three or more amendments; this doubled to thirty in the 86th. During the 1960s, the figure stood at forty—still well below half the membership. Throughout the 1970s and 1980s, however, the great majority—sixty-eight on the average—offered three or more amendments.

Accompanying the increase in participation have been changes in who participates. A decreasing proportion of amendments are offered by members of the originating committee. Even in the 1950s, only about

Table 5.5 Committee Nonmembers' Frequency of Offering Amendments

Congress	Percent of amendments offered by nonmembers	No. of senators who offered one or more amendments	Mean amendments per sponsor	No. of senators who offered given no. of amendments					Maximum no. offered
				1–2	3–4	5–9	10–19	20+	
84th	48.2	33	1.7	27	5	1	0	0	5
86th	51.7	39	2.7	26	7	4	2	0	12
88th	69.2	54	5.0	28	13	8	5	3	37
	(57.2)[a]	(45)	(3.6)						(20)
90th	62.2	64	3.8	41	11	8	2	2	40
92nd	67.2	84	4.8	30	24	19	9	2	21
94th	63.3	83	5.3	35	21	18	6	3	58
96th	61.6	77	4.6	33	12	26	5	1	39
97th	62.3	85	4.2	30	26	23	5	1	22
98th	62.1	72	3.6	41	16	10	5	0	18
99th	62.7	86	3.3	42	22	19	3	0	12

[a]Figures in parentheses are for the 88th excluding the battle over the 1964 Civil Rights Bill.

half the amendments were offered by committee members (see table 5.5). Since the 1950s the proportion of amendments offered by noncommittee members has increased significantly. During the 1970s and 1980s, a bill's floor manager could expect more than six of every ten amendments to come from senators not on the committee that reported the legislation.

In the 84th Congress, only about a third of all senators offered amendments to measures from committees on which they did not serve (see table 5.5). In the 88th Congress, for the first time, over half the membership did. If, however, amendments offered during the battle over the 1964 civil rights bill are excluded, the number drops to below half. (Because the civil rights bill bypassed the Senate Judiciary Committee, all amendments to it are counted as having been offered by nonmembers of the originating committee.) By the 90th Congress, almost two-thirds of the senators were engaging in this behavior, and no single extraordinary legislative battle accounts for the increase. During the 1970s and 1980s, the vast majority of members offered amendments to measures from committees on which they did not sit. Doing so is no longer an unusual act; it has become standard behavior.

Not only do most senators now offer floor amendments to measures from committees on which they do not sit, they sponsor many more such amendments than their predecessors did. In the 1950s, senators who engaged in this behavior tended to practice a restrained activism, offering only a few such amendments. The mean number of amendments sponsored by active senators increased sharply, almost tripling between the mid-1950s and the 1970s. It dropped in the 1980s but remained above the level of the 1950s.

If apprenticeship was a widely observed norm in the Senate of the 1950s, amendment sponsors should be senior members. From the 84th through the 90th Congresses, the typical sponsor was more senior than the average senator by 1.2 years, and the difference was greatest in the 84th Congress.* In the three 1970s congresses, by contrast, the typical amendment sponsor was less senior by 1.5 years than the average senator. Clearly participation patterns have changed in terms of seniority.

In the 1950s and 1960s the typical participation pattern was characterized by low rates of amendment sponsorship among freshmen (those in their first or second year), higher rates among other first termers, and still higher rates among second termers. Participation rates tended to be lower again among the most senior members, many of whom were committee chairmen (see table 5.6). That pattern changed in the 1970s. During the 92nd Congress, freshmen had by far the highest activity rate. Thereafter, the freshmen rate varies, but freshmen as a group are no longer consistently less active than their senior colleagues.

Rates of amendment sponsorship have increased among members at all seniority levels, but clearly the change has been most dramatic among freshmen. In the 1950s and 1960s, freshmen were highly restrained in the offering of amendments, behavior consistent with the serving of an apprenticeship. In the 1970s, freshmen became much more active both in absolute terms and in relation to their senior colleagues. The data strongly suggest the demise of apprenticeship as a behavioral pattern.

An examination of those freshmen who offered at least one amendment confirms that apprenticeship is a thing of the past. The proportion who did so increases monotonically from a little more than a quarter in the 84th to every freshman in the 92nd. The freshmen of the 1970s and 1980s were activists; 87 percent offered at least one floor amendment during his or her first congress. Furthermore, in the 1950s even those freshmen who dared to offer floor amendments were quite restrained in their activism; the four activist freshmen in the 84th Congress offered a total of only five amendments. From the 86th through the 90th, activist freshmen averaged 2.6 amendments each. In the 1970s and 1980s, when most freshmen were activists, the per capita figure was 5.5.

---

* The mean seniority for the typical sponsor is the mean over all amendments; it is thus a weighted mean, with a member's seniority weighted by the number of amendments he sponsors.

Table 5.6   Rate of Amending Activity by Party, Region, Seniority, and Ideology
(Amendments offered per capita)

Congress	All Senators	Republicans	Democrats All	Democrats North	Democrats South
84th	1.2	1.2	1.2	1.2	1.1
86th	2.0	2.2	2.0	1.8	2.4
88th	3.9	4.6	3.6	2.5	6.5
90th	3.9	5.0	3.3	3.5	2.7
92nd	6.1	5.5	6.5	6.5	6.6
94th	7.0	8.1	6.3	5.3	8.9
96th	5.6	7.4	4.6	4.7	4.5
97th	5.8	4.5	7.3	8.0	5.0
98th	4.1	3.7	4.6	4.8	3.9
99th	4.6	3.7	5.6	6.4	2.7

	Seniority Fr.	Seniority First Term	Seniority Second Term	Seniority More than Two Terms	Ideology Lib.	Ideology Mod.	Ideology Cons.
84th	.3	.8	1.9	1.2	2.0	0.9	1.2
86th	1.0	2.4	2.3	2.3	2.3	1.5	2.5
88th	1.2	3.1	6.0	4.0	1.8	3.7	6.3
90th	1.3	2.9	4.5	4.4	5.2	2.6	4.8
92nd	7.5	6.1	6.5	5.3	8.3	4.9	5.5
94th	4.2	9.1	9.4	5.1	5.8	5.2	10.3
96th	5.0	4.5	8.8	4.1	5.2	5.4	6.6
97th	3.2	6.1	6.8	6.6	10.7	5.6	4.3
98th	.5	4.4	4.7	3.8	5.8	4.2	3.5
99th	5.4	4.3	4.8	4.3	7.9	4.8	3.5

During the 1950s and early 1960s, there was a fairly strong tendency for activist freshmen to be liberal northern Democrats; eleven of the seventeen activist freshmen in the 84th, 86th, and 88th Congresses were. Such well-known liberals as Eugene McCarthy, Phillip Hart, Abraham Ribicoff, George McGovern, and Gaylord Nelson offered floor amendments during their first congress. The other six activists were Republicans from either the Northeast or the mountain states. During those congresses, not a single southern freshmen senator offered even one amendment, indicating that southern Democrats were more willing than other freshmen to serve an apprenticeship. During this period the reelection and policy costs of serving an apprenticeship were less for southern than for northern Democratic freshmen, because southern Democrats were still more electorally secure than their northern colleagues and committee leadership was in the hands of senior southern Democrats.

The class of 1966 broke the mold of the 1950s and early 1960s. It included the first activist southern freshman, Ernest Hollings of South Carolina, and the first midwestern and border Republican activists, Charles Percy of Illinois, Robert Griffin of Michigan, and Howard Baker of Tennessee. Thereafter, almost all freshmen regardless of region of origin were activists. A few freshmen even began appearing among the hyperactives who offered ten or more amendments. In the 92nd Congress, for example, Robert Taft, Jr., offered twenty-four amendments and James Buckley offered sixteen. In the most recent congress under study, freshmen Tom Harkin and John Kerry offered ten or more amendments each.

One would expect those members most dissatisfied with the committee version of a bill to be most likely to offer floor amendments. Certainly Republicans' greater frequency of amendment sponsorship from the 86th through the 96th Congresses and the Democrats' greater rate in the 97th through 99th is in part due to dissatisfaction with bills written by committees controlled by the opposition party. Similarly we would expect ideologically extreme senators to be less frequently satisfied and thus more inclined to offer floor amendments. Members at the ideological extremes do tend to be more active than more moderate senators (see table 5.6). In five of the ten congresses under study, liberals and conservatives sponsored more amendments on a per capita basis than did moderates, and the difference was frequently substantial. In the 88th and 96th Congresses, conservatives offered substantially more amendments per capita than either moderates or liberals, whereas in the 97th, 98th, and 99th, liberals were by far the most active of the ideological groups.

Although cyclical phenomena such as the ideological center of gravity of the chamber and partisan control affect activity rates across groups, the extent to which increased floor activity is an across-the-board phenomenon is most striking. Almost all senators, regardless of party, region, seniority, or ideology, are now floor activists.

Not only have senators' rates of participation increased, the character of the participation has also changed. Senators have become more broadly involved across issues. They are less likely to confine their amending activity to a narrow range of areas. Such specialization has declined, and more and more senators have become generalists.

Two measures of specialization were constructed. The primary measure is simply the number of different committees of origin of the bills to which the senator offers amendments. If a senator sponsors

amendments to bills from only a small number of committees, specialization is indicated. Because committees vary in breadth of jurisdiction
and some issues areas fall within the jurisdiction of several committees,
a second measure was also constructed—the number of issue areas in
which a senator offered amendments. Clausen's five issue domains, aug-
mented by an internal category as explained earlier, are used. The two
indicators are quite highly related; the mean correlation over the ten
congresses is .80 if computed on the basis of those senators who offered
at least one amendment, and .87 if the total membership is the base.

The means of both these variables show a clear decline in specialization over time (see table 5.7). The mean of the number of committees
measure stood at .8 in the 84th Congress, indicating a high degree of
specialization. This increased steadily to a high of 3.3 in the 94th. The
mean for the congresses of the 1970s and 1980s is over three times that
of the mid-1950s. The number of issues measure shows the same trend:
away from the specialization norm that prevailed in the 1950s and
toward the pattern of broad participation that had become typical by
the 1970s and 1980s.

Table 5.7   Decline in Specialization and the Rise of the Generalist

Congress	No. of Committees Measure		No. of Issues Measure	
	Mean	No. of Generalists[a]	Mean	No. of Generalists[a]
84th	.8	4	.8	6
86th	1.2	9	1.1	15
88th	1.4	12	1.4	21
90th	1.8	18	1.7	26
92nd	3.0	35	2.4	45
94th	3.3	39	2.2	37
96th	2.9	35	2.2	36
97th	3.0	36	2.2	41
98th	2.2	22	2.2	30
99th	2.7	29	1.9	37

[a]Number of senators who scored 4 or higher (for issue measure 3 or higher) on the
measure. See pp. 85–86 for definition of measures.

If we define as generalists those members who offered amendments
to bills from four or more committees, we find that generalists were
deviant in the 1950s; only four senators in the 84th Congress and nine in
the 86th were generalists (see table 5.7). The number climbed in the
1960s and accelerated in the 1970s. In each of the three congresses of the
1970s under study over a third of all senators were generalists. In the 94th

Congress, one member offered amendments to bills from thirteen different committees. The number of generalists declined a little in the 1980s, but the decline was largely an artifact of the character of the issue agenda, not an indicator that senators' behavior was reverting to specialization. During the 98th Congress (1983–84), conflict focused heavily on budget priorities; half the amendments that came to a roll call vote were offered to Appropriations and Finance Committee bills, two-thirds to bills from these two committees plus Armed Services.

Table 5.8 Partisan, Regional, Seniority, and Ideological Patterns Among Specialists and Generalists (Percent of group that fits the definition of generalist according to number of committees measure)

Congress	Republican	Democrats	
		North	South
84th	6.4	3.5	0
86th	11.1	6.7	10.0
88th	24.2	6.1	5.3
90th	21.6	19.6	5.6
92nd	34.8	39.5	23.5
94th	44.7	34.8	37.5
96th	41.5	34.1	20.0
97th	27.8	47.2	36.4
98th	20.0	22.2	30.0
99th	24.5	40.5	10.0

Congress	Seniority				Ideology		
	Fr.	First Term	Sec. Term	More than Two Terms	Lib.	Mod.	Cons.
84th	0	0	10.8	0	7.7	2.4	4.9
86th	0	8.7	12.9	11.5	11.5	5.1	11.4
88th	0	17.9	14.8	9.7	3.3	12.8	19.4
90th	0	15.8	23.5	18.0	22.7	10.6	25.0
92nd	46.2	43.5	25.0	28.9	51.9	32.4	25.0
94th	18.2	72.0	47.8	19.5	42.4	30.6	45.2
96th	35.0	39.3	39.1	27.6	40.0	41.7	31.3
97th	15.0	30.6	52.6	46.2	62.5	33.3	28.6
98th	0	31.6	21.4	13.8	16.7	32.6	11.9
99th	57.1	36.0	25.6	20.7	54.5	31.1	20.5

Using the issue area measure of specialization, we define as a generalist any senator who offered amendments in half or more of the six broad issue areas. This indicator shows the same trend but produces higher numbers of generalists. Generalists were extremely atypical in the 1950s; by the 1970s, nearly four of every ten senators offered amendments in at least three of the six issue areas. Clearly, senators now are more broadly involved across multiple issues.

Freshmen senators show the most dramatic change in behavior. In the 1950s and 1960s, no freshman was a generalist. An abrupt change occurred during the 1970s. Almost half of the very active freshmen class of the 92nd Congress qualified as generalists. As freshmen became more active participants, they also were more likely to act as generalists.

Members of the minority party are somewhat more inclined to be generalists, as are those at the ideological extremes. However, although the generalist style was frequently preferred by those at the ideological extremes in the 1950s and 1960s, its practitioners became less ideologically distinctive in the 1970s, as the generalist style became more common. Large proportions of moderates were acting as generalists.

The decline in specialization and the development of the generalist closely parallel the increase in participation. The activity measure of number of amendments offered and the number of committees specialization measure are strongly related; the mean correlation over the ten congresses is .80. The increase in senators' floor activity has taken the form of broad participation across a number of issue domains and committees.

In sum, since the mid-1950s, and particularly during the 1970s, a new Senate floor style developed. The modal floor style in the 1950s was one of highly restrained activism. Members who participated on the floor by offering amendments sponsored only a few, and those were in a narrow range of issue areas. By the early 1980s, the modal style was one of unrestrained activism. The typical senator offers large numbers of floor amendments and is little concerned with whether the bill at issue originated in a committee on which he serves. He participates in a broad range of issues. During the 1970s, freshmen increasingly adopted the new style of unrestrained activism as soon as they entered the chamber. The new style is not conditional upon a senator's status. A large proportion of the membership—regardless of seniority, ideology, party, or region—has adopted the new style.

A high rate of offering floor amendments is only one facet of the new Senate style. Increasing use of extended debate is another. As documented below, the number of filibusters rose exponentially from the 1950s to the 1970s. The typical senator became increasingly willing to use his power of extended debate, and on an increasingly broad array of issues.

The floor was added to, but did not replace, the committee as an arena for legislative activity. Senators expanded the supply of valued committee positions because holding a committee position facilitates involvement in the issues within that committee's jurisdiction. At the same time that floor activity was increasing, so was committee activity (see Smith and Deering 1984). From 1955 through 1968, the number of Senate committee and subcommittee meetings averaged 2,633 per congress. It then started a rapid monotonic climb and reached 4,067 by the 93rd Congress of 1973–74 (Malbin 1980, 258).*

The Transformation of Senate Norms

The data on floor activity presented in the previous section indicate that the behavior of many senators no longer conforms to Senate norms. Offering large numbers of amendments in a wide variety of issue areas, for example, would seem to violate both the specialization and the reciprocity norms.

Our theoretical framework suggests that norms will lose their hold when the costs of conformity increase greatly. When P (the payoff when no one conforms) minus the costs of whatever sanctions may be applied is greater than R (the payoff when everyone conforms), the individual senator no longer has any incentive for conforming to the norms. However, the sanctions available to leaders are limited. A senator cannot be deprived of his seat or his vote, nor realistically of his committee assignments. Leaders have more discretion over prospective committee assignments, but the discretion is not wide enough, nor the stock of such assignments large enough, to provide leaders with a reliable tool for extracting norm abidance from large numbers of senators who otherwise would not conform. The critical point is reached, therefore, when P becomes greater than R for an appreciable number of members. Such a change in the payoff matrix represents an increase in the value for goal advancement of the behavior proscribed by the norms.

The transformation of the Washington policy community greatly increased the opportunity cost of conforming to the specialization norm. If a senator confines his attention to only a few issues, he is passing up multiple opportunities for involvement across a broad range of issues and thereby fails to exploit opportunities to advance his goals. Such broad involvement is essential for the senator who wants a shot at the presidency, because it is considered a necessary qualification for the pres-

---

* Aggregate data are, of course, only indirect and possibly misleading indicators of individual activity levels. However, the literature and interview data substantiate the inference that the average senator's total amount of committee activity has not decreased and may have increased.

idency and because it brings visibility. Such involvement enables the policy-oriented senator to extend his impact beyond some narrow policy area. It provides the influence-oriented senator with more frequent opportunities to play a leadership role. The quest for reelection dictates satisfying important constituency groups, and given the growth in the number of such groups, satisfying them, for many senators, dictates involvement across a broad range of issues.

Abiding by the legislative work norm as defined by Matthews is, of course, incompatible with broad issue involvements. No senator can devote himself to the "highly detailed, dull and politically unrewarding" (p. 94) legislative tasks in many different issue areas.

The transformed environment has also altered the costs of conforming to the reciprocity norm. Restraint in the use of the immense powers conferred upon the individual by the Senate rules is more expensive now in terms of opportunities forgone. Skillfully used, those powers provide the instrument through which a senator can extend his involvement in issues far beyond his committee jurisdictions. The powers of extended debate and of offering unlimited numbers of amendments dealing with any topic to almost any bill can be used for agenda setting and policy incubation as well as affecting policy directly. The threat to use these powers can provide leverage to influence legislation before it reaches the floor. The increasing time pressure under which the Senate works has made these tactics more effective (Oppenheimer 1985).

To the extent that the institutional patriotism norm dictates that senators focus their energy and attention inward on the Senate, the costs of conformity have increased. The new environment made an outward-directed style more productive in terms of goal advancement. Within that environment, agenda setting is a more important part of the policy process, and senators' agenda-setting activities are primarily public. The process of shaping the debate on issues is more public than it used to be. By developing an audience outside the chamber, senators can gain leverage within the chamber. In general, because the Senate is now more permeable and more responsive to outside influences, senators are encouraged to cultivate the sources of possible outside pressure.

If the payoffs of nonconforming behavior have increased, what about the costs of violating the norms? Given central leaders' relatively meager stock of sanctions, norm enforcement in the Senate has almost certainly always relied primarily upon the behavior of individual senators vis-à-vis one another. Norm violators were excluded, partly or completely, from the exchange of favors that was so mutually beneficial and, consequently, were less effective than those included, especially in obtaining benefits for their constituency. When most senators abide by the norms, excluding the occasional violator requires no collusion; each individual senator refuses to deal with the violator because the violator is considered neither a reliable nor a productive trading partner. If many senators, including more senior members holding positions of institutional importance, become violators, exclusion will no longer be an effective enforcement mechanism. Not dealing with a large proportion of their fellow senators, especially if that proportion includes members with significant resources, would be costly for the remaining senators. It follows that if the gross payoffs of nonconforming behavior increase substantially for a large group of senators, the costs of violation would almost simultaneously decrease.

What, then, is the current state of Senate norms? This assessment rests on data on floor behavior over time (amending activity and extended debate) and on interview data. Interviews were conducted by the author in the offices of a sample of eighteen senators. Although the sample was not randomly selected, it is representative of the Senate membership in terms of party regional grouping (northern Democrat, southern Democrat, or Republican) and ideology. Because freshmen were purposely oversampled, the sample is significantly less senior than the Senate membership as a whole; it does, however, include a representative proportion of very senior members (those who have served more than two terms). Senior staffers, primarily legislative directors and administrative assistants, were interviewed. At least two interviews were conducted in each office in 1985 and 1986; at least three in the offices of freshman senators. All unattributed quotations are from these interviews or from others conducted over the past several years with longtime Senate observers.

Instead of asking about Senate norms directly, I began my interviews with a series of questions about the senators' current and recent activities. Seventeen of the eighteen senators were reported as currently or recently involved to a significant degree in at least one issue not within the jurisdiction of any of the senator's committees. In the great majority of these cases, such involvements were not confined to matters directly related to constituency interests. A number of senators have a long-term interest and involvement in one or more noncommittee issues. Interview data thus confirm the inferences drawn from the data on the offering of amendments on the floor. The change in modal floor behavior from highly restrained and narrowly focused in the 1950s to unrestrained activism across a broad array of issues by the 1970s signifies that senators' behavior no longer conforms to the specialization norm.

In replying to questions about the senator's activities, these senior staffers very seldom distinguished between issues within and not within the senator's committees' jurisdiction. Furthermore, none displayed any need to justify such extracommittee involvements. That a senator will be broadly involved in a number of issues, some of which do not fall within the jurisdiction of his committees, is taken as a matter of course. If norms are defined as widely shared expectations about appropriate behavior, then specialization is no longer a Senate norm.

In response to a direct question, these staffers readily acknowledged that it is easier for a senator to exercise influence on a matter that comes before a committee on which he serves. "Legislation is written in committee, so being there is important," an experienced aide explained. If you are not on the committee, "you are not there when the detailed decisions are made." "In conference, you are not a player," said another. In addition, being on the committee "gives you a platform to speak from." To have a "sustained, long-term effect" on an issue, "you need to be part of the network and the press needs to know you are a player." Committee membership is the easiest way of accomplishing those objectives (see Evans 1986; for a House comparison, see Hall 1987a). From a practical standpoint, then, a senator is better off choosing a committee issue over a noncommittee issue if the payoffs of involvement are roughly equal. Aware of this, senators are more likely to get involved in issues that come before a committee on which they serve than in those that do not; but this is the result purely of practical calculations concerning likely impact for a given amount of time invested. Extracommittee involvement brings no condemnation. Furthermore, the practical barriers are not so high as to preclude a great deal of such involvement. Expressing the consensus opinion, a staffer said, "To have an impact, it takes less work, less energy if you're on the committee, but it's not necessary."

Given Senate committee assignment practices in the 1970s and 1980s, even if a senator were to confine himself to matters that came before his committees, he would be broadly involved. As we saw earlier, in the 1950s, most senators served on two standing committees; now the majority serve on three or more.

Howard Metzenbaum, a senior Democrat, served on Budget, Energy and Natural Resources, Judiciary, and Labor and Human Resources during the 99th Congress; freshman Democrat John Kerry on Foreign Relations, Labor and Human Resources, and Small Business. Lowell Weicker, a senior Republican, held positions on Appropriations, Energy and Natural Resources, Labor and Human Resources, and Small Business; junior Republican Pete Wilson on Armed Services, Agriculture, Special Aging, and Joint Economic. When senators hold committee assignments of such number and breadth, the notion of specializing in the issues that come before the senator's committees loses much of its meaning.

The feasibility of such broad involvement constitutes an important component of the "lure of the Senate" (Plattner 1985). "I wanted my fingers in as many pies as I could get them in because I think I can be a more effective legislator as a result," said Charles Grassley in discussing what made the Senate attractive to him (ibid., 992). Contemplating a run for the Senate, Dan Glickman, a four-term House member, explained, "I'm a generalist. I like to get involved in everything. The Senate is a forum more suited to that kind of personality" (ibid., 995). Those with House experience particularly emphasized the opportunities for broad involvement across a wide range of issues as one of the Senate's most attractive features. Despite immense changes in the House during the 1970s, that chamber's rules and norms still severely limit a member's ability to involve himself in issues outside the jurisdiction of his committees.

If senators are no longer expected to specialize, what is the status of the norm of legislative work? Senators no longer do the "highly detailed, dull, and politically unrewarding" work, nor are they expected to. Such tasks have been universally delegated to staff.

Between the 1950s and 1980s, senators greatly increased both personal and committee staffs. They did so in order to make possible involvement in a broader range of issues. Even the most junior senator now commands a staff of considerable size.

Once staffs relieved senators of detailed and routine work, it became much more feasible for senators to involve themselves in a broad range of issues. Staff members can do a great deal of the "homework" necessary for effective participation—work that in the days before large staffs the senator would have had to do himself. Effectiveness still requires an understanding of the substance and the politics of the issue. Typically it is now the job of staff members to gather such information and efficiently present it to the senator.

The literature suggests that the apprenticeship norm in its strict sense became defunct in the early 1960s under pressure from the large activist class of 1958 and the additional liberal northern Democrats that entered the chamber in large numbers in the first half of the 1960s (see Ornstein, Peabody, and Rohde 1977, and Foley 1980). The data on floor behavior indicate that a further change came in the 1970s; in the early part of that decade, freshmen became much more active on the floor. Even in the 1960s freshmen were consistently and significantly the least active group in terms of offering amendments on the floor and the least likely to offer amendments in a broad range of areas. In the 1970s and

1980s, freshmen became as active as other members on the floor. Although the expectation that junior senators were to serve an apprenticeship became defunct in the early 1960s, it was not until a decade later that freshmen senators commanded the resources that made high levels of activity on the floor possible. (For a discussion of committee activity, see Price 1972.)

In the contemporary Senate, freshmen are not expected to remain on the sidelines, nor even to be restrained in their participation in committee or on the floor. Since many are attracted to the Senate by the scope it allows for participation, it is not surprising that contemporary freshmen "hit the ground running," in Howard Baker's words (Dewar 1984, 13). All the freshmen in my sample entered the Senate with a list of legislative projects or of issues in which they immediately wanted to get involved. Large staffs make it possible for a senator to involve himself in a variety of issues from the beginning of his service, as all those in the sample did. With skill and a little luck, a freshman can even play a major leadership role in his first year, as Tom Harkin did on agricultural issues and Phil Gramm did on the Gramm-Rudman Bill in 1985.

According to Matthews, the norm of reciprocity dictates that senators employ great restraint in exercising the immense power vested in each by the rules of the Senate. "The spirit of reciprocity results in much, if not most, of the senators' actual power not being exercised," Matthews wrote (1960, 101).

The most obvious indicator of a change in the reciprocity norm is found in the great increase in the use of extended debate. Filibusters are much more frequent than they used to be and are much less restrictive in their target bills.

The period from 1955 to 1960 saw a total of two filibusters, for an average of .67 per congress; from 1961 to 1964, the average per congress was three; for 1965 to 1970, it was five. The congresses of the 1970s (1971–80) averaged 11.4 filibusters each and the congresses of the 1980s (1981–86) averaged 12.3. A rare event in the 1950s, the filibuster had by the 1970s become quite common.

This increase in frequency was accompanied by a broadening of the scope of the targeted bills. Of the seventeen filibusters between 1955 and 1968, almost 60 percent were related to civil rights. By contrast, of one hundred filibusters in the period from 1969 to 1986, less than 15 percent were related to civil rights.

No single issue has replaced civil rights as the primary target of the filibuster. During the 1970s and 1980s, a wide range of issues provoked extended debate on the Senate floor: the Supersonic Transport, the military draft, campaign financing, the genocide treaty, labor law reform, the dispute over a New Hampshire Senate seat, the sale of Conrail, and various nominations were among the measures filibustered. So too were the Rice Production Act and soft drink bottlers' antitrust immunity. (For a list of measures on which cloture votes were taken from 1917 to 1980, see *Congress and the Nation* 1981, 916–17.)

Because in the 1950s and 1960s the filibuster was primarily used against civil rights legislation, it was commonly perceived as a tool of conservatives. Now senators of all ideological hues employ the device. In the 1970s, liberals began to make use of the filibuster with some frequency; and in the 1980s, they did so much more often than conservatives. From 1955 through 1970, there were eighteen filibusters that pitted clearly defined ideological groups against each other; only three were instigated by liberals. During the 1970s, liberals conducted ten filibusters, conservatives thirty-two. In contrast, during the period of Republican control of the Senate in the 1980s, liberals conducted eighteen of twenty-three clearly ideological filibusters.

Not all filibusters are ideologically motivated. Filibusters undertaken because of constituency concerns are on the rise. Of thirty-seven filibusters between 1981 and 1986, five appear to have been motivated by relatively narrow constituency interests. In September, 1984, for example, New York's senators filibustered a banking bill because officers of Citicorp and Chase Manhattan opposed certain provisions (*Congressional Quarterly Almanac* 1984, 275).

The two senators who probably use the filibuster most frequently are Howard Metzenbaum, one of the Senate's most liberal members, and Jesse Helms, one of its most conservative. Although the frequency of use varies greatly, most current senators who have been in the Senate for any length of time appear to have participated in a filibuster at some point. Eleven of the fourteen nonfreshmen senators in my sample were reported to have done so. Of the other three, two are very junior. According to his administrative assistant, the only senior member reported never to have engaged in a filibuster had been so successful with *threats* to filibuster that he never actually had to engage in one. The growth in the number of filibusters is thus not simply the result of a few members increasingly exploiting the great leeway the Senate rules offer the individual. Rather, most members now engage in such behavior at least occasionally.

Furthermore, actual filibusters are simply the tip of the iceberg; threats to filibuster, most informed observers agree, are much more frequent than they used to be. "There are a lot of bills that aren't important enough to the leadership that you can hang the bill up simply by threatening a filibuster. And we do that a lot," a staffer reported. "Getting up on the floor and giving long speeches is not how filibusters are conducted anymore," another staffer explained. "Rather you threaten a filibuster, and then the leader pulls the bill off the floor, and you go behind the scenes to try to negotiate it out."

Clearly senators' behavior has changed; senators are now much more likely to make expansive use of the powers the Senate rules confer upon the individual. But can we conclude that the reciprocity norm is defunct? Could a body like the Senate operate at all without at least a weak reciprocity norm? Interview data suggest that the norm still exists, but that the limits of what is considered acceptable behavior are much broader and considerably more ambiguous than they were in the 1950s and that the sanctions for violating the limits are less. All of the senators in the sample were reported to be willing to engage in a filibuster; none would refrain as a matter of principle. On the other hand, even those who most frequently engage in extended debate agree it should only be used on important matters. "We try not to filibuster just because it's a bad bill," a staffer to a very active senator said. "It has to be a matter of principle, of morality." The senator will filibuster "only if the issue is of paramount importance to this country, if it is something that would have lasting national significance," a senior staff member to another activist senator explained. "He wouldn't do it just to win or on issues of lesser importance." In addition to matters of principle, issues of central importance to a member's state were mentioned as justifying the use of extended debate. "Your colleagues understand and respect you when you're fighting for the life of your constituency," an aide said. "But you have got to pick and choose your shots. You can't filibuster on everything just because you're going to lose."

Despite this seeming agreement that the use of extended debate should be confined to matters of extraordinary importance, filibusters on lesser matters appear to bring little condemnation. At the time I was asking these questions, Senator Paul Sarbanes of Maryland was filibustering a bill to shift management of Washington National and Dulles airports from the federal government to a local authority. Although of importance to the state of Maryland, the bill would not seem to qualify as a life-or-death matter for the state. Yet not once during my interviews was this filibuster mentioned as going beyond the acceptable limits. Those senators best known for frequently engaging in unlimited debate tend to be regarded with a sneaking admiration rather than with condemnation.

When asked how the senator decided when to engage in a filibuster, a staffer replied, "You've got to ask yourself, 'What do my colleagues think?' There are three types of senators around here: the show horses, the work horses, and the horses' asses. On any given day, a senator will fit into one of those categories, and you've got to ask yourself how will you be perceived." The problem is that the distinction between a show horse, now acceptable, and a horse's ass, unacceptable, is a good deal less clear than the old work horse-show horse distinction.

Senators are aware that unrestrained use of unlimited debate would make the Senate completely unable to function as a legislature. Many believe that the Senate is close to that point even now (see, for example, Ehrenhalt 1982). When senators engage in delaying tactics before a recess or adjournment, they are seriously inconveniencing their colleagues. The victims can respond with some pretty strong words; in 1982, when Senators Helms and East kept the Senate in session almost until Christmas by filibustering a nearly universally supported gas tax bill, Senator Simpson attacked Helms on the floor: "Seldom have I seen in my legislative experience of 17 years or more, a more obdurate and obnoxious performance. I guess it's called hardball. In my neck of the woods we call it stickball. Children play it" (Miller 1986, 83).

A senator who frequently engages in such behavior may not be "the most popular guy in the Senate," but most, like Howard Metzenbaum, "can live with that" (Ehrenhalt 1982, 2178). They can live with that because the costs, beyond sporadic criticism, are minimal. "You have to work with these people again next week," an aide to such a senator said, "and *they need you* as much as you need them." A number of the senators who most frequently push the powers inherent in the Senate rules to the limit are senior members who hold committee leadership positions. That greatly raises the costs of attempting to enforce restraint through excluding these senators from the favor-exchange network. In any case, there is no indication that an inclination to apply sanctions exists. Perhaps senators are a little less willing to cooperate with and help out those of their colleagues who most frequently push their powers to the limit. Yet when in early 1985 the Senate made modest committee assignment reforms, several senators known for such activism on the floor were granted waivers allowing them to keep more committee assignments than Senate rules allow.

According to Matthews, another aspect of the reciprocity norm was an admonition to help out a colleague when one was in a position to do so. In return, one could expect repayment in kind (Matthews 1960, 99). Although the interviews yielded little evidence of an imperative to do favors, senators certainly do favors for their colleagues and they expect similar treatment in return. The value of such exchanges is perhaps sufficiently immediate and obvious that no admonition is required. Floor and committee votes are only one and probably not the most important bargaining currency. What goes into the chairman's mark, particularly of appropriations bills, committee staff positions, and authorizations to hold field hearings in one's state can all serve as the basis for implicit or explicit bargaining. Senators even sometimes loan a colleague a sub-committee to allow the colleague to hold a field hearing.

"This mode of procedure requires that a senator live up to his end of the bargain, no matter how implicit the bargain may have been," Matthews wrote (1960, 101). Some senators believe there are more members who do not always keep their word than there used to be. Joseph Biden says that in the early 1970s when he entered the Senate, "there was only one person who, when he gave me his word, I had to go back to the office to write it down. Now there's two dozen of them" (Ehrenhalt 1982, 2176). Another senior senator, Robert Packwood, reports, "It was my experience in the early days that you could count on somebody's word from the beginning on a vote. They'd stick with it, even if it was going to affect them adversely. You didn't figure they were liars. Now, there are more members who are less reliable. They're very honest when they give you their word, but they don't hesitate to change it later on" (Miller 1986, 133).

A story told by the staffer of a junior but not freshman member may explain, in part, this decline in reliability. This senator frequently traded his vote on a given matter to several different colleagues. Asked by the aide what he would do if those colleagues found out, the senator told the staffer not to worry, because "no one talks to anyone else around here." When colleagues in fact do not know each other well and interact primarily on a superficial level, as is the case in the contemporary Senate, the social pressures to keep one's word are somewhat lessened. In addition, since much of the bargaining is done by staff, the chances of misunderstanding are increased.

Nevertheless, implicit and explicit bargaining is still the modus operandi of the Senate. And such a mode of procedure cannot survive unless most members understand each other and keep their word most of the time. The contemporary Senate just makes it a little less likely that partners to a bargain will always agree on its character, and a little less expensive to renege occasionally.

Explaining the Senate norm of courtesy, Matthews wrote, "A cardinal rule of Senate behavior is that political disagreements should not influence personal feelings" (1960, 97). Courtesy is still a norm of the Senate. "Avoid getting personal. Stick to the issues," the aide to a highly ideological senator included among his prescriptions for being an effective senator. On the Senate floor, members still go out of their way to

praise their colleagues, and outrageous compliments are not rare.
Witness the following exchange:

> *Mr. Matsunaga:* Mr. President.
> *Mr. Robert C. Byrd:* I see my good and dear and true friend from Hawaii, a
> man who wears a perpetual smile—
> *Mr. Helms:* And who is also generous.
> *Mr. Robert C. Byrd:* Not only generous, but also a gentleman. A man who is
> clean on the inside, a man who is clean on the outside; a man who neither
> looks up to the rich nor down on the poor; a man whose compassionate heart
> goes out to the young, the old, the maimed; a man who is too honest to cheat
> and too honorable to lie: that man is a gentleman. I speak of none other than
> my friend from Hawaii.
> *Mr. Helms:* Mr. President, I say if that does not gain for the majority leader
> a case of fine pineapple, nothing will (*Congressional Record* February 9,
> 1979, S1421).

Although courtesy is still a norm, it seems to be breached more often
that it used to be. "There's much less civility than when I got here ten
years ago," reports Joseph Biden. "Ten years ago you didn't have people
calling each other sons of bitches and vowing to get each other"
(Ehrenhalt 1982, 2176). Reports of name calling do appear to be increasing. In response to a provocative statement by John Heinz, Lowell
Weicker responded, "Anyone who would make such a statement is
either devious or an idiot. The gentleman from Pennsylvania qualifies
on both counts" (Cohen 1981, 238). These words were stricken and never
appeared in the *Congressional Record.* Annoyed when Christopher
Dodd insisted on a closed session of the Senate on Central America in
1983, Barry Goldwater delivered a multifaceted insult. "I served with
Dodd's father and I have tremendous respect for his father. I think one
of Chris' main troubles is that he's trying to live up to his old man and he
can't do it. And the evidence is that the two men who called for the
session made utter fools of themselves with the information they
thought they had," he said (Miller 1986, 135). Mark Andrews recently
referred to Helms and his supporters on the Agriculture Committee as
"Jesse and his pack of thieves"; Tom Harkin and Robert Dole have had
regular "slanging matches" on the Senate floor (Washington *Post,*
March 18, 1986).

Because the Senate has only one-hundred members, it is said that
senators can get to know one another in ways that members of the much
larger House cannot. It is true that most senators know each other and
even use first names, but these relationships are increasingly superficial
(Baker 1980). Senators do not spend much time together and conse-

quently do not know each other well. "You don't see the other Senators very often and you rarely get a chance to discuss many issues with them," Edmund Muskie said. "You rarely have more than one or two Senators sitting with you during the hearings. Days go by when you don't run into more than one or two Senators" (Asbell 1978, 80). Like many new senators, Pete Domenici was surprised at the lack of camaraderie:

> I think the exclusive club that we thought we were part of implied that we related to one another; mostly club members are supposed to be friends. They are supposed to see each other. I think one of the major frustrations in this institution is that there isn't any time for that. The thrust of this institution is against rather than in favor of that kind of relationship. That is yielding some very strange things, like relationships with staff almost exclusively instead of with fellow Senators (Jones and Woll 1979, 6).

The large staffs, the frequent traveling, and in general the time pressure created by the large number of issues with which they deal were identified as the reasons senators did not get to know each other well. "They don't have time to hang around the cloakroom like they did thirty years ago," a staffer concluded. Senators' increasing tendency to fully exploit the powers inherent in the Senate rules, when combined with senators not knowing each other well, puts considerable strain on the courtesy norm.

To the extent that the institutional patriotism norm dictates that senators focus their energy and attention inward on the Senate, and to the extent that it requires a "total" "emotional commitment to Senate ways" and bars "using the Senate for purposes of self-advertisement and advancement," the norm is defunct (Matthews 1960, 102). Substantial numbers of senators run for president at some time during their senatorial careers or seriously explore the possibility of doing so. Despite the neglect of Senate duties that such a campaign entails, these senators are not condemned by their fellow senators. The expectation that senators will use public arenas to promote their policy interests and themselves is widespread; that senators will attempt to speak to audiences outside as well as inside the chamber is taken as a matter of course. Behavior in committee and on the floor that is thus motivated is considered neither extraordinary nor illegitimate. Using the media to the fullest extent available is considered only good sense. "If you're asked [to appear on network television], you'd be a fool to turn it down," an aide to a senior senator explained. "If you're offered that kind of audience, that kind of possibility, you've got to use it."

Explaining another facet of the institutional patriotism norm, Matthews wrote, "Senators are expected to believe that they belong to the greatest legislative and deliberative body in the world" (1960, 101). If that implies an unwillingness to criticize the institution, then that aspect of the norm is also dead. The Senate has been subjected to a litany of criticism during the last few years, and senators have been prominent among the toughest critics (see, for example, Ehrenhalt 1982; Dewar 1984; Roberts 1984; Grabowski 1987; Calmes 1987; Kassebaum 1988.)

Senators' criticism is, however, often of a different character from the unrestrained Congress-bashing so typical among House members (see Fenno 1978, 164–68). Much of it appears to reflect a true concern about the institution, rather than being simply a form of self-aggrandizement, that is, a way for a senator to make himself look good at the expense of the institution. Thus the norm of institutional patriotism may not be defunct, but it has certainly changed. No longer are "senators. . . fiercely protective of, and highly patriotic in regard to, the Senate" (Matthews 1960, 102). They may criticize it in sorrow, but criticize they do.

The transformation of the Washington policy community, thus, raised the opportunity costs of abiding by Senate norms. It did so not just for a subset of members with special political needs or distinctive goals but for all senators. The opportunities offered by the new environment are broadly useful in the pursuit of the full range of goals.

Senators' behavior did change greatly and relatively quickly. For a time, senators continued to pay lip service to norms that they regularly violated (Ornstein, Peabody, and Rohde 1977). When such behavior occurs repeatedly and without being sanctioned, the norm is defunct. Both in terms of expectations and behavior, the norms of apprenticeship, specialization, and legislative work are defunct; reciprocity and institutional patriotism have undergone major changes; courtesy is still a Senate norm but is more frequently breached in practice.

In sum, both expectations and behavior have changed. A new Senate style, that is, a new behavioral strategy for goal advancement, has replaced the old style based upon specialization, restraint, and an inward-looking institutional patriotism. In contrast, the new style is predicated upon high rates of activity in multiple arenas and across a broad range of issues.

6 // Institutional Consequences of Behavioral Change

How an institution functions, that is, if and how it carries out the tasks with which it is charged, is determined by the behavior of the individuals within it. That behavior, in turn, is determined by the interaction among institutional arrangements, the external environment, and the goals of the individuals. In the previous chapter, I argued that senators, in response to a transformation in the external environment, changed institutional arrangements. They increased the supply and equalized the distribution of committee and staff resources in order to facilitate modes of behavior that the transformed external environment rewards. The altered institutional arrangements and the new external environment both contributed to a change in senators' behavior (see also Ornstein, Peabody, and Rohde 1977; Rohde, Ornstein, and Peabody 1985). A change in behavior of the magnitude that occurred should significantly alter how the institution functions. This chapter analyzes the effect the new behavioral strategies by which senators pursue their goals had on the Senate.

The Change in Committee Functioning

Senators increased the supply of valued committee positions and of staff to facilitate the broad involvement across a range of issues that the new Washington policy community rewards. Beginning in the mid-1960s, and accelerating in the 1970s, committee activity did increase. The average number of committee and subcommittee meetings per congress was 2,530 from 1955 through 1964; this increased to an average of 2,891 in the period from 1965 to 1968 and then rose monotonically to 4,265 during the 94th Congress (1975–76). It then began to decline but still stood at 3,236 in the 97th Congress (1981–82) (Ornstein, *et al.* 1984, 145–46).

Committees, thus, are more active than they used to be. The political environment of the 1980s—characterized by narrow partisan majorities, split control of the chambers, and huge budget deficits—imposed major constraints on legislative initiatives and was responsible for some decline in activity. Yet even in that environment, the level of activity was high and remained well above the level prior to 1969. During the 97th Congress, standing committees averaged 164 hearings each; during the 98th, they averaged 148 (Davidson and Kephart 1985, 65).

The most active committees are the most desirable. The four most prestigious committees were each well above the mean in number of hearings in the period from 1981 to 1984; they averaged 251 hearings each per congress. Commerce, Judiciary, and Labor were the other consistently highly active committees. The service committees were least active; Rules and Veterans Affairs averaged only thirty hearings per congress each in the early 1980s.

When senators have multiple assignments on highly active committees, committee functioning is adversely affected. Most members agree that senators are spread too thin. Senators typically face conflicting committee obligations. Senator Dan Quayle reported that on the morning of July 31, 1984, forty-nine senators had more than one committee or subcommittee meeting they should have been attending and that eleven had three or more (U.S. Congress, Senate 1984, 3). Consequently, simply getting a quorum for the transaction of committee business is often difficult. Committee decisions are frequently made by only a subset of committee members, a subset that may shift erratically over the course of a mark-up as senators run in and out. Because senators cannot develop expertise in the full range of issues under the jurisdiction of their various committees, they may become overly dependent upon staff. Certainly staff are responsible for all of the routine committee work and often for much else.

To alleviate these problems, the 1977 committee reorganization placed limits on the number of committee and subcommittee assignments a senator could hold and on the number of subcommittees a senator could chair (*Congressional Quarterly Weekly Report*, February 12, 1977, 280–81). Even though the limits imposed were quite generous—a senator was limited to serving on a total of eleven committees and subcommittees—by 1984, fifty senators held Senate-approved exemptions from these rules (U.S. Congress, Senate 1984, 8). Another reform effort in 1985 cut the number of slots on major committees from 231 to 214; but, in order to pass this modest contraction, the sponsors had to agree to eleven waivers exempting senators from committee service limitation rules (*Congressional Quarterly Weekly Report*, February 23, 1985, 348). The problem, of course, is that although such limitations may contribute to the efficient functioning of the institution, proliferation serves the interests of individual members. Consequently, senators have been unwilling to impose meaningful limitations upon themselves.

Most committees, particularly attractive committees, are highly active. That activity is not, however, the result of uniform and continuous participation by all the committee's members. Many hearings take place at the subcommittee level and are basically one man shows conducted by the subcommittee chair. Often even mark-ups at the full committee level do not involve the entire membership, certainly not as active participants. It is not necessarily the senior members who play the biggest role, but rather those senators interested enough in the legislation at issue to attend mark-up sessions on a regular basis.

During the 1960s, the distribution of influence within committees began to change; the tight hold of senior committee leaders began to relax, and junior members gained opportunities for meaningful participation. That shift toward more equality accelerated in the 1970s, with junior members becoming much more likely to serve on the most prestigious committees. Staff makes it possible for junior members, even freshmen, to take a meaningful part in committee decision making. By and large, a skillful junior member willing to put in personal time on an issue will be more influential than a senior member who relies primarily on staff. Given the time pressure under which all senators, but especially senior senators, work, junior members can sometimes assume leadership roles by default.

That most junior members of the majority party now hold at least one subcommittee chairmanship has contributed significantly toward the equalization of influence within committees. Some subcommittees are decision-making entities; they have the power to mark up legislation, giving their chairs some obvious clout. Many, however, do not; they hold hearings, but mark-ups are reserved for the full committee (see Smith and Deering 1984, 133–34). Subcommittees, particularly the latter type, are primarily vehicles for their chairmen. The chair has very wide discretion in terms of hearings. A subcommittee chair can use his subcommittee to pursue his own agenda and, by his activities, may influence the parent committee's agenda. Within an environment characterized by diverse and active interest groups and abundant press coverage, he may even be able to pressure a reluctant parent committee to take up his issue.

Because senators, including junior ones, have an array of opportunities for participation from which to choose, committee leaders not infrequently find themselves courting members, junior as well as senior, to get them to participate. Leaders need a quorum to transact business; in addition, leaders have a stake in maintaining a high rate of committee activity because an inactive committee is perceived to hold little influence. Full committee chairs often agreed to the creation of new subcommittees as a lure to increase incentives for participation. On some committees, even minority members are allowed to chair field hearings in their home states. The problem of maintaining participation is, of course, the greatest for the chairs of the least desirable committees; their rank-and-file members are, consequently, in a particularly strong position vis-á-vis the committee leadership. But even chairs of the prestige committees can have difficulty obtaining participation on important but unglamorous legislation.

The 1975 rules change that opened to the public all Senate committee meetings, including mark-up sessions, has had a major impact upon committee functioning. Led by junior senators Lawton Chiles and William Roth, and supported by the citizens' lobby Common Cause, the reform forces won decisively on a 77 to 16 vote (*Congressional Quarterly Weekly Report*, November 8, 1975, 2413–14). Although the new rules allow committees to close meetings by majority vote for certain specified reasons—national security, for example—virtually all committee meetings have been held in open session since the new rules went into effect.

Thus, almost all committee decision-making sessions are now open to the public and the press. Senators' actions are subject to direct scrutiny by lobbyists who compose much of the often large audience for mark-up sessions. Open meetings appear to have stimulated press coverage. Once committee meetings are open, important ones must be covered, and once covered, a story about the meeting is likely to be used. Committee decision making is a much more public enterprise than it used to be.

Open mark-ups and conference committee meetings give interest groups without strong ties to influential committee members a better chance to have an impact on committee decisions. Such groups now have much more access to timely information. The opening of mark-ups changes the dynamics of decision making. With press and lobbyists watching, compromise may be more difficult, and grandstanding may be encouraged. On the other hand, both the process and the outcome have to appear fair and responsible to the press. That constraint is likely to help groups representing the less powerful and those championing diffuse, noneconomic interests. Andrew McFarland explains one public interest group's perspective on open meetings:

> Common Cause is primarily concerned that a few reporters as well as a Common Cause volunteer be present at important committee meetings. Then, if a committee does something unexpected, such as granting tax exemptions to friends of committee members, news of this event will appear in Common Cause bulletins and influential newspapers. Common Cause volunteers attend most meetings of congressional taxation and appropriations committees and report to the organization's lobbyists if there is a sudden move to grant political favors (1984, 173).

The Senate Finance Committee's about-face on tax reform in the spring of 1986 was almost certainly the result of extensive and extremely negative press coverage of an orgy of special interest decision making in which the committee had engaged. (Putting together the reform proposal did take some closed negotiating sessions; see Birnbaum and Murray 1987.) Schlozman and Tierney report that 48 percent of citizens' groups perceive that sunshine rules have made it easier for their organization to operate effectively, well above the 36 percent of all groups surveyed (1986, 308–309).

Citizens' groups, unlike corporations, trade associations, or unions, report that other changes in Congress in the 1970s have made it easier for their organizations to operate effectively as well. Such changes as growth in congressional staff and the increase in the number of subcommittees, in addition to sunshine rules were perceived as making their task easier by 57 percent of citizens' groups but by only 14 percent of corporations, 15 percent of trade associations, and 18 percent of unions. At the other extreme, 63 percent of corporations, 68 percent of trade associations, 56 percent of unions, but only 24 percent of citizens' groups report that the changes have made their tasks more difficult (Schlozman and Tierney 1986, 308). Sunshine provisions and the more equal distribution of influence within committees have benefited those groups least likely to have had ties to powerful senior members, who in the past had disproportionate influence in committee decision making.

As a consequence of the sunshine reforms and changes in the distribution of resources, Senate committees have become more active and more internally democratic, and committee decision making has become more open to a variety of outside influences. Greater activity, openness, and internal democracy are likely to have an impact on the character of committee decisions. An even more important and more direct determinant is the ideological complexion of committee members and committee leaders. Did the changes in the distribution of valued committee positions result in a more ideologically representative committee system?

In the late 1960s, Democratic committee chairmen had been highly unrepresentative of the Democratic membership as a whole (see table 6.1). Since they are chosen on the basis of seniority, the chairs reflected the heavily southern and western cast of the pre-1958 Senate Democratic membership and were much more conservative than the typical Senate Democrat. In the mid- and late 1970s, the top committee leaders gradually came to be representative of the Democratic membership. Thus, twenty years were required for the major compositional change that took place in the Democratic membership between 1959 and 1965 to be reflected in the ranks of the top committee leadership.

Table 6.1 Ideological Representativeness of Committee Leaders
(Leaders' conservative coalition scores minus that for group as a whole)

Congress	Republicans	Democrats		
		All	North	South
86th–93rd (1959–1974) (mean)	4.6	24.4	11.9	2.0
94th	1.3	12.1	6.3	10.5
95th	-10.2	10.2	1.8	5.5
96th	-2.7	-2.3	-2.6	10.9
97th	-1.0	.9	.8	9.1
98th	-1.6	9.0	-.3	3.8
99th	-2.7	14.1	.5	4.8

In the 1980s, the leadership group again became somewhat more conservative than the membership as a whole. Although senior southerners were by no means immune, proportionately more senior northerners were defeated in the elections of 1978 and 1980. Consequently, southerners again held a disproportionate share of the top committee leadership positions in the mid-1980s. Thus during the 99th Congress (1985–86), when southerners made up little more than a fifth of the Democratic membership, they held almost half (seven of fifteen) of the ranking minority member positions on standing committees.

In contrast, the Republican leadership group is representative of the membership as a whole in the 1980s just as it has been since at least the early 1950s. Interestingly, moderate Republicans who assumed chairmanships in 1981 moved significantly to the right during the 97th Congress (1981–82), thus moving toward the ideological center of gravity of the Republican membership. Five Republican committee chairmen had scored below 70 on the conservative coalition index in the previous, Democratic-controlled congress; the scores for Mark Hatfield, Robert Packwood, Robert Stafford, Charles Percy, and Charles Mathias ranged from 19.2 to 50.4 and averaged only 38.9—far to the left of the Republican membership. These five senators increased their conservative coalition scores by an average of 18.7 points, double the 9.3 increase for the Republican membership as a whole. Although still on the left of their party during the early 1980s, they were considerably less deviant than they had been prior to assuming chairmanships. The great majority of Republican committee leaders continued to be strong conservatives. Similarly, Republican subcommittee leaders were representative of the Republican membership in the 1950s and 1960s and continued to be so in the 1970s and 1980s.*

During the 1960s, Democratic subcommittee chairmen were unrepresentatively conservative, and the difference was especially substantial between 1963 and 1968. The expansion in the number of good committees and the northern liberals' increasing seniority worked together to completely erase the difference by the early 1970s. From 1971 through 1986, Democratic subcommittee leaders were highly representative of the Democratic membership.

Although the ideological complexion of committee leaders influences likely policy decisions, the composition of committee memberships is even more important, especially given the equalization of influence within committees. To assess each committee's ideological center of gravity, the median conservative coalition score of its members is used. Committees are classified as unrepresentatively conservative or liberal relative to the chamber membership if the committee median is ten points above or below the chamber median.

The committee system of the 1970s, like that of the 1960s, was characterized by ideologically heterogeneous committees. Between 1971 and 1980, an average of 10.6 committees were unrepresentatively conservative or liberal in each congress—almost identical to the mean of 10.5 for the period from 1958 to 1970. The more conservative congresses of the early 1980s saw some decline in ideological diversity, with an average of 6.3 committees falling 10 points or more above or below the chamber

---

* To assess ideological representativeness, the mean conservative coalition score of subcommittee leaders (weighted by number of good subcommittees chaired) was compared with the mean score for the entire party membership.

median. The change in committee assignment practices did not produce uniformly representative committees.

Some committees show a remarkable continuity in their ideological center of gravity. The Agriculture Committee continued to be much more conservative than the chamber as a whole in the 1970s and 1980s, just as it had been since 1959. During the 1970s, the committee's median conservative coalition score was, on the average, 30.4 points to the right of the chamber median; during the 1980s, it averaged only 12 points more conservative than the full membership. However, the declining deviance was the result of the chamber becoming more conservative with the big Republican gain in 1980, not of the committee moving to the left. In contrast, the Labor Committee was consistently and significantly to the left of the Senate membership as a whole in the period following 1970, as it had been in the 1950s and 1960s. From 1971 through 1986, the Labor Committee's median conservative coalition score was, on the average, 30.2 points below the chamber median. Banking also continued to be a relatively liberal committee; in five of the eight congresses between 1971 and 1986, its center of gravity was more than 10 points to the left of the chamber median, and the average deviation over the eight congresses was -13.9.

These committees' ideological skew, it was argued earlier, is the result of differential member preferences. Liberals find Labor and Banking especially attractive committees; members from rural states who often are conservatives are attracted to the Agriculture Committee. Changes in committee assignment practices have further increased the likelihood that senators will receive their preferred assignments; consequently, these committees continue to be ideologically unrepresentative.

Differential attractiveness may account, at least in part, for the unrepresentativeness of two of the four prestige committees. Conservatives probably were more attracted to the Armed Services Committee than liberals during the 1960s and 1970s, and may have continued to be during the 1980s. Certainly the committee was unrepresentatively conservative from 1959 through 1986 (the 88th Congress excluded). From 1971 through 1980, the committee's ideological center of gravity was, on the average, 33.2 points to the right of the chamber median. During the more conservative congresses of the 1980s, Armed Services was relatively less unrepresentative than it had been during the 1970s; the difference between the committee and the chamber median averaged 12.9 points. Foreign Relations, arguably as a consequence of differential attractiveness during the early part of the period, was unrepresentatively liberal from 1969 through 1982; the committee's center of gravity was on the average 25 points to left of the chamber median during those years. A concerted effort to balance the committee by conservatives produced a representative committee in the 98th and 99th Congresses, during which the mean deviation was only 3 points.

The unrepresentatively conservative cast of Appropriations and Finance in the 1950s and 1960s cannot be attributed to liberals' lack of interest in those committees. These committees are broadly attractive to senators. The expansion in the number of assignments and changes in distribution transformed the money committees from conservative strongholds to representative forums. Appropriations was consistently more than 10 points to the right of the entire Senate from 1955 through 1970, its ideological center of gravity averaging 14.5 points to the right of the chamber median during those years. In the early 1970s, as a result of membership replacement, the committee became representative and has remained so ever since. In fact, the Appropriations membership in the 1970s and 1980s was more apt to be slightly to the left than to the right of the chamber membership (the mean difference was -3.1). Conservative dominance of Finance lasted from 1955 through 1978; during those years, the committee's average center of ideological gravity was 22.6 points to the right of the chamber median. A leftward shift in the committee's membership when the Senate itself moved to the right produced an unrepresentatively liberal committee in the 96th Congress (1979–80). During the 1980s Finance has been representative of the Senate membership, with a mean deviation of .9.

The change in the distribution of committee positions has not increased committee representativeness uniformly. Committees that are differentially attractive to liberals and conservatives for reasons of policy or reelection continue to be ideologically unrepresentative. However, Finance and Appropriations—the two prestige committees that are the most desirable and probably the most important of all Senate committees, and therefore extremely attractive to members of all ideological hues—have become representative of the chamber membership.

Overall, then, the current committee system is more ideologically representative than that of the 1960s. Three of the four prestige committees, including the two crucial money committees, are representative of the chamber membership. So too is the Budget Committee; unrepresentatively conservative during its first Congress (the 94th), Budget has been representative ever since. The Democratic and Republican subcommittee leaderships closely reflect the party contingents from which they are drawn. As is typical for their party, Republican committee leaders as a group are representative of the Republican membership. On the Democratic side, however, committee leaders, after becoming a faithful reflection of the membership in the late 1970s, began to diverge again in the mid-1980s. However, the current leaders, although more conservative as a group than the typical Democrat, are not as deviant as the chairmen of the 1960s and early 1970s were. The sort of intraparty conflict generated by the unrepresentativeness of the powerful chairs of the 1950s and 1960s is also less likely to reoccur because committee chairmen are less powerful now.

In sum, committees are more active, more internally democratic, and more open to a variety of external influences. The committee system is, on balance, more ideologically representative. To be sure, high activity rates in combination with the proliferation of assignments has produced problems of erratic participation. Yet, on balance, these changes should have enhanced the ability of committees to make decisions acceptable to a majority of the Senate and to major external actors. However, as the next two sections will show, committees have become *less* autonomous, and Senate decision making *less* committee centered.

The Senate Floor as a More Active Decision-making Arena

In the 1950s, Senate decision making was committee centered; to a large extent, the floor functioned to ratify decisions made within highly autonomous committees. By the 1970s, the Senate floor had become a much more active decision-making arena. Committees could no longer expect to have their decisions accepted as a matter of course. More—and more consequential—decisions were being made at the floor stage.

If the Senate's contested workload is defined as consisting of all measures that elicited at least one floor roll call vote, then the workload approximately tripled between the mid-1950s and the mid-1970s (see table 6.2). In the 1980s, the contested workload shrank to about the level that was characteristic of the 1960s. The decrease is a little misleading, however. During this period, Congress was passing fewer but longer and more complex bills. Thus, the average length of public bills enacted in the 1950s and 1960s (1955–68) was 2.7 pages, rising to 4.4 pages in the early 1970s (1969–74), and 7.9 pages for the later 1970s and early 1980s (1975–83) (Ornstein, *et al.* 1984, 150).

Between the 1950s and the 1970s, there was a dramatic increase in contested bills as a proportion of all bills passed. In the 84th Congress, only 2.2 percent of bills that passed elicited even one floor roll call vote (see table 6.3). That figure rose steadily through the late 1960s, reaching 8.3 percent in the 90th Congress (1966–67), and averaged 18.5 percent in the 1970s. Although it fell in the 1980s to 12.5 percent, that figure is well above

Table 6.2 Composition of the Senate's Contested Workload

Type of Measure	84th	86th	88th	90th	92nd	94th	96th	97th	98th	99th
					Congress					
Bills	55	115	97	114	170	218	176	116	99	106
Treaties	19	15	10	34	34	12	12	9	7	6
Nominations	6	8	2	4	6	17	26	37	13	27
Constitutional Amendments	1	1	1	0	2	0	1	1	2	1
Senate Resolutions	8	6	12	12	10	26	24	20	3	5
Totals	89	145	122	164	222	273	240	183	124	146[a]
No. of Roll Calls	217	422	534	596	955	1290	1027	948	646	735

[a]Impeachment votes on Judge Claiborne are included as one measure.

Table 6.3 Increase in Bills Contested on the Senate Floor
(Bills subjected to one or more roll call votes as a percentage of all bills passed)

Congress	Percent Contested
84th	2.2
86th	6.8
88th	7.2
90th	8.3
92nd	16.4
94th	21.0
96th	18.0
97th	14.4
98th	10.6

Source: Number of bills passed in the 84th through 97th Congresses taken from Ornstein, *et al.* 1984, 145–46; in the 98th from Davidson and Kephart 1985, 72.

the level prior to 1970. In the 1970s and 1980s, bills were much less likely than in previous decades to pass without at least one recorded floor vote. No longer are committee decisions perfunctorily ratified on the floor.

Of course not all measures that elicit at least one roll call get much floor attention. A large proportion elicit only one recorded vote (table 6.4). Although treaties, nominations, and Senate resolutions occasionally provoke great controversy, in general bills are more likely to be contentious than other types of measures. Nevertheless, a significant though declining proportion of bills that elicited at least one roll

Table 6.4 Increase in Highly Contentious Measures

No. of Roll Calls Per Measure	All Measures Congress									
	84th	86th	88th	90th	92nd	94th	96th	97th	98th	99th
1	59.6[a]	54.5	43.0	50.0	51.4	43.2	43.8	56.8	42.2	50.7
2	16.9	16.6	22.3	12.8	14.9	18.3	11.7	9.3	13.7	8.2
3–4	13.5	13.1	16.5	17.0	9.5	17.3	14.5	9.9	13.7	8.2
5–9	7.8	12.5	9.9	12.2	15.3	11.3	19.6	9.8	10.5	11.6
10+	2.2	3.4	8.3	7.9	9.0	9.9	10.4	14.2	15.3	13.7
	Bills Only									
1	40.0[a]	47.8	40.2	33.3	40.6.	35.3	30.1	36.2	34.3	38.7
2	25.5	18.3	22.7	16.7	17.1	20.6	11.9	12.9	17.2	9.4
3–4	18.2	14.7	17.5	23.7	11.8	19.7	19.3	15.5	16.2	19.8
5–9	12.7	10.5	9.3	14.9	19.4	12.8	25.0	13.8	13.1	13.2
10+	3.6	4.3	10.3	11.4	10.6	11.5	13.6	21.6	19.2	18.9
Maximum[b]	31	44	121	31	79	130	60	52	46	43

[a]Percent of measures (bills) on which only one roll call was taken.
[b]Maximum number of roll calls on a single bill.

call in fact elicited only one or two. In the 1950s, about two-thirds of contested bills were subject to only one or two roll calls; by the 1980s, half of contested bills were.

If many bills still receive only modest floor attention, an increasing proportion receive a great deal. By the end of the 1970s, almost one bill in seven could be expected to be subject to ten or more roll calls on the Senate floor; during the 1980s, one in five bills elicited ten or more roll calls.

Given the growth in the number of measures that make up the contested workload, the increases in the proportion of measures that elicited many roll calls represent very large increases in absolute terms. In the 84th Congress, nine measures elicited five or more roll calls, and only two elicited ten or more; in the 96th, the number subject to five or more roll call votes had grown to seventy-two, and the number eliciting ten or more stood at twenty-five. During the 1980s, when the contested workload had shrunk somewhat, an average of twenty-two measures per congress were subject to ten or more roll calls.

These data clearly show a major increase in activity on the Senate floor. But are the decisions being made consequential, or is this activity largely symbolic? One indicator that can be employed to distinguish real from symbolic decisions is vote margin. A very wide margin usually indicates that the outcome was not in doubt and that a recorded vote was taken for reasons other than deciding the issue; senators may, for example, want to be on record as supporting a popular position or program.

Whether all measures or bills only are considered, no trend in the proportion of close roll calls is evident (see table 6.5).* The 84th Congress, with its very close party balance, produced by far the highest proportion of close votes; since then, just under 20 percent of roll calls have been close, on average. Symbolic roll calls as a proportion of all roll calls showed little trend during the period of Democratic control; the 1980s saw a modest increase. The increase in floor activity, then, was not primarily an increase in symbolic activity. Not only are many more decisions made on the floor; these decisions are as likely as those made in the 1950s to be real rather than symbolic decisions.

Furthermore, the more roll calls a measure elicits, the more likely those votes are to be close and the less likely they are to be symbolic. Those measures that provoke a high rate of floor activity also tend to be the most controversial measures.†

Table 6.5 Real versus Symbolic Decisions

Vote Margin	All Measures Congress									
	84th	86th	88th	90th	92nd	94th	96th	97th	98th	99th
Close	27.6[a]	18.5	17.4	19.3	19.7	17.7	19.1	20.6	18.3	19.6
Symbolic	23.0	24.2	12.9	23.7	26.8	24.3	25.3	32.2	30.7	29.7
	Bills Only									
Close	32.8	20.3	17.8	20.2	19.4	18.1	20.3	22.2	19.2	20.9
Symbolic	14.7	22.4	10.7	20.2	25.2	24.0	22.9	27.5	28.6	25.8

[a]Percent of roll calls on which margin was close.

---

* Close votes have been defined as those on which the margin was ten votes or less, and symbolic votes as those on which the margin was sixty or more; that is, if the full membership is voting, a split of 80–20 or greater is a symbolic vote.
† Measures were classified into three categories of activity level (one roll call; two to four; five or more). The percent close and the percent symbolic roll calls were computed for each activity level category for each congress. The between-group difference on percent symbolic was significant at the .05 level in nine of ten congresses; on percent close roll calls, it was significant at the .05 level in six of ten congresses.

The growth in the mean number of recorded votes per measure is largely due to a huge increase in the number of amendments offered and forced to a recorded vote. The number of amendments, excluding committee amendments, on which the Senate took a roll call vote stood at 115 in the 84th Congress; it increased to 204 in the 86th Congress (1959–60). The titanic struggle over the 1964 Civil Rights Bill accounts for much of the very large increase in the 88th Congress, during which 392 amendments came to a floor vote. The figure is, however, almost equally high—390—in the 90th Congress, even though no single legislative battle accounts for the large number of amendments. The 1970s saw another big jump in amendments; during the 92nd Congress (1971–72), 606 amendments came to a recorded vote on the Senate floor; the figure increased to 698 in the 94th Congress (1975–76), stood at 555 in the 96th Congress (1979–80), and averaged 486 in the congresses of the 1980s—a decrease but nevertheless a much higher level than those of any of the congresses of the 1950s or 1960s.

Floor tactics changed as the number of amendments increased. In the 1950s and 1960s, amendments were typically simply voted up or down. In the 1970s, an amendment's foes frequently first moved to table the amendment, hoping to benefit from the procedural nature of such a vote. Amending activity is here defined as votes on amendments (other than committee amendments), on amendments to amendments, and on motions to table amendments. The change in amending activity on bills in the congresses under study is shown in table 6.6.[*]

Table 6.6 Increase in Amending Activity on Bills

No. of Amending Roll Calls per Bill	Congress									
	84th	86th	88th	90th	92nd	94th	96th	97th	98th	99th
0	27.3[a]	47.0	29.9	26.3	42.4	38.5	26.1	30.2	34.3	34.9
1–2	50.9	33.0	42.3	42.1	26.4	34.4	34.1	32.8	32.3	25.5
3–4	10.9	10.4	13.4	12.3	14.1	11.0	14.2	6.0	8.1	14.2
5–9	9.0	6.1	6.2	10.5	7.7	8.8	18.2	14.7	10.1	12.3
10+	1.8	3.5	8.2	8.8	9.4	7.3	7.4	16.4	15.2	13.2
Maximum[b]	24	20	110	29	74	114	41	45	41	39

[a]Percent of bills on which no amending roll calls were taken.
[b]Maximum number of amending roll calls on a single bill.

---

[*] On the average, 95 percent of amending activity occurred on bills.

The proportion of contested bills subject to no amending activity displays no trend over time; it varies a good deal within the range of just over one-quarter to nearly one-half of contested bills, and averages about one-third. The proportion of bills on which there is either little or no amending activity (one or two amendments that reached to a roll call) has declined whereas the proportion subject to high amending activity has increased considerably. In the 84th and 86th Congresses, about 10 percent of contested bills were subject to five or more amending roll calls. This figure increased to 14.4 percent in the 88th and 19.3 in the 90th Congress; in the 92nd and 94th, it declined slightly but remained well above the level of the 88th Congress. During the 96th through 99th Congresses, over one-quarter of contested bills were subjected to five or more amending roll calls; in the congresses of the 1980s, about 15 percent were subjected to ten or more amending roll calls. Given the increase in the number of contested bills, these increases in percentages represent very large increases in absolute numbers. In the 84th Congress, six bills were subject to five or more amending roll calls; in the 96th Congress, forty-five bills were. The congresses of the 1980s saw an average of sixteen bills on which ten or more amending roll calls were taken.

Amending marathons are much more frequent than they used to be. On the 1964 Civil Rights Bill, 110 roll calls on amendments were taken. This bill aside, however, the most highly contested bills of the 1950s and 1960s provoked fewer than thirty amending roll calls. In the 92nd Congress, the maximum was seventy-four; in the 94th, 114; and the average for the 96th through 99th was 41.5. In all three congresses of the 1970s and the first two congresses of the 1980s, tax bills provoked the maximum amending activity. The first budget resolution of 1985 and the farm program authorization (S. 1714) elicited the highest level of amending activity of the 99th Congress.

These data again show the increase in floor activity. Before we can conclude that this increased activity represents a rise in the number of consequential decisions made on the floor, vote margins must be examined. If most of the increase in amending activity is accounted for by amendments that pass or fail by very wide margins, we can conclude that the increased activity is largely symbolic.

An examination of passage votes on amendments shows no secular trend in the proportion decided by a close margin. If the 84th Congress is set aside as atypical because of its very close party balance, then throughout the period under study around one-fifth of passage votes on amendments were decided by a narrow margin (that is, ten votes or less). the proportion decided by a very large margin (sixty votes or more) increased from an average of 10 percent in the 1950s and 1960s to an average of almost 17 percent in the 1970s, and about 25 percent in the 1980s. More of the floor decisions on amendments are symbolic than in previous decades; nevertheless, the proportion of such decisions that are symbolic remains relatively low. The increase in amending activity is by no means simply a symbolic show without policy consequence.

A classification into issue areas of those measures that elicited at least one roll call provides a picture of the Senate's contested floor agenda. An examination of the contested agenda over time may allow us to gauge whether the increase in floor decision-making activity is related to change in the issue agenda.

The issue classification used is that of Clausen (1973). His five categories are supplemented by a sixth "internal" category, which, as its name implies, includes such internal Senate business as rules changes and decisions concerning ethics and other measures that affect senators very directly, such as campaign finance legislation.*

Government management of the economy and international involvement dominate the contested Senate floor agenda in terms of frequency of measures (see table 6.7). The relative importance of the two issues varies, but neither their relative importance nor their combined importance shows any trend over time. Agricultural assistance is a small and declining proportion of the Senate agenda. In terms of proportion of measures, civil liberties—which includes matters such as subversive activities regulation and criminal justice procedure, in addition to black civil rights—makes up only a small proportion of the contested agenda. Social welfare measures generally account for a moderate proportion of the agenda; that proportion is somewhat erratic but exhibits no secular trend.

Thus, as the contested workload increased, the distribution of measures across these broad issue categories did not change in any consistent fashion. These findings strongly suggest that the increase in floor decision-making activity is not due simply to one or a few hot issues rising to great prominence. If one or a few such issues accounted for most of the increase in the contested agenda, we would expect more change in the distribution of measures across issue areas.

The mean number of roll calls per measure in each issue area over the ten congresses under study provides an indicator of which were the most and least conflictual issue areas and how this has changed over time (see

---

* Particularly because Senate amendments need not be germane, all the roll calls on a given measure may not fall into the same issue category. A measure was classified into a given category if more than half of the votes on the measure fell into that category.

Table 6.7   The Senate Agenda

	A. Distribution of Measures Across Issue Areas					
Congress	Government Management	International Involvement	Social Welfare	Civil Liberties	Agricultural Assistance	Internal/ Mixed
84th	31.5	37.1	7.9	5.6	10.1	7.9
86th	39.3	27.6	11.7	4.8	6.2	10.3
88th	33.1	24.8	14.9	2.5	7.4	17.4
90th	29.3	37.8	11.0	4.3	3.0	14.6
92nd	31.1	30.6	20.3	5.4	3.2	9.5
94th	42.5	18.7	14.7	2.9	4.4	16.8
96th	38.3	25.4	12.9	6.3	3.7	13.3
97th	39.3	27.3	12.0	6.6	5.5	9.3
98th	35.5	21.8	16.1	12.9	3.2	10.5
99th	41.5	28.3	7.5	8.5	6.6	7.6

	B. Roll Calls Per Measure Within Issue Areas					
Congress	Government Management	International Involvement	Social Welfare	Civil Liberties	Agricultural Assistance	Internal/ Mixed
84th	1.8	2.3	3.6	1.0	5.2	2.0
86th	2.4	2.3	4.6	8.0	3.6	1.9
88th	2.7	3.7	4.5	41.3	6.0	2.8
90th	3.0	2.3	5.8	11.3	3.4	4.5
92nd	4.2	4.1	3.5	10.0	2.6	4.0
94th	5.4	3.1	3.0	15.3	2.9	4.9
96th	5.1	2.5	4.0	6.4	3.9	3.8
97th	5.3	3.0	4.0	10.7	5.4	8.4
98th	4.5	6.4	3.8	3.5	6.0	7.9
99th	5.5	4.5	2.6	3.1	7.2	9.9

table 6.7B). In the mid-1950s, agricultural assistance was the most conflictual issue area; by the 1970s, activity on farm measures was consistently below the mean for all measures, and usually considerably below; in the 1980s, farm legislation became highly controversial again. Social welfare measures consistently provoked more activity than the mean from the mid-1950s through the late 1960s—a period of the incubation and then passage of New Frontier and Great Society social programs. In the 1970s and 1980s social welfare measures produced lower than average levels of activity. In the mid- and late 1970s, as first energy policy and then economic policy in general moved to the center of controversy, government management measures surpassed the mean for activity level. Civil liberties measures provoked a high level of amending activity during most of the congresses under study.

The internal/mixed category in the 1980s provides a particularly interesting example of the effect of political environment on Senate decision making. Intended as a residual category, it includes those measures
on which less than half the roll calls could be categorized into one of the
other five issue categories. Despite the Senate's lack of a germaneness
rule, most measures subjected to a significant number of roll calls could
be classified into one of the issue categories—until the 1980s. The budget
deficits and the narrow partisan majorities of the 1980s combined to
make passing legislation, especially legislation involving the spending
of money, much more difficult. This, of course, accounts for the shrink-
ing of the contested workload in the 1980s. Another consequence was
that "must" bills, ones that had to pass to keep the government functioning, became vehicles for all sorts of extraneous provisions. Massive
continuing appropriations resolutions were regularly subjected to
amending marathons as senators attempted to catch the last (and often
the only) train leaving the station.

Although variations in the agenda of political issues and in the political climate clearly influence "where the action is," the Senate floor has
become a more active decision-making arena across the full range of
issue areas. Measures in all areas are fair game on the Senate floor.

Certainly no committee is exempt from having its legislation subjected to challenge at the floor stage. Most committees now face many
more floor roll call decisions than they did in the 1950s. The number of
floor roll calls taken on its measures has increased significantly for ten
of the eleven major committees in existence for the entire period under
study (see table 6.8). Only the Agriculture Committee shows no such
trend. For most of the other committees, the number of roll calls to
which their legislation was subjected increased from the 1950s to the

Table 6.8 Increasing Floor Challenge to Measures From Most Committees (Mean
number of roll calls per congress on measures, by committee of origin)

Committee	1950s	1960s	1970s and 1980s
Appropriations	50	90	175
Armed Services	3	22	71
Finance	35	72	136
Foreign Relations	55	76	82
Agriculture	33	30	32
Banking	27	16	45
Commerce	15	21	44
Interior/Energy	5	11	40
Judiciary	36	43	93
Labor	24	44	45
Public Works/Environment	12	7	27

1960s, and then again in the 1970s and 1980s. The increases were frequently very large, particularly for the prestige committees. During the 1950s, decisions of the Armed Services Committee were very seldom challenged on the floor; in the 1970s and 1980s, its legislation was subjected to about 70 roll call votes per congress. Measures from Appropriations, Finance, and Foreign Relations were subjected to a considerable number of roll call votes in the 1950s; all now confront still more frequent floor decisions. In the case of the two money committees, the increase has been large, and legislation from the two is the target of a great many more floor roll call votes than any other committee. The only committees that rival the prestige committees as targets of such high levels of floor activity are Judiciary and Budget.*

Of course, many of these roll call votes are decisions on amendments offered to the committee's legislation on the floor. During the 1980s, the prestige committees have had to contend with large numbers of such attempts to alter their measures on the floor. Appropriations confronted 109 amendments per congress on the average; Finance, seventy-nine; Armed Services, forty-nine; and Foreign Relations, thirty-one. Of other committees, only Judiciary with forty-six and Budget with sixty-eight were in the same range; the next highest committee was Agriculture, with twenty-three. For Appropriations, Finance, Armed Services, and Judiciary, these figures represent very large increases over the 1950s; measures from these committees faced three or more times as many floor amendments in the 1980s as they did in the 1950s.

What impact has the increase in amending activity had on legislative outcomes? The percentage of first degree amendments subjected to a roll call vote that passed is shown in table 6.9.† Except for the 88th Congress, amendment success rate has been remarkably stable at around thirty percent.** Therefore, as amending activity increased, the amendment success rate did not fall. Consequently, many more floor amendments are now accepted. During the entire 84th Senate, only thirty-three first degree amendments won on floor votes. By and large, the Senate showed great restraint in altering legislation on the floor. The number of successful amendments increased in the late 1950s and

---

* The mean number of roll calls per congress on measures from the Budget Committee was 75.9 for the 94th through 99th Congresses.
† Committee amendments are excluded. Including second degree amendments does not appreciably change success rates and would complicate interpretation.
** The 88th Congress is an anomaly in terms of the success rate of amendments. The unusually low rate is in part but by no means completely explained by the large number of unsuccessful amendments offered to the 1964 Civil Rights Bill.

the 1960s, and then again very significantly in the 1970s. During the 1970s, the Senate accepted on the average 183 floor amendments per congress—about 5½ times as many as it had during the mid-1950s. Although this dropped in the 1980s, the mean number of amendments accepted—141—was over four times the figure of the mid-1950s. Clearly, the Senate now is much more willing to alter measures on the floor.

Table 6.9 Outcomes of Amending Activity

| Congress | Amendments that Passed (first degree only) | | Percent of Bills Amended of | |
	Percent	Number	All Contested Bills	Those with Amending Activity
84th	30.0	33	23.6	33.3
86th	29.8	59	29.6	57.6
88th	14.4	54	24.7	35.3
90th	30.8	113	42.1	57.1
92nd	35.3	187	33.5	58.2
94th	28.5	182	31.7	53.1
96th	35.1	179	50.6	68.5
97th	29.3	161	44.0	63.0
98th	31.8	127	39.4	60.0
99th	31.0	136	42.5	65.2

Bills are less likely now than in the past to escape the floor stage unscathed. Although the trend is somewhat erratic, the proportion of contested bills amended on the floor has increased significantly. During the 1980s, 40 percent or more of all contested bills had at least one amendment added on the floor. If we restrict our attention to those bills subjected to some amending activity, the trend is similar but the figures are considerably higher. Once floor amendments are offered, a bill is increasingly unlikely to emerge from the floor stage unchanged.

Many more floor amendments are approved and many more bills are now amended on the floor. Although a definitive assessment of the legislative impact of these trends would require judgments about the importance of the amendments accepted and of the bills amended, an examination of amendment success rates by measures' committee of origin does provide some basis for inferences about the importance of the bills at issue. Are the presumably less important bills from minor committees more frequently amended than the presumably more important bills from major committees?

By and large, the minor committees, which also have small contested workloads, tend to be most successful in warding off amendments on the floor. The District of Columbia Committee, for example, did not have a single amendment added to one of its bills on the floor during the congresses under study. Roughly, committee success rates vary inversely with committee workloads; those committees which handle the largest number of contested measures tend to be least successful in warding off floor amendments. That relationship, although evident throughout the period under study, seems to strengthen in the 1970s.

Finance, Appropriations, Foreign Relations, and Armed Services, the Senate's prestige committees, also tend to be its busiest, and, during the 1970s and 1980s, generally were less successful than average in protecting their bills on the floor. The average committee success rate for the 1970s and 1980s was 68.2 percent; that is, committees were unsuccessful in warding off floor amendments to their bills a little more than 30 percent of the time. For the same period, the mean success rate of the four prestige committees was 61.9 percent; almost four of ten floor amendments offered to bills from these top committees passed. To the extent that the bills handled by these four committees are on the average more consequential than those handled by other committees, the prestige committees' below-average success rates imply that the more important bills are more likely to be amended on the Senate floor than the less important bills.

That it fosters the development and application of expertise has always been a primary justification for the committee system. By the same token, marking up a bill on the floor has been frowned upon because less expertise will be brought to bear in that arena. Presumably, expertise is most critical in the crafting of legislative language, and the quality of legislation may be affected by whose amendments are accepted. One might argue that amendments offered by committee members are likely to reflect more expertise than those offered by nonmembers.

In the 1950s and 1960s, committee members consistently had a significantly higher success rate than nonmembers on amendments they sponsored (see table 6.10). However, the difference in success rates narrowed in the 1970s and 1980s, and, in the 99th Congress, nonmembers were more successful than members. Senate majorities are increasingly willing to support amendments offered by nonmembers of the committee of origin. Either expertise is valued less, or, because of the increase in staff, it is less associated with membership on the originating committee.

Table 6.10 Floor Success Rates on Amendments Offered by Committee Members and Nonmembers (Percent of first and second degree amendments that passed)

Congress	Member	Nonmember
84th	32.2	25.5
86th	35.0	26.2
88th	23.1	12.1
90th	36.1	27.2
92nd	38.5	34.5
94th	32.4	27.9
96th	45.5	31.8
97th	32.7	29.6
98th	34.4	30.7
99th	27.8	34.3

Nonmembers, it will be recalled, offer a growing proportion of the increasing number of Senate floor amendments. Combined with the increasing success by nonmembers in obtaining passage of their amendments on the floor, these trends almost certainly signify a major increase in the influence of non-committee members on Senate legislation. If, in fact, non-committee members (and their staffs) bring less expertise to bear in the drafting of amendments than do committee members, the result may be sloppier legislation. The involvement of senators not on the committee, on the other hand, is likely to bring a broader perspective to the questions at issue.

One might argue that the influence of nonmembers has not increased; rather the arena in which it is exercised has changed. Perhaps committee members in the past were better at anticipating what was acceptable to their chamber colleagues or perhaps they were more amenable to accommodating those colleagues in behind-the-scenes bargaining (see Hall 1987b). Both possibilities may be partly valid, but that does not necessarily mean that there has been no increase in the influence of nonmembers. In the 1950s, when the issue agenda was relatively small and stable, when the Senate membership was ideologically homogeneous by later standards, and when many senators' interests were relatively narrow (often being confined primarily to the issues within the jurisdiction of their own committees), committee members probably found it relatively easy and not very costly in policy terms to craft legislation acceptable to a large majority of their colleagues. Within the framework here employed, committee autonomy could not have survived for long if it resulted in large numbers of senators having to accept policy outputs they found abhorrent. The weakening of committee autonomy in the 1960s can be traced to the increased ideological heterogeneity of the membership. Ideologically unrepresentative committees were unwilling and unable to report legislation acceptable to the great majority of the now deeply polarized Senate. Thus, conflicts frequently spilled out on the floor.

The more representative committees of the 1970s and 1980s should have been better able than the skewed committees of the 1960s to produce broadly acceptable legislation, yet their legislation was more, rather than less, subjected to being amended on the floor. To be sure, the selective participation of senators in the work of their committees may have resulted in the actual decision makers on the particular bill being far from representative. Furthermore, in a Senate that is ideologically fairly polarized, representative committees also tend to be polarized, and such committees may be less inclined to compromise. In addition, and crucially important, given a more crowded and less stable issue agenda and a Senate membership characterized by broad and varied issue interests, the information on senators' preferences necessary to anticipate their reactions and write a broadly acceptable bill may be hard to come by. Even to the extent the information is available, fashioning a bill acceptable to such a large number of interested senators may be difficult. Similarly, when a great many senators have a variety of interests in a bill, accommodating them all through behind-the-scenes bargaining may be too complex, too time consuming and too expensive in policy terms. Thus, contemporary Senate committees may be less adept at anticipating what is acceptable to their colleagues; they may even be less willing to accommodate all their interested colleagues in behind-the-scenes bargaining. If so, the expansion of senators' involvement in issues is a primary cause, and one is led to conclude that senators do have more influence on legislation from committees on which they do not serve than they used to.

One can argue that contemporary committees try harder to anticipate their colleagues' reactions and to accommodate them through behind-the-scenes bargaining. In the 1950s the combination of norms bolstering committee autonomy, closed committee proceedings, and senators' small staffs made challenging a committee on the floor difficult for senators not on the committee, even if their views were not taken into account. Knowing this, committees might have been inclined to engage in the minimum amount of accommodation necessary to prevent a challenge. Lacking all these advantages, committees now have a greater incentive to accommodate interested nonmembers. Because the number of interested nonmembers tends to be so much larger, accommodating them has become more difficult; however, committees make very serious attempts to do so. Interview data suggest committees attempt to anticipate what will be acceptable to a broad majority of the Senate, and they bargain extensively with individual interested nonmembers. Because of what nonmembers may be able to do to a committee's bills once they reach the floor, committees are now more open to influence by nonmembers than they used to be.

Certainly, Senate decision making is characterized by much broader participation than in the past. Many more decisions are now made in an arena—the Senate floor—where the full membership can participate. Also, both the framing of alternatives (via the introduction of amendments) and the selection among them are increasingly broad-based enterprises.

In sum, as senators became increasingly active on the floor, they changed Senate decision making. The floor has become a more active decision-making arena. More decisions are made on the floor, and these are consequential rather than symbolic decisions. Committees can no longer expect their decisions to be accepted by the chamber without question. Attempts to alter committee decisions through floor amendment are now routine and often successful. Measures from the prestige committees, because they are consequential and often controversial, are especially likely to be targets of amending attempts. These committees' prestige does not produce deference to their decisions.

Increased levels of amending activity on the floor have reduced committees' control over the Senate agenda within their jurisdictions and increased the influence of nonmembers. Committees cannot keep issues from being considered by refusing to report legislation; the issue will simply be brought to the floor as an amendment.

As a result, Senate committees are less autonomous in decision making than they used to be, and Senate decision making is less committee centered. Participation in the processes by which Senate agenda is determined, and Senate outcomes are arrived at, is much more broadly based than in the past.

Obstructionism as Standard Operating Procedure

"There is today more power in the hands of a single person, more leverage to impede the process, than there used to be," says Russell Long, a senator from 1948 to 1987. "We've given far too much power to the impeders" (Ehrenhalt 1982, 2178). The Senate has done so not by changing its rules but by being unwilling and unable to prevent senators from fully exploiting the power those rules grant to each of them.

Senate rules put few constraints upon senators' floor activism. A senator can hold the floor indefinitely unless the Senate is willing to invoke cloture, which requires an extraordinary majority. A senator may offer an unlimited number of amendments, and in most cases those amendments need not even be germane. In the 1950s norms restrained senators from fully exploiting the powers granted to them by the rules of the Senate. The transformation of the Washington policy community since then has greatly increased senators' incentives to exploit those resources; in response, senators' behavior changed. In this section, the impact of senators' greater use of extended debate upon the decision-making process will be examined.

Like high levels of amending activity on the Senate floor, frequent use of extended debate has become more attractive because it is a high visibility strategy and one that allows a senator to broaden the range of his involvement in issues beyond the jurisdiction of his committee. But, as Bruce Oppenheimer (1985) argues persuasively, the filibuster has also become more attractive because it has become more effective. During the 1960s and 1970s, as the number and complexity of issues on the political agenda grew rapidly, the Senate's workload increased. The expanding workload and senators' increased amending activity on the floor put great pressure on floor time (see Oppenheimer 1985, 396–97). As floor time became an increasingly precious commodity, a filibuster's impact upon the Senate's functioning intensified; when floor time is scarce, a senator need not obstruct the flow of business for long to have a devastating impact upon the Senate's schedule. Consequently, the filibuster, actual or threatened, became a more powerful weapon.

Filibusters are much more frequent than they used to be.* The period from 1955 to 1960 saw a total of two filibusters, for an average of .67 per congress; from 1961 to 1964, the average per congress was three; for 1965 to 1970, it was five. The 1970s congresses (1971–80) averaged 11.4 filibusters per congress, and the 1980s congresses (1981–86) averaged 12.3. A rare event in the 1950s, the filibuster had become commonplace by the 1970s.

This increase in frequency was accompanied by a broadening of the

---

* When Senate debate becomes a filibuster is, to some extent, a subjective judgement. The analysis here is based upon the following lists: for 1955–76, Paul S. Rundquist, "Filibuster and Cloture Related Delays in the Senate, 1947–1976," Congressional Research Service, 1977; for 1977–78, United States Senate, Committee on Rules and Administration, *Senate Cloture Rule* (Washington, D.C.: U.S. Government Printing Office, 1979), pp. 50–54; for 1979–80, Mildred Amer, "Senate Filibusters in the 96th Congress," Congressional Research Service, 1981; for 1981–86, *Congressional Quarterly Almanac*, annual list of issues on which cloture votes were taken. In addition, the Meese confirmation filibuster in 1985 is included although no cloture vote was taken.

scope of the targeted bills. Of the seventeen filibusters between 1955 and 1968, seven concerned civil rights bills; another three dealt with attempts to change Rule 22, the cloture rule—attempts very much tied to the struggle to enact civil rights legislation. Thus, almost 60 percent of the filibusters were related quite directly to civil rights legislation. In contrast, only five of sixty-three filibusters in the period from 1969 to 1980 concerned civil rights bills. Another four were aimed at attempts to change Rule 22, but that struggle was less closely tied to civil rights after the mid-1960s. Even if these are counted as civil rights filibusters, less than 15 percent of filibusters in the latter period were related to civil rights. Four of thirty-seven filibusters between 1981 and 1986 concerned issues related to civil rights.

As the filibuster changed from an extraordinary tactic reserved for the most momentous of issues to a relatively common device, targeted bills became more diverse both in subject matter and in significance. The majority continued to involve ideologically charged issues of considerable importance—the genocide treaty, the consumer agency debate, labor law reform, natural gas pricing, "social issues" such as school prayer, and the imposition of sanctions on South Africa. Internal institutional questions other than Rule 22 also became more prominent. The battle over Senate Resolution 60 giving junior senators more staff provoked a filibuster that pitted junior against senior members; proposals to broadcast Senate proceedings were filibustered at several points during the 1980s. The New Hampshire Senate seat dispute occasioned a filibuster that split the Senate along partisan lines. Narrower and less consequential bills also were subjected to filibusters. Perceptions of adverse constituency effects motivated the filibusters of the Rice Production Act by Louisiana's senators in 1976, the Financial Services Competitive Equity Act by New York's senators in 1984, the Surface Transportation and Uniform Relocation Assistance Act by Illinois' senators in the same year, and the Metropolitan Washington Airports Transfer Act by Maryland Senator Paul Sarbanes in 1986.

From 1955 through 1970, when filibusters were rare and almost all concerned ideologically charged issues, most filibusters pitted clearly defined ideological blocs against each other; 87 percent of the instances of extended debate pitted southern Democrats against advocates of civil rights, or conservatives more generally against liberals. In only three cases, none before 1965, was there no such clear ideological division: for example, although conservative southern senators were prominent in the opposition to the constitutional amendment abolishing the Electoral College, the 1970 battle could not be classified as simply a fight between liberals and conservatives; a number of senators from small states also opposed the change. During the 1970s, the proportion of filibusters that pitted liberals against conservatives declined to 76 percent; thirteen filibusters were not thus classifiable. During the early and mid-1980s (1981–86), 67 percent of filibusters involved a clear liberal versus conservative split; in five of the remaining thirteen cases, a relatively narrow constituent interest motivated the filibuster.

Given the increasing time constraints under which the Senate works, frequent filibusters present serious problems for senators who need to pass legislation in order to advance their goals as well as for the Senate as a legislative institution. The Senate membership has attempted to alleviate those problems through rules changes, but with limited success. The initial impetus for overhauling Rule 22 to make cloture easier to invoke came from frustrated civil rights supporters in the 1950s and 1960s. Except for a minor change in 1959 establishing a two-thirds vote of those present and voting rather than two-thirds of the total membership as sufficient to cut off debate, their efforts met with no success. Not until the explosion in the number of filibusters in the 1970s did sufficient support to alter the rules develop. The campaigns to change the filibuster rule during the 1970s and 1980s were led by Senate party leaders, an indication of the problem that the increased use of extended debate created for them. In March, 1975, the Senate approved a compromise change in the cloture rule on a 56–27 vote (U.S. Congress, Senate 1979, 27–28). Cloture on all measures other than those amending the rules of the Senate would henceforth require three-fifths of the total Senate membership—sixty votes if there are no vacancies. Rules changes would still require two-thirds of those present and voting.

Although the change did make cloture easier to invoke, it did not solve the problem. Senator James Allen of Alabama, an adept parliamentarian and a strong conservative who philosophically opposed most of the legislative initiatives of the 1970s, showed his colleagues that the invoking of cloture need not end a filibuster. If a senator is willing to make full use of his individual powers, he can continue to prevent Senate action by calling up amendments offered before cloture was invoked, by demanding roll call votes on those amendments and insisting on repeated quorum calls, and by calling for the reading of amendments, conference reports, and the *Journal*.

Allen was the first and the most frequent practitioner of the post-cloture filibuster, but other senators quickly picked up the tactic. In 1977, liberals Howard Metzenbaum and James Abourezk conducted a post-cloture filibuster of President Carter's energy bill. Having filed more than five hundred amendments before cloture was invoked, they were able to delay action by insisting on their reading and on roll calls. Majority Leader Robert Byrd eventually broke the filibuster but only by using a questionable and much criticized procedure.

In response to the postcloture filibuster, the Senate again changed its cloture rule in 1979. The new rule specified that a final vote must occur after no more than one hundred hours of postcloture debate, with time spent on procedural motions and votes counted as part of the total (*Congress and the Nation* 1981, 917–18). In 1986, when the Senate agreed to broadcast its proceedings on television, it further reduced the maximum to thirty hours (*Congressional Quarterly Weekly Report,* March 1, 1986, 520). The one-hundred-hour limit had little impact because, in an environment of time constraints the threat to consume one-hundred hours is almost as effective as the threat to delay indefinitely. Even the more stringent thirty-hour limit is likely to make a significant difference only on "must" legislation.

The increase in filibusters has had a number of important effects on the Senate's decision-making processes. Attempts to invoke cloture have become routine and are usually sponsored by party leaders. In the 1950s and 1960s, an attempt to invoke cloture would usually be made only once; for that period, the number of cloture votes per filibuster was 1.2. In the late 1960s, the leadership occasionally began to force multiple cloture votes; there were four such votes on the 1968 Civil Rights Bill, for example. In the 1970s, multiple cloture votes became routine; from 1971 through 1986, the Senate voted on cloture motions 178 times. The number of cloture votes per filibuster averaged 1.9. The Senate voted on cloture six times each on the New Hampshire Senate seat dispute in 1975, labor law reform in 1978, and the gas tax in 1982, and seven times on antibusing amendments to the Justice Department authorization in 1981 and 1982.

As cloture has become an almost routine procedure, it is being used for purposes other than breaking a filibuster. Amendments considered after cloture has been invoked must be germane, and cloture has occasionally been sought to force germaneness (U.S. Congress, Senate 1979, 47). Leaders sometimes seek cloture to speed action, even when no filibuster is threatened. As the 1986 session neared its end, Senator Alan Simpson used cloture as a preemptive measure to forestall potentially deadly delays in approval of the conference report of the immigration reform bill. Although Senator Phil Gramm had engaged in some delaying tactics, no filibuster had developed or was threatened (*Congressional Quarterly Weekly Report,* October 18, 1986, 2595).

Extended debate is being used for new purposes as well. In August, 1984, Congress had still not passed a budget resolution. Democrats were frustrated by Senate Republicans' unwillingness to negotiate a defense figure but, as a minority, were unable to force action directly. When the agriculture appropriations bill was brought to the floor, Lawton Chiles, senior Democrat on the Senate Budget Committee, objected to waiving the Budget Act provision that prohibited consideration of money bills prior to adoption of the conference report on the first budget resolution. By use of extended debate, he delayed action for a week, making it clear that his purpose was to get Republicans to resume negotiations on defense spending. Cloture was successfully invoked on the second try. Chiles, however, threatened to begin another filibuster on the next scheduled appropriations bill. At that point, Majority Leader Howard Baker agreed to Chiles' suggestion of a "summit" meeting of party and committee leaders to negotiate an agreement on military spending (*Congressional Quarterly Weekly Report*, August 11, 1984, 1984). In February, 1985, farm state Democrats blocked the confirmation vote on Attorney General-designate Edwin Meese, and all other Senate business. Their purpose was to force action on a totally unrelated issue—aid to farmers. To end the filibuster, newly elected Majority Leader Robert Dole had to promise the senators engaging in the filibuster prompt floor action on emergency farm credit legislation that the administration opposed (ibid., February 23, 1985, 335–38; March 2, 1985, 371–74).

Probably the most important change in the Senate's decision-making process is considerably less visible. Full-blown filibusters are vastly outnumbered by threats to filibuster (see, for example, Calmes 1987, 2118). When floor time is tight—before a recess or near the end of the session—a single senator's threat to engage in extended debate is often sufficient to prevent the leadership from bringing up any bill that is not "must" legislation. As a tacit recognition of this fact, the meaning of "holds" has changed. According to a Republican leadership manual of procedure: "When a senator has particular concerns about a measure, he may ask that a 'hold' be placed against it. It will be honored for so long as the majority leader can do so, but at some point the leadership may move the legislation notwithstanding the hold which has been placed against" (Gold 1981).

However, over time, holds have become more nearly absolute. As a long-time staffer explained:

> It used to mean that putting a hold on something meant simply that you would be given twenty-four hours notice that this thing would come up, so you could prepare for that. And, of course, when you put a hold on something, it puts the people, the sponsors, on notice that you had some problems and it would be in their interest to come and negotiate with you. But four or five or six years ago it started to mean that if you put a hold on something, it would never come up. It became, in fact, a veto.

The party leaders have repeatedly attempted to return to the former interpretation of holds. On December 6, 1982, Majority Leader Howard Baker announced on the floor: "In these final two weeks . . . holds will be honored only sparingly and under the most urgent circumstances. . . . Senators are aware, of course, that holds . . . are matters of courtesy by the leadership on both sides of the aisle and are not part of the standing rules of the Senate" (*Congressional Record*, S13901). On February 25, 1983, the Washington *Times* reported that Baker and Minority Leader Byrd had agreed to restrict the use of holds; a hold would simply entitle a senator to notification. In early 1986, Senator Dole asserted that henceforth holds would not constitute vetoes. Few of the staffers interviewed believed that Dole would be more successful than previous leaders in making this change stick. As long as members are willing to back their holds with actual extended debate, the leaders are faced with an impossible situation when floor time is short. Assuming that the bill at issue is not "must" legislation, calling it up is likely to consume scarce time unproductively, time for which the leaders have multiple and clamorous requests.

Party and committee leaders' control of the flow of business to and on the floor is more tenuous than it used to be. Because of the looseness of Senate rules, Senate majority party leaders have always had less control over the floor schedule than their House counterparts do. With members now so much more inclined to exploit the possibilities inherent in the Senate rules, controlling the schedule has become even more problematic. Rank-and-file senators can disrupt the planned flow of business through filibusters, amending marathons, or lesser actions. In the spring of 1983, Senator Christopher Dodd requested a secret session of the Senate on Nicaragua. Rules specified that Dodd's request had to be granted if the motion received a second, which Paul Tsongas agreed to furnish. "Thus begins Howard Baker's week," a chronicler of the episode wrote. "Two freshman minority senators dictate a major change in the Senate's schedule, and the majority leader is unable to do anything to stop them" (Miller 1986, 33).

Because of senators' capacity and willingness to disrupt leadership plans, scheduling has increasingly become an exercise in accommodating all interested parties. It has always been necessary for the majority leader to confer with the minority leader on scheduling; other senators known to have an interest in the legislation have also been consulted. That process has become institutionalized. A Republican manual of procedure states:

In addition to holds, other notifications are commonly used by senators to alert the leadership to their interest in a measure. Thus, when legislation has been reported and hits the Calendar, senators may notify the leader that they wish to be consulted before the measure is called up, or before a time agreement is entered into, or any one of a host of possible considerations. In this fashion, the leadership is aware of whom to contact whenever it appears likely that some action will take place involving that legislation (Gold 1981).

Senators also expect the leadership to schedule around their own personal schedules. Alan Ehrenhalt tells a story that illustrates the problems leaders face in scheduling when everyone must be accommodated. In 1980, then-Majority Leader Byrd was on the Senate floor trying to find a time the following Monday for a vote on the budget resolution. "One senator after another announced that a particular time would be inconvenient. Byrd was reduced to writing all the preferences on a long yellow legal pad, a process that made him look more like a man sending out for sandwiches than the leader of a deliberative body" (1982, 2182). As veteran Senate staffer William Hildenbrand explains, "Everyone who wants to be accommodated is accommodated. If someone doesn't want a vote on Monday, there's no vote on Monday. The leadership just coordinates the individual requests" (ibid.).

Maximum accommodation of the individual member extends even to such matters as how long votes last. In June, 1983, Howard Baker complained on the floor of the Senate: "The Senate has not performed a single regular roll call vote within the 15 minutes allowed. . . . It is getting to the point where Members just feel that the vote is going to be held up for them and we have delayed announcement of a vote 7, 8, 10 minutes or more" (*Congressional Record*, June 10, 1983, S8223).

Party and committee leaders have considerably less ability than they once did to keep measures from reaching the floor. Senators feel no compunction about offering measures blocked in committee as floor amendments. A precedent now exists for using the filibuster to force unrelated matters onto the floor despite strong opposition from the majority party leadership, as occurred with agricultural legislation in early 1986. In 1985, the Rules Committee voted 10–0 to report out Mack Mattingly's line-item veto bill with an unfavorable recommendation; the committee reported the bill only because Mattingly threatened that otherwise he would offer it as an amendment to the "must pass" supplemental appropriation bill (*Congressional Quarterly Almanac*, 1985, 468). Strong opposition from Majority Leader Howard Baker, Finance Committee Chairman Robert Dole, and President Reagan was not sufficient to keep junior Republican Bob Kasten from getting his proposal to repeal interest withholding considered on the floor (*Congressional Quarterly Weekly Report*, March 12, March 19, April 23, 1983).

Roll call practices have contributed to the increasing tenuousness of leaders' control over the floor. Senators now consider it their right to obtain a roll call vote at will, even when they cannot muster the one-fifth of the membership present that the rules specify. In the 1940s and 1950s, according to an expert on Senate procedure, the leaders decided when there would be a roll call. Most senators would not second a request for a roll call unless the leader signaled his agreement. In the 1960s, under the extremely permissive leadership of Mike Mansfield, it became a courtesy and then a right of any senator to get a roll call at will. During the 1982 gas tax fight, the leadership, under severe time constraints, did deny roll calls on some amendments. This, however, provoked an outcry, and there has been no attempt to curtail this "right" since then (however, see Granat 1985, 2569).

The Senate has always done most of its work by unanimous consent. As fewer members became unwilling to give their consent automatically, as more insisted on having a say on more issues, the floor proceedings of the Senate became increasingly complex. In August 1986, just before the scheduled recess, an extension of the federal debt limit and the 1987 defense authorization bill were on the floor. A large majority of the membership, certainly more than the sixty needed to invoke cloture, wanted to bring up and pass a bill imposing sanctions on South Africa. A smaller number, probably not enough to cut off a filibuster but led by Majority Leader Dole, wanted a vote on President Reagan's request for aid to the Nicaraguan Contras. The Senate faced a double-barreled "invisible filibuster"; "nobody was actually filibustering either South Africa or Contra aid, but opponents on each side stood ready to do so, jeopardizing the recess" (*Congressional Quarterly Weekly Report*, August 16, 1986, 1879). It took more than two weeks for Dole and Minority Leader Robert Byrd to negotiate a unanimous consent agreement providing for a vote on both measures. The agreement was so long it took Dole almost an hour to read it aloud and "so complicated that many senators admitted they could not understand it even after two or three readings" (ibid., 1878). The agreement even specified a vote on David Boren's proposal to limit contributions by political action committees in congressional campaigns. Earlier in the year Dole had promised Boren floor time for his bill, and Boren called in the promise in the midst of this imbroglio. "It shouldn't take a parliamentary wizard to pass a supplemental appropriation," a weary Senate staff director said in 1982. "It's gotten too difficult to do anything" (ibid., September 4, 1982, 2178). The bill to which he was referring had been subjected to an ultimately successful attempt by Richard Lugar to attach to it a $5.1 billion emergency housing assistance program, a filibuster by William Armstrong against the Lugar amendment, and two presidential vetoes as well as a number of lesser difficulties.

With the leaders' control of the flow of business to and on the floor being so tenuous, the allocation of time on the Senate floor is largely unplanned and, consequently, often irrational. The expectation that leaders will maximally accommodate individual senators results in much wasted time on the floor. In June, 1983, Majority Leader Baker complained, "We have wasted hours upon hours, tens of hours in the Senate waiting for Senators to arrive on the floor to cast their vote" (*Congressional Record*, June 10, 1983, S8223). Under pressure from members, leaders have increasingly stacked votes, that is, postponed roll calls and then bunched them together. The result has not been a saving of the Senate's time. Rather, as Howard Baker lamented, "what has happened today . . . is . . . typical of what happens when you stack votes. That is, everybody leaves town. Nobody will call up amendments. We end up with hours of quorum calls and wasted time" (ibid., 8219). During the first nine months of the 99th Congress, the Senate spent 247 hours—23 percent of its time in session—in quorum calls (Dewar 1985, 14). Quorum calls are used when the principals in a floor fight are engaged in behind-the-scenes negotiations. They are also employed to fill time while waiting for a senator who is scheduled for some form of floor activity but has not arrived.

Leaders have little control over how much time is spent on a measure. Some measures consume inordinate amounts of floor time; others, many senators believe, are given short shrift. Thus, the Temporary Select Committee to Study the Senate Committee System, which was appointed in the 98th Congress, concluded that cloture was often invoked too soon, before measures are fully debated (U.S. Congress, Senate 1984, 16). Because filibusters are so frequent, sponsors of bills file cloture petitions at the first hint of trouble. "Years ago, even Lyndon Johnson would not try to get cloture until after a week," senior Senator Strom Thurmond says. "But now, after one day, if the leaders see you are going to fight, they will apply cloture immediately" (Calmes 1987, 2120).

Extended debate, the accommodation of individuals in scheduling, and high levels of amending activity consume so much time that the usual rush at the end of the session has worsened. As the session draws to a close, large numbers of often consequential bills are passed after only the most perfunctory scrutiny. Senator Howard Metzenbaum claims that the rush at the end of the session is used to shield egregious special interest legislation from any real review (Washington *Post*, February 16, 1983).

In the contemporary Senate, minorities, even very small minorities, can and do influence the Senate's agenda and Senate decisions to a greater extent than they did prior to 1970. To be sure, members of the Senate are much more willing to invoke cloture now than they were in the 1950s and 1960s. Cloture motions were rarely successful during the 1960s; in the first half of the 1970s, the success rate shot up, and then increased again after the rules change that reduced the number of necessary votes to sixty (see table 6.11). In the 1980s, however, the success rate on cloture motions fell to near its level of 1971–75. Highly charged issues and deep ideological divisions had made invoking cloture more difficult again.

Table 6.11   Changes in Frequency and Rate of Invoking Cloture in the Senate

Years	Number of Issues on Which Cloture Was		
	Invoked	Never Invoked	Successful
1955–60	0	2	0 %
1961–70	4	16	18.2%
1971–75[a]	14	11	56.0%
1975–80	26	6	81.3%
1981–86	22	15	59.5%

[a]Through March 8, 1975, when the cloture rule was changed.

As Bruce Oppenheimer (1985) points out, in assessing the success of filibustering as a tactic, the percentage of cases in which cloture is successfully invoked is less relevant than the number of cases in which it fails. From 1971 through 1986, there were thirty-two cases in which cloture was never successfully invoked. Some highly consequential legislation failed as a result: bills establishing a consumer agency (1972 and 1974), labor law reform (1978), the fair housing amendments (1980), anti-abortion and school prayer amendments (1982), the anti-apartheid bill (1985), and the line-item veto (1985). In each of these cases, more than a majority but less than the sufficient number supported cloture.

Increasing time constraints and the development of the postcloture filibuster have made the relationship between invoking cloture and breaking the filibuster less than perfect. Thus, in late September, 1984, cloture was invoked on the Byrd amendment to overturn the Supreme Court's Grove City decision that narrowed the interpretation of certain civil rights laws. Opponents led by Senator Orrin Hatch then offered a series of controversial amendments to the continuing appropriations bill that was the vehicle for the Byrd amendment, and the parliamentary

snarl that ensued resulted eventually in the killing of the Byrd amendment (*Congressional Quarterly Almanac*, 1984, 241). In late 1986, the Senate successfully invoked cloture on the motion to consider product
liability reform legislation. Senator Ernest Hollings, the lead opponent,
then threatened to filibuster the bill, and Majority Leader Dole pulled
the bill from the floor. It was too near the end of the session to spend
large amounts of floor time on discretionary legislation (*Congressional
Quarterly Weekly Report,* September 27, 1986, 2316). Conversely, some
filibusters are unsuccessful even though cloture is never invoked. For
example, Finance Chairman Dole attempted to block the repeal of interest withholding by using a variety of techniques, including a filibuster,
but failed even though cloture was not invoked.

If a filibuster is defined as successful only if it kills the provision at
which it is aimed by blocking or delay, then twelve of thirty-seven, or
almost one-third, of the filibusters waged between 1981 and 1986 were
successful. In another three cases, the filibusterers succeeded in extracting major concessions. The Radio Marti bill, for example, passed in 1983
but only after sponsors worked out a compromise with opponents who
had blocked the measure for more than a year. Much of the opposition
was based on fears that Cuba would interfere with commercial radio sta-
tions in the United States in the process of jamming Radio Marti broadcasts; thus constituency, not policy, was the primary motivation (*Congressional Quarterly Almanac,* 1983, 138). Constituency interests also
underlay Illinois senators Percy and Dixon undertaking a 1984 filibuster
of a bill to release highway funds to the states. Percy and Dixon opposed
a change in the funding formula that, they claimed, shortchanged Illinois. Although cloture was voted, Dixon persisted with other delaying
tactics, and, because the end of the session was fast approaching, the
sponsors were forced to work out a compromise (*Congressional Quarterly Weekly Report,* September 29, 1984, 2367).

In sum, fifteen of thirty-seven filibusters between 1981 and 1986 ultimately rendered the Senate's decision on the measure at issue more
favorable to the filibusterers than it would have been otherwise. When
the chance of having such an impact is 40 percent, the incentives to engage in extended debate are obvious. Furthermore, some of the cases
classified as failures according the strict definition used would probably
be judged differently by those involved. From June, 1981, through February, 1982, Senator Lowell Weicker filibustered antibusing riders to the
Justice Department authorization bill. Weicker gave up his attempt to
block passage of the bill after eight and one-half months and seven
cloture votes, three of which succeeded. He promised, however, that
should the measure pass the House he would filibuster the conference

report and that other "social issues" such as abortion and school prayer could expect the same treatment. "His success in protracting the busing debate already has made the Senate leadership wary of ensnarling the Senate in another lengthy controversy," *Congressional Quarterly Weekly Report* reported (March 6, 1982, 522).

Because the Senate operates in an environment of heavy time constraints, filibusters conducted by a handful of senators, or even one senator, are frequently successful, especially toward the end of the session. Many of Senator James Allen's filibusters during the 1970s were one-man operations, and, in a number of cases, he at least extracted concessions. In 1976, Senator Jake Garn killed an extension of the Clean Air Act by a filibuster on the last day of the session. Probably the most successful solo filibusterer in the contemporary Senate is Howard Metzenbaum. At the end of a session, he uses the full arsenal of Senate prerogatives to block legislation he considers to be special interest giveaways. He claims to have prevented passage of twenty-six separate measures during the 1982 lame-duck session alone (Washington *Post,* February 16, 1983). A day-long filibuster of a water rights bill undertaken when senators were eager to leave for the weekend yielded a number of concessions, even on matters on which Metzenbaum had previously been defeated on recorded votes (Ehrenhalt 1982, 2178).

The impact upon Senate outcomes of senators' increased willingness to engage in extended debate is almost certainly much greater than an analysis of full-blown filibusters and attempts to invoke cloture indicates. Although Metzenbaum has taken part in a number of the filibusters on our list during his time in the Senate, neither of the above examples qualified for the list; they did not last long enough and did not provoke a cloture vote. Holds, direct threats to filibuster, and short but strategically timed instances of extended debate probably have much more cumulative effect on Senate outcomes than the more dramatic and easily documented full-blown filibuster. Such lesser actions influence the floor agenda of the Senate; some measures never reach the floor because of such actions. They also influence the form in which measures pass. To ward off such obstructionist actions, sponsors often make concessions to their opponents.

The increased willingness of senators to exploit fully their right to extended debate, like their increased willingness to offer floor amendments, has reduced committee autonomy. By skillful use of his powers to obstruct, a senator can make himself a major player in issues beyond the jurisdiction of committees on which he serves, as Howard Metzenbaum has done with tax legislation. Committees must concern themselves not only with how a majority of the Senate membership will receive their product, but also with the reactions of intensely motivated minorities, even minorities of one. Substantive concessions are often the price that committees must pay to buy off obstructionist minorities.

The Institutional Consequences of Behavioral Change: A Summary

The change in Senate styles—in the behavioral strategies by which senators pursue their goals—has made the contemporary Senate a more active body than the Senate of the 1950s, or even that of the 1960s. In terms of the number of hearings and other meetings, committees are more active than they used to be. The floor is a much more active arena as well. More amendments are offered, more roll calls are taken, and more filibusters are waged. To be sure, adverse political conditions dampened activity in the 1980s, reducing rates on most but not all indicators below their very high levels of the 1970s; yet activity levels remained higher than they had been in the 1960s.

The change in Senate styles has also altered the distribution of influence in the Senate. As senators expanded the supply of resources and increasingly exploited the powers that Senate rules vest in individual members, influence shifted from party and committee leaders to individual senators. Junior status no longer bars a senator from playing a major role, even a leadership role, within a committee. Party and committee leaders have much less control over the agenda of the Senate than formerly, while rank-and-file senators influence the agenda, positively and negatively, more than they did in the past. Senior leaders can no longer dominate the decision-making process, either in committee or on the floor. The contemporary Senate accords its members very wide latitude; maximum accommodation of the individual member has become the overriding expectation.

Senate decision making is less committee-centered than it used to be; committees are no longer autonomous. Senators are much less willing to accept committee decisions with only perfunctory review. The floor has become a significant decision-making arena, one in which legislation is subjected to scrutiny and, frequently, to alteration. Because members may be able to block committee legislation from reaching the floor or amend it drastically once on the floor, committees must attend to and accommodate the preferences of nonmembers. Committees perforce are more open to influence by nonmembers than formerly.

Senate decision making is also less segmented; it is characterized by broader participation than in the past. More decisions are made in an arena—the Senate floor—in which the full membership can participate; even the framing of alternatives through the introduction of amendments is increasingly a broadly based enterprise. To be sure, a great many of the hundreds of decisions the Senate makes do not involve the participation of a large part of the membership; many are effectively made by small groups of people, sometimes primarily by staff. In the contemporary Senate, however, narrow participation is the result of lack of interest. When senators perceive a decision to be truly consequential, they can and do participate in the decision-making process.

Senate decision making is now a much more public enterprise than it was in the 1950s and 1960s. Sunshine reforms have opened committee mark-ups to public scrutiny. More significant decisions are made on the Senate floor. Press coverage has increased, as have the number and diversity of groups tracking the legislative process.

These changes in how the Senate functions have, in a number of ways, made it a more democratic institution with a greater capacity for representing the interests of the full citizenry and, one might suppose, for making decisions responsive to those interests. Thus, individual senators' greater influence over the agenda of the Senate has expanded the range of interests that have some access to institutional agendas. The range of interests, issues, and ideas that find articulation by senators appears to represent a considerably greater proportion of the range found among attentive publics than was the case in the 1950s. Because a senator's adoption of a cause confers a modicum of legitimacy, fewer groups and ideas are beyond the pale. The contemporary Senate provides a superb forum for the articulation of interests.

Senate decisions may have become more reflective of the preferences of the entire membership and more responsive to public opinion. On balance, the committee system is more representative of the membership as a whole than it was in the 1950s and 1960s. With committees more internally democratic and more open to influence from nonmembers, and with the floor having become a more active and significant decision-making arena, participation in Senate decision making is broader and less segmented than it used to be.

Although the process of reaching a decision in the glare of press scrutiny may be more time consuming, the result will almost certainly have to take more account of public opinion, potential as well as actual. In addition, more and more diverse interests can have an impact on Senate decisions. Interests that were outside the system in the 1950s are more likely to find a senator to champion their cause, and the more open decision-making processes make it much easier for those interests— both directly and through their Senate champions—to have an impact upon decisions.

The change in Senate styles, and the impact of that change upon how the institution functions, has, however, also created problems for the Senate as a legislative body. The Senate finds it more difficult to get its essential legislative business done. The Senate's slowness in passing legislation and its difficulty in making decisions are, in part, the result of senators' broader participation. When more senators representing a greater diversity of interests and opinions take part in legislative battles, decision making will be more difficult. Narrow partisan margins, conflicts with the president, and the constraints imposed by huge budget deficits have contributed to this difficulty. So too have the ability and willingness of senators to pursue their own agendas at the expense of the institution's agenda.

Senators' unrestrained pursuit of their own agendas can be highly divisive. When Senator Jesse Helms and his like-minded colleagues force other senators to go on the record over and over again on such emotional issues as busing, school prayer and abortion, resentments are created. That the point is often not to win but to provide ammunition for future electoral opponents of senators who disagree with Helms makes the tactic that much more divisive. When Senator William Armstrong keeps the Senate in session most of the night with an amendment to repeal a tax deduction for members of Congress, Senate comity is severely strained. When Senator Howard Metzenbaum uses publicity and the Senate rules to kill large numbers of special interest, constituency-oriented bills, the mutual accommodation that contributes to smooth working relationships is disrupted.

More seriously, the growth of obstructionism and the Senate's tolerance of it greatly complicates Senate decision making. Senators regularly hold "must" legislation hostage and extract a ransom in policy concessions. One senator or a small group of senators may be able to block altogether consideration of less-than-top priority legislation. A large minority may be able to stop passage of even major legislation favored by a Senate majority. Thus minorities, even small ones, can wield inordinant influence over legislative decisions.

The very wide latitude that the contemporary Senate accords its members results in a decision-making process characterized by broad involvement but one in which small minorities can be decisive, a seeming paradox that will be further explored in the final chapter.

7 // Contemporary Senate Styles: The Choice of Issues

In a January 6, 1987, press release, Senator Alan Cranston announced his introduction of the legislation to which he would give highest priority during the 100th Congress. The eleven bills dealt with the environment, education, trade, child care, emergency medical care, veterans' benefits, and fair treatment for women in the job market and in the Social Security System. Clearly Cranston is a legislative activist and a generalist who involves himself in a broad range of issues. This, we will see, is the characteristic style of the contemporary Senate.

The typical member of the contemporary Senate is endowed with considerable resources, particularly committee positions and staff, and is little constrained by norms in their use. He operates in an environment that offers an immense range of opportunities for involvement. The number of issues is almost unlimited, and issues can be pursued in a variety of arenas.

Senators and those aspiring to be senators are very much aware of the broad range of opportunities; as was shown earlier, it constitutes one of the Senate's major attractions. "When he first came," a staffer to a junior senator said, "he felt like a kid in a candy shop." Explaining his willingness to give up a House seat to run for the Senate, Toby Moffett said, "I thought there was a better opportunity to talk about issues that I care about and to bring them onto the national stage" (Plattner 1985, 998).

How a senator chooses the issues in which he will involve himself constitutes a critical element of a senator's style, for choose he must. Senate norms no longer dictate specialization, but the day is still only twenty-four hours long. Although the supply of staff and other resources

141

available to senators is generous by the standards of previous decades, it is nevertheless limited. The environment offers far too many opportunities for involvement for a senator to take up all of those with some payoff related to his goals.

Choosing Issues

Broad involvement is not simply an option open to senators. The pressures on a senator for involvement start immediately and come from individuals and groups of all sorts. When asked whether groups come to their senator and ask him to get involved in their issue, staffers almost to a person replied, "It happens all the time." An aide to a freshman reported requests from "half a dozen every day. And it's everything from people who want a week dedicated to some cause or another to those who want to change the way we elect presidents." Freshman senators tend to get most of their serious requests from state-based groups and individuals. However, if the freshman, through his previous career, is associated with some issue, nonstate-based groups interested in that issue are likely to seek him out. Known for his involvement in human rights issues during his House service, Tom Harkin was immediately importuned when he entered the Senate. "We have people from all kinds of countries coming to him and wanting him to help on their particular issue." Another senator known as a New Right ideologue found a wide variety of conservative groups asking him to lead their fights. "He's a fighter," an aide explained, "so many groups come to him and ask him to lead the fight on their issue."

Because groups need Senate allies and because the number of senators and their time is so limited, even freshmen will sometimes find major groups coming to them on an issue with which they have no previous association. In March, 1987, for example, freshman John Breaux offered a floor amendment to a bill to recapitalize the fund that insures savings and loan deposits. The amendment, which deleted the moratorium on most banks' entry into securities, insurance, and real estate, was supported by a coalition of banking groups led by the American Bankers Association and occasioned a major floor battle. Why did Breaux, who does not serve on the Banking Committee and who himself said he knew little about banking, get involved? "I was approached by the banks and they made a good point about equity," Breaux explained (*Congressional Quarterly Weekly Report*, March 28, 1987, 564).

As a senator becomes more senior, such importunings increase. A senator's previous choices on issues may lead to his becoming identified with an issue; frequently productive working relationships between a senator and a group may solidify into an alliance. The result is more pressures and more opportunities for involvement.

Senators are aware that they must make choices. "From all the things he has as possibilities, somehow you have to choose," a staffer explained. "And if you don't, in fact, establish your own priorities and let yourself just be jerked around, you will not be a success and you will be very unhappy." Effectiveness requires "priority setting, discipline, a plan," "not getting spread out over one-hundred different issues," "not scattering your shots too much." "It's critical that you set goals and priorities; otherwise, you will be jerked around all over the place. It's very easy here to work very hard and accomplish absolutely nothing." The temptation to become involved too broadly is great. Said a staffer for a junior senator, "During the first months he was bouncing all over the map. He'd get interested in something, want the staff to brief him on it and then tomorrow it would be something else." Choosing which issues to get involved in is "his biggest problem," said the aide to a senior member. "His tendency is always to do more. He likes to get involved and it's hard for him not to get involved in a lot of other issues."

Over time, senators develop routinized ways of making these decisions. It is among more junior members that one can best observe the struggle to cope. Formal priority-setting meetings are common. "We had a retreat in late December," the aide to a freshman senator said. "This was all the staff from his office and from [the state], and we spent that time setting up goals and priorities and objectives, coming up with a strategy. It's critical that you do that." The administrative assistant to another freshman also reported meeting at the end of the first year to consider future involvements. "We have talked about the issue areas he should be involved in. We've talked about getting two or three more . . . for him to develop, and in the next two or three months we'll pick those." A number of staffers identified the end of the first year as being a critical time for taking stock and for long-range planning. Some offices institutionalize the process. "We have a couple of planning sessions a year to discuss long-term strategy," the aide to a senator in his fourth year of service explained. The legislative director of a senator finishing his first term explained the procedure followed in his office: "The staff tries to organize priorities. At the beginning of the year, the LAs [legislative aides] have a meeting, and they come up with a laundry list of proposals, and then the senior staff goes through that; and then they go through it with the senator to try to come up with an actual priority list." As a senator becomes more senior, the decisions made at such meetings are increasingly at the margin; the senior senator already has a lengthy list of issue commitments that cannot be easily abandoned.

The need to choose is closely bound up with the widespread belief that the successful senator pursues his own agenda; he does not allow the Senate agenda to dictate his issue involvements. "A senator can decide what he wants to work on and they're foolish if they don't," a staffer explained. "It's a mistake for senators to let their agenda be dictated by committee agendas or by outside forces. That's not the way to be effective." Another aide said, "It is very easy to just react. That is an impulse we have to resist all the time." However, to be effective, he continued, a senator must have his own issue agenda. "Those that you've heard of do. It's necessary for effectiveness." Of course, senators cannot ignore the Senate agenda. The trick is finding a way of using the Senate's agenda to further their own. "While you have to deal with the issues that the Senate agenda throws up, you have to vote on them, you always should think, 'Can I use the issue to promote my own agenda in some way or another?'" an aide explained.

How, then, do senators choose the issues in which they will become involved? What are the criteria used? The extent to which involvement in a given issue will advance the senator's goals should, according to our framework, be a central criterion. For two of the eighteen senators sampled, the decision to get involved appears to be almost completely dominated by constituency interests. The questions they ask about an issue are: Does it significantly affect the state? Will involvement pay off in reelection terms? Within the typology of goals, these senators can be classified as primarily oriented toward reelection. In neither case, however, does the orientation to their constituency appear to be purely instrumental; both appear to be motivated also by a genuine sense of obligation to serve the state.

Reelection is a goal of almost all senators; and, under certain circumstances, constituency considerations will dominate the decision to get involved for all. Every senator's office is involved in a bewildering array of constituency-related matters that range from policy issues to major projects to casework. The goal of reelection dictates that few of the myriad individuals and groups that come to the senator for help can be turned down flat. How high a priority an issue is given will, of course, vary. How important is the issue and the group to a senator's reelection? When an issue seriously affecting a key state interest arises, especially if that state interest is threatened, the senators cannot stay on the sidelines; they have no choice but to become involved. Thus, when policy questions relating to tobacco arise, the senators from Kentucky and North Carolina perforce play an active role. Given the agricultural crisis in the Midwest in 1985, Tom Harkin, newly elected senator from Iowa, could not have stayed out of the battle over the farm bill. Legislation affecting the auto industry will involve the senators from Michigan.

Promises made during a senator's campaign may influence his involvement in issues for years to come. Campaign promises concerning issues often are pledges of vigorous involvement; senators believe that reelection dictates following through on such promises. The issues the candidate emphasized during the campaign often link him to specialized constituencies that can provide important electoral support. To maintain those linkages, the senator must maintain his involvement in the issues of interest to those groups (see Fenno 1986).

Most senators pursue multiple goals and must choose the issues in which they will become involved in that more complex context. There are, of course, dream issues—ones that promise positive payoffs in terms of the full set of goals. For Orrin Hatch, chairman of the Subcommittee on the Constitution of the Judiciary Committee during the period of Republican control, the constitutional amendment to require a balanced federal budget has this property: it conforms with his own deeply held policy beliefs, is popular with his Utah constituents, and reinforces his close ties with national conservative groups. For moderate and liberal members, education has much the same character, especially since the revival of educational quality as a salient issue.

Dream issues that have major across-the-board payoffs are not sufficiently prevalent that a senator can confine his involvement to them. By and large, senators satisfy their multiple goals by choosing a range of issues. Some issues are chosen primarily for reasons related to reelection; others because they will yield payoffs in terms of policy and influence. (For a comparison with the House, see Hall 1987a.)

Having positive payoffs in terms of more than one goal clearly increases the attractiveness of an issue. Breaux's decision to offer the antimoratorium amendment discussed earlier was probably affected by its likely payoff to him in terms of both influence and reelection. It gave him, a freshman in his first months of service, an opportunity to play a leadership role; because he succeeded in forcing a compromise on the moratorium issue, it established him as someone to be reckoned with. The bankers in Louisiana and the American Bankers Association will presumably be grateful and contribute to Breaux's reelection.

When an issue that a senator is attracted to for policy reasons provides an opportunity for an alliance with usually antagonistic but important constituency groups, its attractiveness is greatly increased. For William Armstrong, conservative Republican of Colorado, the sodbuster bill (to be discussed further later) allowed him to work with rather than against important environmental groups. Liberal Democrats find many small business issues attractive because they can work on them with a segment of their constituency that is significant yet often antagonistic.

Issues that promise a large positive payoff in terms of policy or influence, but a possibly negative payoff in terms of reelection present senators that pursue multiple goals with their most difficult choices. Junior senators whose policy interests are in the foreign relations area believe that the publicity they receive for involvement in policy decisions concerning Nicaragua, the Philippines, or some other far-off place is at best a two-edged sword in terms of reelection. Many constituents who have no particular views on the policy questions nevertheless resent the senator's seeming concentration on "foreigners' " problems at the expense of their own. "The press is a great deal more responsive on foreign policy issues," an aide explained. "[The senator] had an hour's meeting with [Soviet dissident] Yelena Bonner and that got us months of media attention. So we find that when we go home, the people will say 'Why don't you worry about our problems?' " This senator's response is to emphasize his involvement in domestic and especially state-related issues in his press releases and other publicity efforts.

Decisions regarding involvement in issues entail more than a yes-or-no choice. The senator must also choose how deeply to become involved. He has to decide whether "to try to play a leadership role or just a participatory one." Related to that decision, he has to decide whether his involvement will be primarily via staff or whether he is willing to invest any appreciable amount of personal time in the issue. It is the large staffs that make possible the broad involvement in issues by contemporary senators. A significant proportion of every senator's involvement consists primarily of staff activities. "There are a lot of things where he is only nominally involved and, in fact, it's mostly a staff operation," an aide explained.

For the senators in the sample that pursue multiple goals, considerable differences in the apportionment of staff time and the senator's own time are apparent. Staff spend much more time on issues that primarily promise a payoff in terms of reelection. These senators commit significant amounts of their own time to such an issue only if it is perceived as a life-or-death matter for the state. By and large, these senators reserve their own time for issues that interest them personally, that they believe to be of national significance, and that are also likely to contribute to the establishment or maintenance of a national reputation. Many of these also have some payoff in terms of reelection, but this is not their primary attraction.

Whether involvement in a particular issue will in fact contribute to a senator's achieving a given goal depends, in part, upon the likelihood that the senator's involvement will have an impact. Senior staff frequently mentioned the probability of impact as a consideration in the decision of whether to get involved: "Is it an issue on which the senator can make a difference?" "Is there an effective part for you to play on that issue?"

Often it is the probability of winning that is of concern. The aide to a junior senator said:

> The staff certainly also asks "What are our chances of success on this issue?" He will just ask "Is it right?" and if he thinks it's right, he's willing to charge ahead even if there's not much chance of winning. But we feel that given that there are so many issues, we might as well spend our time and energy on ones where we have a good chance of being successful.

Having an impact is not always defined as winning. A senator may be satisfied with making a good showing and thereby enhancing his reputation, or with simply expressing a point of view with the hope that it will eventually have some impact. "We don't want to tilt at windmills all the time, but we will do that sometimes," an aide explained. "We'll sometimes get involved in something where we know we're going to lose, but maybe over time that will change the process a little."

Senators are more likely to become involved in issues that come before their committees than in those that do not because "having a committee base" maximizes a senator's chance of having an impact for a given amount of time invested. Of course senators request certain committees because they want to get involved in the issues within the jurisdiction of those committees. Nevertheless, committee assignments have independent impact upon the choice of issue involvements. It is easier and less time consuming for a senator to influence an issue that falls within the jurisdiction of his committees and subcommittees because he can be there when the "nitty gritty" decisions are made. In addition, the committee provides a senator with "a platform to speak from"; it makes him part of the "network" of governmental actors, interest groups, and outside experts who interact and share information regularly.

Because being on the committee that deals with an issue does significantly increase a senator's chances of influencing the issue, senators seek multiple committee assignments. Most senators are seriously overextended in the sense that they cannot possibly attend all the meetings of their committees or take a significant part in all of the major decisions of their committees. Yet most are loath to give up any assignments. The more assignments a senator has, the more likely he is to have a committee base for dealing with an issue he wants to get involved in. And that is the way that senators think about their assignments. A junior senator in the sample served on one minor and two major committees his freshman term and added the Joint Economic Committee in his third year. Asked why, a senior staffer explained that "it rounded out his portfolio," that there were now almost no issues that did not fall into the purview of one of his committees.

"The way the Senate is set up," William Armstrong says, "it rewards a member who gets involved in everything, even though he or she may not be a very active participant. By being a member you get a certain leverage on a lot of deals, in a lot of different ways. So, even though it's impossible really to participate in three committees, four committees, ten subcommittees—whatever it is—if your interest is in affecting the outcome of legislation, there's an incentive to be on every committee you can get on" (Miller 1986, 65).

Although involvement in committee issues is more time effective, almost all senators are also involved in issues outside the jurisdiction of their committees. What circumstances will trigger such an issue choice? What justifies the extra effort necessary to have an impact? A vital state interest being at stake will perforce lead to such involvement. Although not a member of the Agriculture Committee, Wendell Ford of Kentucky was a major player in the passage of tobacco legislation during the 99th Congress. Strom Thurmond and Ernest Hollings of South Carolina, a leading textile producing state, were chief sponsors of legislation restricting textile imports that passed the Senate in late 1985. This bill never went through committee at all. Thurmond and Hollings attempted to add the provision as an amendment to other legislation. Their doggedly pursued strategy plunged the Senate into such a procedural morass that the leadership, although it opposed the legislation, agreed to quick consideration of the House-passed textile bill (*Congressional Quarterly Weekly Report,* November 16, 1985, 2370–71). An issue need not be a life-or-death matter for the state to justify some involvement. During floor consideration of the immigration reform bill in 1985, James McClure of Idaho offered an amendment requiring a warrant before federal immigration officers can search an open field. Not a member of either the Judiciary or the Agriculture Committee, McClure was responding to pleas from Idaho growers. When a measure primarily affects only one state, the senators from that state are expected to assume the leadership role even though they do not sit on the committee of origin. Pete Wilson, Republican of California, explained in his newsletter the process that produced the compromise California wilderness bill in 1984: "Senator Cranston and I, after an exhaustive acre-by-acre review of all the lands under consideration, selected the areas we felt were appropriate for wilderness."

The goals of setting policy and gaining influence may also motivate involvement in issues outside the jurisdiction of a senator's committees. An enduring policy interest frequently leads to such involvement. Tom Harkin had been involved in human rights questions, especially as they pertain to Central America, during his House service. Despite the lack of a committee base, he continued that involvement in the Senate. During the spring of 1985, he and fellow freshman John Kerry took a highly publicized trip to Nicaragua, and he was active during floor debate on aid to the Contras, offering several amendments. Although Phil Gramm was denied a seat on the Budget Committee, he did not abandon his interest in budgetary matters. His activities resulted in the Gramm-Rudman legislation by the end of his first year in the Senate. James McClure's conviction that the Soviets were not complying with arms control agreements led him to sustained involvement in that issue. Since 1981, Bill Bradley has taken a lead role on the floor in attempting to protect education funding from Reagan Administration budget cuts. His dedication to tax equity has led Howard Metzenbaum to be a regular participant whenever tax bills are considered on the floor.

Sometimes the desire to stake out a role in an area of interest is a crucial determinant. Mitch McConnell is interested in foreign and defense policy questions, but his committee assignments in the 99th Congress, his freshman term, provided only a very limited basis for involvement. Through reading he became interested specifically in the situation in South Africa in the summer of 1985 and decided to sponsor, with Senator William Roth, a bill imposing sanctions on South Africa (Green 1985, 1085). It was his bill that, after some modifications, passed the Senate. McConnell's activities resulted in considerable publicity—extensive articles with pictures in the Washington *Post* and in *Congressional Quarterly*—and served as a signal to his Senate colleagues and to others in the Washington community of his interest in such issues. In the 100th Congress, McConnell received an assignment to the Foreign Relations Committee. Over the last several years, Jeff Bingaman has been engaged in staking out a role for himself on the issues of foreign trade and the competitiveness of the United States. He has sponsored legislation, served on one Democratic task force, was instrumental in the formation of and chaired another Democratic task force, and has given numerous speeches including a reply to one of President Reagan's Saturday radio talks. When Democrats took control of the 100th Congress, Bingaman became ad hoc chairman for National Competitive Strategy of the Government Affairs Committee, a position created especially for him.

McConnell and Bingaman were intent upon establishing a claim to a share in the making of decisions on issues of particiular interest to them. Despite the lack of a committee base, each managed to do so; for both, one of the payoffs was a committee assignment that would facilitate further involvement in the issue of interest.

The perception that a leadership vacuum exists is often important in the decision to get involved. "It's a matter of where he sees something others don't see," a staffer explained. "Where he sees the need for leadership in an area where he is very interested and where he believes something can get moving, something can get done, where no one else is taking it up." For example, Lowell Weicker took on "the role of protector of constitutional rights against attacks from the New Right on social issues"; after "Ed Brooke was defeated, there wasn't anyone willing to take up that fight—there was a vacuum, especially among Republicans." On the issue of aid to the Contras fighting in Nicaragua, Jim Sasser seems to have perceived a vacuum in the middle of the ideological spectrum and stepped into the position (Tumulty 1986). Gramm's success with Gramm-Rudman was largely the result of his figuring out how to exploit a vacuum. Gramm "knew that we needed to do something about balancing the budget. Everybody knew we needed to do something about balancing the budget. But he didn't see anybody doing anything at a time when he thought something could be done. And so he took it on."

Despite the belief that the effective senator pursues his own agenda, the Senate agenda cannot be ignored. Senators must at least vote on the issues that come up in committee and on the floor. Moreover and more importantly, hot issues—highly salient issues thrown up by the external environment—offer senators opportunities to garner publicity, to lead, to have an impact upon policy. According to a staffer who had previously been a Capitol Hill reporter, there are issues that senators "ride" and issues that they "create." Riding an issue that is already hot has the advantage that the senator need not attempt to create interest; it is already there. Thus, if his goal is to garner publicity, whether to impress the folks at home or to establish a Washington reputation as a leader, persuading reporters that the story is worth covering is relatively easy. If his goal is having an impact upon policy, persuading other senators that his is an issue worth focusing on is less difficult. If an issue a senator has been working on becomes hot, he will almost always move it up on his agenda.

Robert Kasten had attempted to pass product liability legislation for several years without success. "One of the problems with this issue," a staffer said, "has been that in the past it was just not a pressing problem to enough people." The soaring cost of liability insurance and, in some cases, the total inability of some entities such as cities and day-care centers to get coverage led to increasing complaints to members of Congress. By the spring of 1986, the media had declared a "liability crisis"; *Time* magazine ran a major article, and other print and electronic media covered the issue extensively. Although product liability was not at the heart of the problem, Kasten used the momentum generated by the publicity to get his legislation moving. He got a bill out of committee, but it died on the floor during the rush at the end of the session. (By then the furor had died down considerably.)

Kasten's risk-retention legislation, which makes it easier for businessmen, state and local government units, and other organizations to form self-insurance cooperatives, did become law. Many other senators got involved in the issue as well. When in late 1985 some Kentucky day-care centers complained of not being able to get liability insurance, Mitch McConnell perceived the issue as likely to become hot and developed a comprehensive tort reform bill. He was thus ready when a crisis atmosphere developed. Although a freshman, he chaired hearings of the full Judiciary Committee on his legislation in late March. By early May, Orrin Hatch held hearings of the Labor and Human Resources Committee on the impact of the current insurance liability crisis on the availability of health care in America and on his bill to alleviate the problem.

Some involvement in hot issues is purely grandstanding, most often aimed at the folks back home via the local media because reporters for the national media are sensitive to and frequently unwilling to cover such behavior. One of the two reelection-oriented senators was reported by his staff to base his choice of issues in which to involve himself heavily upon current issue salience. "There are the hot news stories and he tags along and gets his picture taken," the staff said, simplifying a highly sophisticated operation. During the period when concern about drugs was at its height, one senator participated in a Drug Enforcement Administration undercover operation, demonstrating how easy it is to buy the drug Crack on the street by doing so. If the senator's goal is purely good publicity for reelection reasons, issues must be chosen carefully. Hot issues on which there is really only one side—drugs and terrorism, for example—are ideal.

Hot issues offer opportunities to policy- and influence-oriented senators as well. The aide to an oil state senator gave an example:

There are some issues that have a life of their own and that force themselves upon you, like oil prices, for example. If oil prices were still $30 a barrel, that wouldn't be an issue. Now, it has to be dealt with, and that's where our comprehensive energy program comes in. Now, that's both a problem and an opportunity. It's an opportunity in the sense that [the senator] always thought that the windfall profits tax was a mistake, but ordinarily there would be no opportunity to open that issue back up. Now there is.

Many senators have made quick reputations for themselves as leaders through their involvement in hot issues. In 1985, freshmen Tom Harkin and Phil Gramm made it clear that they were people who would have to be reckoned with on agricultural issues and budget policy, respectively.

Although senators try to choose their issue involvements rationally, the highly unpredictable environment in which they operate works against an optimal result. Hot issues emerge suddenly and windows of opportunity open unexpectedly, but a senator may simply be too deeply committed to other issues to take advantage of the new situation. An aide concluded his discussion of the decision to get involved by saying that "another consideration is time. If he's deeply involved in four issues, and a fifth comes up, you just can't do the fifth."

Coping Strategies for Legislative Activists

The quantity and breadth of senators' issue involvements result in severe strains on senators' time. All senators, even those who were House members, complain of time pressure. "You sometimes feel that you're a billiard ball," said the aide of a senator without previous legislative experience. "You'll be in a committee hearing, you'll be called to the floor to vote on something that, God knows, you may get five minutes of briefing from your staff on, you go back and there's a different witness talking about something else at the hearing." According to a long-time staffer of a former House member, time "is the biggest problem and the biggest difference between the House and the Senate. As much as having your time chewed up is a problem in the House, it's much worse in the Senate."

All agree that efficient time management is crucial. Efficient time management in the context of the contemporary Senate means delegating as much as possible to staff: if an aide can do it, the senator should not. (On the role of staff, see Foxx and Hammond 1977; Malbin 1980).

"There's such a thing as issues being ripe for decision. [The senator] pays attention to those," an aide to an activist senior senator explained.

"Up till then, the senator has been working on other things; the staff has been working on issues that are not yet ripe. So it's ripeness of issues for decision that determines the senator's time allocation to some extent." This senator's large, experienced, and highly competent staff make his involvement in a broad range of issues possible. They monitor the process on a myriad of issues, alert the senator when his personal involvement is required, and provide him with the substantive and political information necessary to make that involvement effective. In many instances, an experienced staff member can act in the senator's stead.

Most senators attend committee hearings and often mark-ups only when and for as long as they have something specific they want to do. The same rule applies to appearances on the floor. A senior senator's aide explained: "At any given time, he will have three to five simultaneous committee meetings on his schedule. So we must choose. With hearings, the rule is: is his attendance essential—is he chairing or must he be there to represent some viewpoint? With the floor it's the same test: is one of his issues up?" The aide to a junior senator from a large state said, "He only goes [to committee meetings] if there's something specific that he's got to participate in. If he's comfortable with it, he gives his proxy to the chairman. He just doesn't have time to attend them all."

Staff monitor committee proceedings, brief the senator on the matter at issue, and make sure he is at meetings when his personal presence is essential. During 1986, the budget resolution and the tax reform bill were in mark-up simultaneously. The aide to a senator who serves on both the Budget and Finance committees explained how the senator handled the conflict:

> The only way he can do that is by having very good staffers, and we have very good staffers in both those areas. So he tries to be at each committee meeting when he needs to be; that is, he tries to be there when decisive actions are taken. So we have very good staffers who not only keep up with the substance and go through the entire mark-up, but they also are very good at providing intelligence to him, that is, to keep him up with what is happening politically. That's a very important function of staffers. So they sit through the entire mark-up and make sure to get him there when his personal presence is needed.

The aide to a busy senior senator explained, "It's just lucky that we have an excellent staff member who follows the Budget Committee. That makes it possible for us to pop [the senator] in when it's absolutely essential that he take part himself."

Staff do a great deal more than simply monitor and report. Most legislative staff are on the lookout for issues that the senator can become productively involved in; in most interviews staff initiative was listed as one of the sources of involvement in issues. "Staff know what a senator is interested in," an aide explained. "And on trade, for example, the staff is always looking out for things." Legislative staff interact on a regular basis with constituent-based and national interest groups, which are often the source of legislative proposals.

On many issues, the senator's involvement is completely via staff. "There are a lot of things we as a staff do on trade that he probably doesn't even know about," one aide confirmed. Frequently, staff members will deal on their senators' behalf with interest groups, people in the Executive Branch, staff of other members in both chambers, and occasionally directly with other senators, often without specific instructions. The senator is brought in only if and when his personal presence is essential. An aide gave an example:

> Not long ago, the supplemental appropriations bill for the CCC [Commodity Credit Corporation] came over from the House, and the plan was to hold it at the desk and simply pass it without going to committee at all. But it turned out that Whitten had written into the bill a provision that the conservation reserve that we had gotten in the agricultural bill would not get automatic funding through the CCC. And we got a call from the Department of Agriculture saying "Can you help us on that? If this language stands, then basically the conservation reserve won't get off the ground this year." So, I called the environmental groups and told them to get busy, to put some pressure on. I called some Senate subcommittee chairmen. We put a hold on the bill. We really got the environmental groups stirred up. Now he [the senator] did very little on this. I did get him to call Cochran, chairman of the Senate agriculture appropriations subcommittee, to talk to him on that. And what happened was that bill, instead of being held at the desk, was sent to the committee where we won 14 to 2 and then Whitten gave in. So, we got our money for this conservation reserve.

By historical standards, the staff resources available to contemporary senators are extremely generous. Yet few senators believe they have enough staff. The more staff a senator has, the more issues he can become involved in, and contemporary senators can best advance their goals by being active in a broad range of issues.

8 // Committees and the Floor as Arenas for Legislative Activism

A second important element of a senator's style is the choice of arenas in which issues are pursued. Access to a given arena may lead a senator to become more involved in certain issues. Thus some issue involvements are primarily a function of the senator's committee memberships; that is, he would not have become involved with the issue if he did not serve on the appropriate committee. For example, Alan Simpson's involvement in immigration reform stemmed from his assignment as chair of the Judiciary Committee's Immigration Subcommittee. Immigration reform was not a pressing concern for a senator from Wyoming, nor did Simpson have a personal policy interest in the issue. When he assumed the chairmanship, the issue offered him the opportunity to play a leadership role on a matter of considerable importance, and he took it. More often issue choice precedes and determines the choice of arena. Senators and their senior staff first consider the issue and the potential payoffs of involvement; then they consider how and where to pursue the issue. However, because the costs and benefits of involvement in a given issue are strongly related to whether an appropriate arena for pursuing that involvement is readily available, the choice of issues and the choice of arenas are closely intertwined.

Committees and Subcommittees

For many senators, committees are arenas for pursuing specific issue interests, not work groups in which they participate on a continuous basis. "He spends time in committeee doing what *he* wants to do," an aide to a senior senator explained. "He's there when whatever he's concerned with and wants to affect comes up, and when the committee moves on to other issues, he leaves." The multitude of committee and subcommittee assignments that senators have encourages this perspective. No senator can attend all such meetings; he must pick and choose. Choices are made "according to your goals and priorities at a given time." Most staffers tell horror stories of the senator being confronted with major mark-ups in several committees simultaneously. "He needed roller skates to go back and forth," an aide said of one such situation. "Staff kept calling that they *really* needed him in this or the other committee room." Although such instances are not rare, "most of the time, only one of the committees has something of major concern to you," a staffer reported. "And you concentrate on that. Staff covers the other."

Committee and subcommittee leaders have somewhat less freedom to pick purely on the basis of their perception of the importance of the issue. Although they do, of course, have considerable power in setting the agenda of their committee, chairs are more constrained to attend meetings, even if the subject matter is not of burning interest.

Although most senators choose which committee meetings to attend on the basis of perceived importance of the issue being dealt with, the result in terms of committee participation patterns varies considerably across members. At one end of the spectrum are senators who participate in most or all of the business of a committee on a sustained basis. The goal of reelection or, more often, the goals of policy and influence dictate continuous involvement in the issues of that committee over those of the senator's other committees. In many but not all cases, these senators hold leadership positions on the committee. Sam Nunn, for example, spends the largest share of his time on matters before the Armed Services Committee and did so even before he became the top ranking Democrat on it. As chair of the Environment and Public Works Committee in the 99th Congress, Robert Stafford perforce concentrated on that committee's extensive workload. However, because he also chaired the Education, Arts and Humanities Subcommittee of the Labor Committee, which was charged with reauthorization of the Higher Education Act, some of his time had to be diverted to that committee. Only the chairman's power to set meeting times makes it possible for senior members to meet their multiple leadership responsibilities. When a senator does devote a great deal of time to one committee, staff have to pick up the slack on the senator's other assignments.

At the other end of the spectrum are those senators who frequently shift their emphasis among their committees depending upon "where the action is." Wendell Ford serves on Commerce and Energy, both committees with jurisdictions consisting of a range of disparate issues, many of them important to his home state of Kentucky. Where he concentrated his attention depended upon the agendas of the two committees at a given time. During the 99th Congress, Howard Metzenbaum served on Budget, Energy, Judiciary, and Labor. His allocation of time among these committees varied from week to week, depending upon the issues the committees were considering. Of course, senators' committee participation patterns can fall at various intermediate points along this spectrum. A number have a "favorite" committee to which they devote more personal time than to others; they do not, however, participate actively in all the decisions of their favorite committee, but pick and choose depending upon the specific issue. This leaves enough time for some personal involvement in the work of their lesser committees on issues of particular interest.

Most senior and many junior members have at least one committee to which they devote little personal attention. A senator from a state with an important but not dominant agricultural sector sought assignment to the Agriculture Committee purely for constituency reasons. He participates in the committee's work only when it deals with matters directly affecting his state' agriculture. During the 99th Congress, Lowell Weicker chaired the Small Business Committee, the Labor, Health and Human Services, and Education Subcommittee of Appropriations, and the Handicapped Subcommittee of Labor. He had little time left over to devote to his assignment to Energy. Small Business, Veterans' Affairs, and the Special Committee on Aging are fourth assignments for many senators; accordingly, they often get short shrift in terms of personal time. Senators hold on to such assignments, however, because the more arenas a senator has access to, the more likely he will have available an appropriate arena in which to pursue a chosen issue.

Committees offer senators various sorts of opportunities to pursue issues. Committees are still the preeminent arena for shaping legislation. The major committees, of course, offer their members the opportunity to participate in making highly consequential policy decisions—an opportunity that can pay off not just in advancing policy goals but also in terms of reelection and influence.

In 1986, a subset of the members of the Finance Committee wrote the tax reform legislation that ultimately passed the Senate (see Birnbaum and Murray 1987). The open mark-up session had gotten completely out of hand; majorities had approved tax breaks for special interests that cost billions and made a mockery of the reform label. Chairman Robert Packwood, attempting to salvage the bill and his own reputation, called together a group of members he believed were interested in producing true reform. This small group, meeting informally and in private, produced a bill that they were able, with a good deal of help from the media, to push through the committee and the Senate. Bill Bradley, an early advocate of tax reform, was a member of Finance and of the working group and, consequently, was able to play a major role in shaping the legislation. Robert Kasten, another early advocate, did not serve on the committee and was not able to influence directly the shaping of the bill.

The Appropriations Committee gives its members and especially its subcommittee chairs the opportunity to make large numbers of spending decisions, most of which will not receive serious review in full committee or on the floor. These opportunities can be used to further the senator's policy goals, to advance his reelection prospects by making sure his state does well, and to increase his influence by doing favors for other senators. Thus, during the period of Republican control, Lowell Weicker used his position as chairman of the Labor, Health and Human Services, and Education Subcommittee to protect social programs generally and aid to the handicapped—his special interest—specifically from the worst of the Reagan budget cuts. The position also gave him the opportunity to do favors for his colleagues. The 1986 bill, for example, earmarked $5 million for the Oregon Hearing Institute, an item of special interest to full committee chairman Mark Hatfield; $750,000 for a physical therapy clinic in Ernest Hollings' South Carolina; and $750,000 for the Robert A. Taft Institute for Government in New York, as requested by Alphonse D'Amato (*Washington Post National Weekly Edition*, October 14, 1985, 13). Undoubtedly Weicker's home state of Connecticut was not slighted.

Decisions made in committee can, of course, be challenged on the floor. If committee members want their bills to pass the Senate they must be sensitive to the preferences of their fellow senators. Not only can a majority defeat their legislation, an intense minority, sometimes a very small one, can raise insurmountable barriers to passage. Nevertheless, the time pressures on senators are such that most of the decisions made in committee stand. Consequently, if a senator wants to influence policy in a given area on a sustained basis, the committee with jurisdiction over that area provides the best arena for doing so.

In addition to participating in the making of legislative decisions, committees and subcommittees offer other opportunities for pursuing issues that can also contribute to a senator's goals of reelection, policy, or power. The positive agenda-setting powers of committee and subcommittee chairmen are extensive, especially with respect to hearings. Basically, a committee chairman can hold hearings on any matter that under the broadest definition falls within the committee's jurisdiction. Although committee chairmen must approve subcommittee hearings and occasionally will deny a request (usually by claiming no room is available), subcommittee chairmen also have very wide discretion in holding hearings.

Hearings can contribute to a senator's prospects for reelection by shoring up his relationships with specialized constituencies in his state and by generating good publicity. Field hearings in the state are particularly useful for these purposes. During the 1985 Easter recess, Pete Wilson held hearings at Fort Ord to examine the status of military housing. They came in the wake of a small boy's suicide because of his army father's inability to afford housing in which the family could live together and received considerable press coverage. Wilson then proceeded to Fresno, where he held hearings on the trade problems facing California farmers. Senators sometimes "borrow" subcommittees from their chairs for the purpose of holding field hearings. Alphonse D'Amato, for example, has held hearings in New York under the auspices of the Labor, Health and Human Services, and Education Subcommittee, the Agriculture Subcommittee of Appropriations, the Judiciary Committee, and the Armed Services Committee. D'Amato, at that time, chaired none of these entities and did not even serve on the latter two.

Some minor committees, like Small Business and the Special Committee on Aging, are attractive because they lend themselves to field hearings. Both committees, in order to encourage member participation, have very permissive policies on field hearings. Both allow minority party members to chair field hearings in their home states. In September, 1986, for example, Democrat Jeff Bingaman held a field hearing of the Senate Special Committee on Aging in Santa Fe. The topic—the health needs of elderly Indians—nicely combined a constituent service orientation with his policy interest in health matters.

For Democrats, Small Business is also an attractive committee because it allows them to work with and develop ties to an important group of constituents that often supported their opponent in their first successful Senate campaign. Of course, liberal Democrats are unlikely to convert the entire small business community into fervent supporters; they can realistically expect to gain support from some, while lessening the intensity of opposition among others.

Committees and subcommittees provide forums well suited to agenda setting, and hearings are a useful vehicle for publicizing problems. Some hearings—for example, those on obscene lyrics in popular music, at least when one of the witnesses is a senator's wife—will receive extensive media coverage, and information about the problem will be widely disseminated as a result. Of course, most senators' attempts to publicize an issue do not have this sort of media appeal. During the 99th Congress, James McClure, chairman of the Energy Committee, held several sets of hearings designed to warn that current United States energy policies were likely to lead to another energy crisis. The staff dubbed one set the "When the Lights Go Out" hearings. Although McClure would undoubtedly have welcomed heavy coverage by the mass media, the hearings were aimed primarily at a more restricted attentive public and especially at decision makers in Washington. One purpose of seven days of hearings in early 1987 on national security strategy by new Armed Services chair Sam Nunn was to publicize among the national security issue public what Nunn saw as the Reagan administration's lack of a coherent strategy. Howard Metzenbaum, who had long been concerned about the safety of the artificial sweetener aspartame, used the occasion of a negative scientific report about the sweetener to announce hearings on the issue—hearings that, he hoped, would further publicize the issue.

Hearings can be employed as instruments of policy promotion—the publicizing and legitimating of a policy position that are also aspects of agenda setting. John East's hearings on abortion in 1981 provide a notorious example of such use—and an indication of the limits of a subcommittee chairman's autonomy. East invited only witnesses who agreed with his position that life begins at conception and, thus, that abortion is murder. Severely criticized for the one-sidedness of the testimony, he was pressured into holding further hearings during which alternate views were presented. Hearings held by Edward Kennedy, new chairman of the Labor and Human Resources Committee, in early 1987 represent a more typical example of policy promotion. After six years of Republican control of the Senate, Kennedy used a series of high-profile hearings to reestablish a liberal agenda. By mid-April a dozen hearings had been held on a wide range of subjects that included health care for catastrophic illnesses, mine safety, education, unemployment, and AIDS.

Some subcommittees are ideally suited for focusing on dramatic problems and thereby (and not incidentally) publicizing the subcommittee's chair. During the 99th Congress, the Subcommittee on Children, Family, Drugs, and Alcoholism held hearings on drug abuse in the military, missing children, international narcotics control, dependent care programs, effects of domestic violence, the impact of drug education, runaway children, designer drugs, Nicaraguan involvement in drug trafficking, and alcohol abuse programs. Paula Hawkins, the subcommittee chair, reaped considerable media coverage from these hearings, particularly in her home state of Florida.

In the Senate, subcommittees are often designed to meet the needs and interests of their chairs. Thus, the Labor and Human Resources Committee's Subcommitttee on Children, Family, Drugs, and Alcoholism was created especially for Paula Hawkins; the Security and Terrorism Subcommittee of Judiciary was created for Jeremiah Denton. When the Democrats regained control of the Senate in 1987, a new subcommittee on Defense Industry and Technology was established on Armed Services. The subcommittee was designed for Jeff Bingaman, its chair, and provided him with a forum in which to pursue his interest in defense research and development. Although Bingaman had not served on the Governmental Affairs Committee during the 99th Congress, a special position of ad hoc chairman for National Competitive Strategy was devised for him when he was assigned to the committee in the 100th Congress. This was, in part, an acknowledgment of his status as a significant actor on the issue, and it gave him a forum for further involvement. Accordingly, Bingaman chaired major Government Affairs Committee hearings on the competitiveness of the United States in world trade in the spring of 1987.

The distribution of committee and subcommittee assignments in the Senate is governed by powerful tendencies toward accommodation. To the extent possible, senators get the assignments they want, and because the supply of assignments is so large, conflicts are minimized. To be sure, conflicts over policy occasionally dictate deviations from the norm of accommodation. When the Republicans organized the Senate in 1981, new Judiciary Committee Chairman Strom Thurmond abolished the antitrust subcommittee rather than see it chaired by liberal Charles Mathias, second ranking Republican. However, accommodation is the rule, and the result is that all but the most junior members (and often them as well) possess committee and subcommittee positions well suited to involvement in issues of special interest to them. For example, during the years of Republican control, Orrin Hatch chaired the Constitution Subcommittee of Judiciary, an ideal forum for playing a leadership role on a variety of New Right social issues of intense interest to him. Lowell Weicker's chairmanship of the Handicapped Subcommittee of Labor allowed him to become still more active on an issue of deep personal concern. During the 99th Congress, Weicker successfully shepherded to passage a bill overturning a Supreme Court decision that denied attorney's fees to the parents of handicapped children suing for their education rights. Through his chairmanship of the Labor, Health and Human Services, and Education Subcommittee of Appropriations he was able to protect handicapped programs from the most severe of the Reagan Administration budget cuts.

Because of the chair's extensive powers to set his subcommittee's agenda, a given subcommittee may be useful to senators with very different interests. When Republican Robert Kasten became chair of the Consumer Subcommittee of the Commerce Committee, he was not interested in consumer legislation as traditionally defined. Instead he used the subcommittee to develop uniform product liability legislation. When Christopher Dodd succeeded Paula Hawkins as chair of the Subcommittee on Children, Family, Drugs, and Alcoholism of Human Resources, he made childcare legislation the subcommittee's top priority.

Being a member of the committee with jurisdiction over an issue facilitates involvement in that issue, most obviously because the senator can participate directly in the making of committee decisions; he has a vote. "If you're not on the committee, you can lobby committee members," a senior staffer explained, "but you are not there when the decisions are being made." In addition, committee membership and even more a committee or subcommittee leadership position results in the senator becoming a part of the network of those perceived to be concerned with and active on the issue. Interest groups will have to deal with the senator, and if he shares their views, they may look to him for leadership; experts will bring their ideas to him; the media will perceive him as a player and will come to him for comments. By active involvement in an issue within a committee, the senator establishes an identification with the issue and legitimates himself as a significant actor on the issue.

For the junior senator who does not serve on the standing committee with jurisdiction over the issue of interest, some of the minor committees provide a substitute. In 1981 and again in 1986, the Small Business Committee held extensive hearings on the impact on small business of the tax changes being considered by the Finance Committee. Many of these hearings were chaired by junior members who were able by this route to get involved in a hot issue. Because small business is arguably affected by almost everything of importance, the committee provides a vehicle through which its members can become involved in any of a wide range of issues.

Similarly, the Special Committee on Aging can be used to pursue a variety of policy interests and thereby establish an identification with an issue. Jeff Bingaman used his membership on the committee to pursue his interest in health promotion programs. Hearings of the committee (along with other activities, including floor amendments and a state-wide voluntary program to change lifestyles in New Mexico) have established him as a leader on the issue even though he serves on no committee with legislative jurisdiction over health matters.

Minority party senators, who do not chair committees or subcommittees, are at a real disadvantage. Some of the chairs of minor committees do allow minority party members to chair hearings, mostly in the field, but the subject matter is tightly constrained. Only nonideological, nonpartisan issues can be pursued.

During the years of Republican control, the Democratic conference set up task forces in an attempt to provide substitute forums. These task forces were charged with developing Democratic alternatives in major policy areas and were intended to serve purposes similar to those of subcommittees for their chairs. The task force on trade did yield considerable publicity for its members, especially for its chairman, Lloyd Bentsen. The task force on competitiveness gave its chairman, Jeff Bingaman, standing in the Washington policy community to participate in the debate on a set of issues in which he is deeply interested. However, such substitutes are clearly inferior to a subcommittee with official status.

The Senate Floor

The Senate floor provides another arena in which senators may choose to pursue issues. Norms place few restrictions on floor activism. "He's been surprisingly active on the floor," a staffer said of his boss, a former House member. "It's much more possible to participate on the floor in the Senate." According to an aide to another former representative, "There's a different atmosphere here than in the House. There's much more latitude to legislate from the floor."

As we saw earlier, the Senate floor has become a much more active decision-making arena since the 1950s. Most senators now are at least occasionally active on the floor, and many are frequently active.

Senators use floor amendments to attempt to alter decisions made in their committees. A senator may have lost in committee but believe his chances are better with the entire membership. The balance of forces in a committee may be such that it is "not worth the effort to try to have an impact in committee"; he may thus concentrate his efforts on the floor.

The 1985 floor battle over the Department of Defense authorization bill, for example, saw seven different members of the Armed Services Committee offering nine amendments that resulted in roll call votes. Most were minority party members hoping to reverse adverse committee decisions on the floor. Thus John Glenn proposed reducing from

$2.96 billion to $2.8 billion the authorization for research on antimissile defenses; James Exon proposed cutting funds for the reactivation of the battleship Wisconsin and prohibiting future spending to reactivate battleships. Both amendments failed. Edward Kennedy attempted to reverse a committee decision exempting most military construction projects from the Davis-Bacon Act's prevailing wage standards, but his amendment lost on a 49–49 vote.

Sam Nunn, ranking Democrat on Armed Services, offered an amendment to cap the number of MX missiles at fifty, half the number the Reagan administration wanted. He had proposed a cap of forty within committee, but it had failed. Aware that the committee membership was more conservative than the Senate membership as a whole, Nunn decided to take the fight to the floor. On the day Nunn was to offer his amendment, members of the administration approached him with offers of compromise. Having become convinced that Nunn had the votes, they hoped to salvage something. In three days of negotiations between Reagan aides and Nunn and his principal cosponsors, Majority Leader Robert Byrd, Albert Gore (a freshman senator involved in MX battles when a House member), and David Boren, an agreement was reached. The number of missiles was raised from forty to fifty (*Congressional Quarterly Weekly Report*, May 25, 1985, 982–89). When Nunn offered his amendment (now endorsed by the president), it passed easily on a 78–20 vote. Although the agreement allowed the president to save some face, it was in fact a defeat for his position. Nunn had taken on the committee majority, the Republican leadership, and the president and had won.

Senators also use floor amendments to influence legislation reported by committees on which they do not serve. More than six of ten amendments are offered by nonmembers of the originating committee. Senators often attempt to influence legislation in committees on which they do not serve by informal means before it reaches the floor. If they fail, they feel free to take on the committee on the floor. Thus, Pete Wilson tried to persuade Judiciary Committee members involved in writing the immigration reform bill that an agricultural worker program was a needed component. He even invited Alan Simpson, chair of the Immigration Subcommittee and the bill's chief sponsor, to come to California to talk to growers about their problems. When such efforts failed, Wilson proposed a guest worker program as a floor amendment to the bill. On his first attempt, he was defeated; but a second amendment containing a revised program passed.

The floor provides an arena in which a senator can pursue policy interests that do not fall into the jurisdiction of his committees. During floor consideration of the Department of Defense authorization bill discussed earlier, twenty-two amendments were offered and pushed to a roll call, thirteen by senators who were not Armed Services Committee members. Most of those represented attempts to significantly influence major policy decisions. Thus, David Pryor and Charles Grassley offered as an amendment a comprehensive procurement reform proposal. Pryor also sponsored an amendment to delete funds for production of nerve gas. Dale Bumpers and Patrick Leahy drafted an amendment calling on President Reagan to abide by the SALT II and ABM agreements. Closed-door negotiations with hard-liners James McClure, Malcolm Wallop, and Steven Symms—who opposed abidance by the United States with the pacts because of allegations of cheating by the Soviets—produced compromise language acceptable to McClure (though not to the other hard-liners), and the Bumpers-Leahy amendment passed easily. A number of Democrats proposed cutting SDI funding by varying amounts, while Wallop proposed earmarking a portion of SDI funds for development of antimissile weapons that could be deployed within five to seven years.

Policy decisions made by legislation such as the Department of Defense authorization bill are wide-ranging and highly consequential. Many senators have strong views about the issues involved. For those not on the appropriate committee, the floor provides an arena for involvement in those issues. Senators may be able to affect policy directly by getting an amendment adopted. Failing that, nonmembers may still be able to influence the debate, increase their chances of winning the next time the issue comes up, or persuade their opponents to compromise.

Success rates on floor amendments are sufficiently high to encourage use of the floor as an arena for influencing legislation. About 30 percent of amendments subjected to a roll call vote pass. On the Department of Defense authorization bill, eight of twenty-two amendments passed.

Of course, winning is not always the point; agenda setting and policy promotion are sometimes the real aim. Thus, when Jeff Bingaman offered an amendment establishing a teacher training corps to the higher education reauthorization bill on June 3, 1986, he did not expect to win. The floor debate, however, gave the proposal some visibility, and the amendment's good showing—it lost 56 to 37—put pressure on the Labor and Human Resources Committee to act on the free-standing version of the legislation.

Anti-SDI forces did not expect most of their amendments directing funding cuts to pass during consideration of the 1985 Department of Defense authorization bill. Rather, they hoped a good showing would strengthen their position in future battles on the issue.

Amendments are also sometimes used to force senators to go on the record, usually on highly emotional issues such as abortion and busing. The senators who offer such litmus test amendments hope the results can be used by their ideological allies to defeat senators who vote incorrectly. Using roll call votes to create campaign issues, while certainly not new, was perfected in the 1970s and 1980s by members of the New Right. Senators affiliated with the New Right, especially Jesse Helms, offered dozens of such amendments, which New Right groups such as the National Conservative Political Action Committee then used in their campaigns against liberal senators. As Paul Weyrich, a leading New Right strategist, explained:

> [Helms] made the social issues enough of an issue within the GOP to defeat all those liberal Democrats [in 1980]—a course of action Dole had resisted for years. He got those dozens of roll calls on the record. And with those votes, we were able to pin the pro-abortion, pro-busing, pro-pornography, pro-whatever label on those senators who otherwise would have gotten away with those views for years and years to come (*Congressional Quarterly Weekly Report*, March 6, 1982, 500).

By passing a committee altogether and using the floor as the primary legislative arena is considerably easier in the Senate than in the House. James McClure, long an advocate of weakening gun control laws, succeeded early in the 99th Congress in by-passing the Judiciary Committee and having his bill weakening gun controls placed directly on the Senate calendar. Majority Leader Dole, an ally of McClure, promised to bring the bill to the floor whether or not a time agreement could be reached. Realizing that a filibuster might nevertheless jeopardize the bill, McClure sought a compromise with gun control supporters that would assure a vote on the bill. After days of negotiation, McClure, Dole, and Orrin Hatch came to an agreement with opponents of the bill, including Edward Kennedy. For a time Howard Metzenbaum held out for further concessions, something he was able to do because time agreements require unanimous consent. Metzenbaum did finally agree that gun control advocates had gotten the best deal possible. McClure then shepherded the bill to passage on the Senate floor.

In using the floor as the principal arena for legislating, McClure had a number of advantages that contributed to his success. The Judiciary Committee had approved the legislation in previous congresses, a senior majority party member of Judiciary, Orrin Hatch, was a fervent ally, and the Majority Leader was highly supportive.

Because Senate rules allow nongermane amendments to most bills, such advantages are not prerequisites to by-passing a committee and legislating successfully on the floor. A senator can offer his legislation as a rider to an unrelated bill. In the case of the interest withholding repeal battle in 1983, a junior senator succeeded in doing so despite formidable opposition.

The 1982 tax bill contained a provision mandating a 10 percent withholding levy on interest and dividend income. When that bill was on the floor, freshman Republican Robert Kasten's amendment to delete the provision lost narrowly. Once the provision passed, lobbyists for adversely affected financial institutions formed a coalition and mounted an extensive grass-roots lobbying campaign for repeal. According to the Democratic Study Group Report on the withholding controversy:

> In inserts to year-end statements sent to millions of depositors, banks have told their customers that "10% of your savings is going to disappear" because of the withholding law, and that "the government is going to loot your savings." Bank statements have also included form letters and preprinted postcards addressed to Members of Congress urging repeal of the new law. As a result, Congress has been inundated with the biggest flood of letters ever on an issue—even larger than Watergate or the Vietnam War (No. 98-7, April 15, 1983).

The Senate Republican leadership, Finance Committee Chairman Robert Dole, the president, and the House Democratic leadership all opposed repeal. Kasten was nevertheless determined to push the issue, but the nature of the opposition and the fact that Kasten did not sit on the Finance Committee dictated that he carry his fight to the Senate floor. In March, 1983, Kasten offered interest withholding repeal as an amendment to a jobs and recession relief bill that the Senate leadership wanted to pass quickly. Dole vowed to kill the jobs bill rather than allow a vote on Kasten's amendment, which he knew he could not defeat. "I don't have the 51 votes to table this amendment," Dole acknowledged, "but one thing we can do is discuss this for a few days or weeks so the American people can understand what it's all about" (*Congressional Quarterly Weekly Report*, March 12, 1983, 491). Majority Leader Baker warned that the president might well veto the jobs bill if it contained the Kasten amendment. Kasten twice tried to cut off the filibuster by invoking cloture but failed to amass the needed sixty votes. After a week of deadlock and delay, a compromise was struck that allowed a vote on the jobs bill. In return for withdrawing his amendment from the jobs bill, Senate leaders promised Kasten that his amendment would be the first item considered when a trade reciprocity bill was brought to the floor on April 15, the deadline for filing income tax returns.

When the reciprocity bill was called up, Dole, with the help of several liberal Democratic allies, mounted another filibuster. Kasten had filed a cloture petition, and the Republican leadership, aware that he had the votes to cut off debate, moved to adjourn the Senate. Despite intense party pressure not to do so, Kasten contested the motion. The adjournment motion failed on a 63–31 vote, a major defeat for the leadership. Dole realized he could not stop repeal and agreed to talk; after hours of intense negotiations, a compromise was reached that gave Kasten most of what he wanted but was formulated in terms that saved face for Dole. The compromise measure passed the Senate by a large margin. As Kasten had hoped, the big Senate victory provided sufficient pressure to force a repeal measure onto the floor of the House, where it passed handily. Consequently it was unnecessary for him to offer repeal as an amendment to the debt ceiling bill, as he had threatened to do.

The legislative purpose Kasten hoped to accomplish on the floor was straightforward—repeal of a provision in a previously passed bill. Although the compromise resulted in more complicated language, the decisions that senators faced on the floor were not particularly complex. By contrast, the 1985 Gramm-Rudman amendment is a case in which the floor was used as the primary legislative arena for highly complex legislation that made major structural changes in how the Congress makes spending decisions.

Phil Gramm, an economist by training, made his mark in the House on budget issues; he was the prime Democratic sponsor of the 1981 Reagan budget. The Reagan-supported budget resolution and the reconciliation bill to carry it out became known as Gramm-Latta I and II, respectively. Elected to the Senate as a Republican in 1984, Gramm sought assignment to the Budget Committee but was passed over. However, the lack of a committee base did not deter Gramm from focusing on budget issues. In the spring of 1985, only a few months into his first year in the Senate, he criticized the Budget Committee's budget in Op-Ed articles in major newspapers. A few months later, he held a news conference to deplore the compromise on the budget between members of the Reagan administration and Senate Republicans (*Congressional Quarterly Weekly Report*, March 15, 1986, 613).

In mid-1985, most Republican senators felt that members of the administration had let them down on the budget. They had made the tough decisions, including voting to hold down increases in Social Security, but the administration, rather than backing them up, had given in to the House Democrats on the social security issue. Gramm, in response, began to think about changes in the budget process that would force deficit reductions. In July, 1985, when he directed his staff to begin the appropriate research, he was already considering the debt limit bill as a possible vehicle for this purpose. Gramm settled on a mechanism of legislating decreasing annual deficit targets, resulting eventually in a balanced budget; failure to meet a given target would trigger automatic across-the-board spending cuts.

Gramm presented his proposal at a GOP Policy Committee lunch following the August recess. Senate Republicans, deeply concerned that the huge deficit would become a major campaign issue, greeted the proposal with enthusiasm; the bill seemed to offer a way of turning a political liability into an asset. This widespread rank-and-file enthusiasm appears to have convinced Majority Leader Dole and Budget Committee Chairman Pete Domenici—who reportedly were initially wary—to support the legislation. The president also endorsed the plan. After Gramm agreed to exempt Social Security from the automatic cuts, a number of Democrats signed on as cosponsors.

Gramm and his primary cosponsors Warren Rudman and Ernest Hollings offered the plan as an amendment to the debt limit increase bill. Republican leadership support proved to be crucial, because Minority Leader Robert Byrd and Senators Lowell Weicker, J. Bennett Johnston, and Gary Hart all threatened to filibuster. For a week, including rare Saturday and Sunday sessions, the Senate debated in public while negotiating behind closed doors. Two amendments were adopted; one reduced the great discretion given to the president, and the other broadened the impact of the automatic cuts. On October 9, by a vote of 72 to 24, Gramm-Rudman was agreed to by the Senate.

Thus highly complex legislation making major changes in the budget process was adopted by the Senate approximately two weeks after it was first introduced. Its primary author, a first year senator, persuaded the Senate to accept such consequential and complex legislation without subjecting it to committee scrutiny. The measure's great political appeal overshadowed the doubts that most senators had about making changes of this magnitude in a manner their predecessors would have considered cavalier.

Floor activism is sometimes aimed at exacting concessions or killing legislation outright. Given the time pressure under which the Senate works, the leadership is loath to even schedule a bill that will consume large amounts of floor time unless it is "must" legislation. The threat to delay is thus a powerful one and is used by all senators at least occasionally.

Holds, threats to filibuster, and even actual filibusters are often invitations to negotiate. Offering or threatening to offer large numbers of amendments is another frequently employed tactic for exacting concessions from a bill's sponsors. As a committee staff director explained, "I can't count the number of times there have been that Senator X, usually Hatch or Armstrong, has 100 amendments in his pocket. So we had to start by watering the bill down" (Ehrenhalt 1982, 2180).

Negotiations often take place before the legislation reaches the floor; in fact, the leadership will often insist that a time agreement is reached before scheduling a bill for floor action. In addition, much bargaining takes place during floor consideration. "You can accomplish a lot on the floor," a senior staffer explained. "A lot of things are worked out on the floor or just off it in the cloakroom."

When the aim is to kill the legislation outright, the tactics employed are similar—extended debate, actual or threatened, and sometimes a plethora of amendments. The prospects of success are very much affected by how constrained the Senate's time is. Success is much more likely when the end of the session looms than it is earlier in the year.

The use of holds and of threats to filibuster to encourage a bill's sponsors to negotiate is standard operating procedure in the Senate. All senators use these tools, and they are used on all kinds of legislation—on minor bills with an impact on some fairly narrow state interest as well as major legislation with a broad policy impact. Full-fledged filibusters, especially those aimed at killing legislation, are most frequently but by no means always aimed at major, ideologically charged bills and motivated by policy concerns.

Although most senators occasionally make full use of their powers to obstruct, for some such behavior constitutes a major element of their style. Orrin Hatch first made his name in the Senate in 1978 when, as a freshman, he took a lead role in the successful filibuster against labor law reform legislation. Hatch, Jesse Helms, and Richard Lugar organized a filibuster in which a dozen senators held control of the Senate floor, preventing all but routine business (U.S. Congress, Senate 1979, 53). Six times between June 8 and June 22, Majority Leader Robert Byrd sought to impose cloture; each time, he fell short of the needed sixty votes, though twice by only two votes. The opponents had won. Time pressure and dim prospects of success kept Byrd from making further attempts to break the filibuster. Late in the congressional session of 1980, Hatch was again instrumental in killing major legislation he opposed, as a bill to strengthen federal enforcement of open housing laws succumbed to his filibuster.

When Republicans took control of the Senate and Hatch assumed the chairmanships of the Labor and Human Resources Committee and of Judiciary's Constitution Subcommittee, his emphasis shifted from blocking to passing legislation. Although less frequently appropriate, obstructionism as a strategy was not abandoned.

In early 1984, when the Supreme Court, in its Grove City decision, narrowed the interpretation of 1972 legislation barring sex discrimination in education and, by implication, that of other major civil rights laws, civil rights proponents immediately began attempts to overturn the decision. The House passed a bill in June, but the Senate Labor Committee did not act. Hatch, the chairman, strongly opposed the language that sponsors wanted because, he claimed, it would broaden the reach of the original legislation. He was supported by the Administration. Majority Leader Baker refused to bring up the House-passed bill until sponsors and opponents agreed on a compromise version. After three months of futile negotiation and with time running out in the session, proponents decided to force the issue. Minority Leader Byrd offered the Grove City legislation as a substitute amendment to a continuing appropriations resolution. Hatch responded by offering proposals on school busing, gun control, and tuition tax credits as perfecting amendments to the substitute. As Hatch had intended, forcing senators to vote on those highly controversial matters, especially so soon before an election, plunged the Senate into a parliamentary morass. At several points, the chamber came close to abandoning its rule requiring that amendments considered after cloture is invoked be germane, a course that both Baker and Byrd warned would lead to legislative chaos. At this point, Robert Packwood, a major supporter, threw in the towel. He moved that the Byrd amendment be tabled and a relieved Senate voted 53 to 45 to do so (see *Congressional Quarterly Weekly Report*, October 6, 1984, 2430–33). Thus Hatch killed a bill that almost certainly had majority support: sixty-three senators were cosponsors of the Senate companion bill to the House-passed version. He did so even though the Senate had voted overwhelmingly to invoke cloture. By creative use of the Senate rules, Hatch was able to raise the price of passage beyond what a majority was willing to pay.

Despite this case and some other well-publicized instances (such as the gas tax filibuster by Senators Helms and East that kept the Senate in session until almost Christmas in 1982), the senators that have employed obstructionism as a major element of their style have, in the 1980s, more often been liberals than conservatives. With a conservative Republican majority in control of the Senate and of most of its committees from 1981 through 1986, liberals more often had reason to use the floor in this way.

During those years, liberal Republican Lowell Weicker regularly employed all the procedural tools available to him to block New Right initiatives on so-called social issues. He waged, sometimes alone and sometimes with allies, a series of filibusters aimed at blocking passage of legislation or constitutional amendments on school busing, school prayer, and abortion. His filibuster against antibusing legislation in 1982 and 1983 stretched over eight months. That legislation eventually passed the Senate but never emerged from the House. A six-week filibuster waged with Robert Packwood and Max Baucus killed anti-abortion and school prayer provisions in 1982. Weicker took a lead role in the successful effort to defeat a proposed school prayer amendment in 1984. During six years of Republican control of the Senate and the presidency, none of the New Right's major legislative goals in the area of social issues became law.

Howard Metzenbaum was accomplished at using Senate rules to delay and extract concessions before the change in Senate control. In 1977, he and James Abourezk led a two-week filibuster against President Carter's energy bill. When the Republicans took control, however, there were "more things to be against" and Metzenbaum dedicated himself to a watchdog role, using the Senate rules (of which he has an excellent command) to block as much "bad" legislation as possible. "We're the lobbyist for the people who can't afford to have a lobbyist here, for the average taxpayer, for the average consumer," an aide explained. "We're basically against subsidies for special interests."

Energy, intelligence, and an excellent staff make possible Metzenbaum's extremely broad involvement in issues. "He is all over the lot. He has his nose in lots of things," aides report. When asked what the main things are that the senator has been working on recently, staff will list several dozen items. One aide concluded, "If you've looked, you'll see there are just not very many major issues that we are not involved in." Although Metzenbaum is also very active in his committes, the floor has been an important legislative arena for him. According to an aide, "We have a rule here in this office that our business is to know about every bill that's passed in the chamber, and we do know just about every bill. And by looking at every bill, you often find important issues. You find things that are going through that shouldn't, and that gets you involved in various things."

In his battle against special interest bills and other legislation he thinks unwise, Metzenbaum has mounted numerous filibusters and threatened many more. By using holds, by objecting to unanimous consent agreements, and, if necessary, by offering a spate of amendments when senators want to go home for the weekend, he often extracts concessions. "Many are little things," an aide explained, "but they add up." Furthermore, other senators know he will examine their proposals.

"When you prepare an amendment or a bill, subconsciously you're thinking about Howard Metzenbaum. Will it pass the Metzenbaum test?" David Pryor explained (*Congressional Quarterly Weekly Report*, January 3, 1987, 16).

Metzenbaum is most active on the floor toward the end of the session and immediately before recesses. It is then that senators attempt to slip through their more egregious giveaways, he believes. And the time pressure gives extra leverage to a senator willing to delay. "He really gears up towards the end of the session and before recesses," a staffer explained. "We put a watch on the floor. We have staff on the floor and in the galleries all the time. We put a hold on anything that we don't know what it is." On October 1, 1983, the New York *Times* reported:

> For more than a week now, Mr. Metzenbaum has had a "hold" on a wide range of legislation: Granting antitrust immunity to the beer and shipping industries; a limited antitrust exemption for the National Football League; making major changes in the bankruptcy law; leasing oil shale lands; helping the timber industry; and other measures dealing with tariffs, drug manufacturers and dam repairs.
>
> In his seat when the Senate convenes, still there when the Senate adjourns, sometimes far into the night, the Ohio Democrat has, thus far, prevented floor consideration of all these and other bills.

By being active on the floor, Metzenbaum directly and indirectly influences legislation in a broad range of areas. In order to get their bills to the floor, senators must often make concessions to him. Thus he was the toughest bargainer among the gun control supporters who forced James McClure to compromise in order to get a time agreement for his bill. He is among the most active sponsors of floor amendments and often influences legislation in that way. In addition, to the extent that other senators consider his likely reactions in making their legislative decisions, he indirectly influences policy decisions. In essence, he raises the price to others of certain kinds of decisions.

In sum, whatever the issues a senator wishes to pursue, his committees or the floor are likely to provide him with a serviceable arena. Committee assignment practices result in senators holding multiple positions, usually on those committees of most interest to them. Subcommittees to a large extent are personal vehicles for their chairs. There are few constraints on using the floor to pursue issues.

9 // Legislative Activism: A Quantitative Analysis and a Case Study

For senators, pressures and incentives are heavily weighted toward high levels of activity and broad involvement in issues both in committee and on the floor. This chapter provides two perspectives on the resulting widespread legislative activism. First, legislative activism is analyzed quantitatively through an examination of floor amendments offered and bills sponsored. Second, a case study of senators' activity on one particular hot issue provides another perspective.

Activists and Generalists: A Quantitative Analysis

Floor amendments offered and pushed to a roll call vote provide a measure of one facet of legislative activism. A senator who offered five or more such amendments during a congress can be considered a floor activist. By examining a senator's behavior over time, one can determine whether activism so defined is a stable element of the senator's style.

Table 9.1 displays, for all senators and for those who served in the 97th, 98th, and 99th Congresses (1981–86), the number of congresses in which they were floor activists. Thus thirty-one of the eighty-seven senators who served in all three congresses were never floor activists; an identical number were activists in two or more of the three congresses. For these senators, activism or nonactivism on the floor appears to be a stable element of their style. In contrast, for those senators who offered five or more amendments in one of the three congresses, floor activism appears to be an option, the choice of which is dependent upon circumstances. Four of the seven freshmen first elected in 1984 were floor activists in their first congress; a high degree of such activism in a senator's first congress probably indicates a strong inclination toward an activist style. Of the six senators who first entered the chamber in the 98th Congress, half were activists in one of their first two congresses but none in both; thus no conclusions about their styles are possible.

Table 9.1 Floor Activism in the Senate (Measured by number of Congresses, 97th through 99th, in which senator offered five or more amendments)

No. of Congresses	All Senators	Those Who Served 97th–99th	North Dem.	South Dem.	Republicans
0	37	31	10	4	23
1	32	25	12	1	19
2	18	18	7	3	8
3	13	13	8	2	3

In the mid-1980s, then, over one-third of the Senate's members were regularly active on the floor in offering amendments; over one-quarter were occasionally activists on the floor. Only about one-third of senators were consistently restrained in their floor behavior.

Floor amending activity measures only one facet of legislative activism. The number of bills sponsored provides another indicator that is not so closely tied to activity at the floor stage. In 1985, the average senator was prime sponsor of 22.7 substantive bills and resolutions (symbolic measures dedicating a day to some cause and the like were excluded); thirty-three senators sponsored twelve or fewer bills; thirty-two, between thirteen and twenty-two bills; and thirty-five senators sponsored twenty-three or more.

These measures, to be sure, do not capture all possible facets of legislative activism. A senator could be deeply involved in the legislative process at the committee stage without necessarily sponsoring many bills; he might be actively engaged in working out disagreements at the floor stage without being a regular offerer of amendments. Nevertheless, these measures do tap important and somewhat different facets of legislative activism. The measures are only moderately related (gamma = .35 when the number of bills is collapsed into three categories as indicated above).

Although both measures indicate high levels of legislative activism, they also indicate considerable variation among senators. What are the determinants of legislative activism? We expect legislative activism to be a broadly attractive style, but do certain types of senators find it particularly attractive?

Floor activism is not related to seniority. If the least senior members—who, by the definition of the measure, cannot score high—are removed from the analysis, junior and senior senators do not differ in their propensity toward activism on the floor. Liberals are somewhat more likely to be activists than conservatives, but the relationship is moderate to weak (gamma = -.34). Northern Democrats are more likely to fall into the most active group and less likely to fall into the least active group than the average senator, whereas Republicans are somewhat more likely to fall toward the inactive end of the spectrum. These tendencies are not, however, very strong, and senators from each of the regional party groupings are to be found at every activity level.

Liberals' and northern Democrats' tendency to be especially active in offering floor amendments appears primarily a result of situational factors. Because the 97th through 99th Congresses were conservative and controlled by Republicans, liberal northern Democrats were most likely to be dissatisfied with the legislation reported by committees and thus most likely to challenge it on the floor.

Certain formal positions in the Senate require their occupants to be activists on the floor while others may discourage activism. Thus the majority and minority leaders, whose jobs revolve around activism on the floor, both are in the highest activity category (see Peabody 1981). Committee chairmen are distributed across all the activity categories but are more likely than the average senator to fall into the lowest. Chairmen are, of course, likely to be busy protecting their legislation from amendments. Ranking minority members might be expected to be particularly active in offering floor amendments because they often will have lost in committee. Contrary to this expectation, however, ranking minority members were distributed across activity categories very much like the membership as a whole.

The larger the number of subcommittee ranking minority member positions a Democratic senator holds, the more likely he is to be a floor activist (tau b = .37, gamma = .52). Because ranking minority members of committees are no more likely than other members to be activists, the relationship for subcommittee ranking members is probably not primarily the result of position dictating activism. Rather, senators particularly inclined toward activism are also particularly likely to stockpile subcommittee leadership positions.*

---

* A senator's inclination to activism is assumed to be a function not of personality characteristics but of the senator's goals and of situational factors such as his electoral

In sum, activism on the floor in the form of amendment sponsorship is, in part, a response to the political context; those senators most likely to have lost in committee are most likely to try again on the floor. Position in the chamber also influences activism; the floor leaders are perforce highly active. Yet more impressive than such differences among senators is the extent to which activism on the floor is a broadly attractive strategy to all types of senators.

Bill sponsorship taps a somewhat different facet of legislative activism than offering amendments on the floor, and the determinants are different. The mean number of bills sponsored in 1985 was much lower for freshmen than for more senior members; the freshmen mean was 8.9, that for all senators except Majority Leader Dole was 21.8. Clearly the development of bills takes more time than the development of amendments. That process takes place during a senator's first two years in the chamber; thereafter, there is no relationship between seniority and number of bills sponsored. Bill sponsorship is also unrelated to ideology. There are, however, differences between party regional groupings. Republicans score highest, averaging 24.9 bills each (Dole excluded), whereas northern Democrats average 20.3 and southern Democrats score a low 11.5. The overall party difference is probably a function of partisan control of the chamber. For those in the majority, legislative activism is more likely to take the form of bill sponsorship, just as, for those in the minority, it is more likely to involve floor amendments. The strong tendency of southern Democrats to sponsor fewer bills than other senators appears, however, to be a choice of legislative style distinctive to this group of senators and not explainable by other variables.

Position in the chamber does influence bill sponsorship. The majority leader sponsors a much larger number than any other member; in 1985 Dole sponsored 108 nonsymbolic bills, while the next most active senator sponsored 79. (Because of this, Dole was removed from the analysis before the relationship between bill sponsorship and other variables was assessed.) The minority leader, although well above average, does not sponsor an extraordinary number of bills, indicating that bill sponsorship at very high levels is a majority function. As one would expect, committee chairmen sponsor many more bills than other senators; they averaged 31.6 in 1985. Ranking minority members averaged well below other members (14.6) but this is the result not of their position but of their being disproportionately southern Democrats. In sum,

---

situation. Data on the full membership that would make it possible to completely disentangle this complex set of relationships are not available.

Table 9.2 Legislative Activism in the Senate

Activism[a]	All Senators	Those Who Served 97th–99th	North Dem.	South Dem.	Republicans
Low	26	20	9	4	13
Medium	25	18	11	1	13
High	49	49	17	5	27

[a]See below for definition of measure.

the majority leader and committee chairmen sponsor large numbers of bills; freshmen and southern Democrats sponsor modest numbers.

Among Republicans, when Dole, the committee chairmen, and freshmen are set aside, there is a modest relationship between number of subcommittees chaired and number of bills sponsored. The duties of subcommittee chairmen explain this relationship in part. It may, however, also reflect a stockpiling of these positions by senators particularly inclined toward activism.

The offering of amendments and the sponsorship of bills thus tap somewhat different facets of legislative activism, with the differences being related to political context and position in the chamber. A combination of the two produces a measure that taps general legislative activism with the effects of political context and chamber position removed. Those senators who were defined as activists on one or both measures are classified as activists on this combined measure (that is, they fell into the highest category on bill sponsorship and/or their floor amending activity was high in two or three of the last three congresses). Senators whose bill sponsorship rate is medium or low and who were never floor activists in the last three congresses were classified as inactive. All others were placed in an intermediate category.

Half the Senate membership falls into the most active category; these senators are legislative activists according to one or both of the measures (see table 9.2). One-quarter fall into each of the other categories. This combined measure thus portrays a Senate of activists. Democrats and Republicans, liberals and conservatives are about equally likely to be activists. Junior members are less likely than more senior members to be in the most active category, but the overall relationship is not strong. Most committee chairs fall into the most active category but so do almost half of other senators. In sum, legislative activism is a broadly distributed Senate style.

Not only does a high level of legislative activity characterize the

Table 9.3 Floor Generalists and Specialists In the Senate
(Measured by number of congresses, 97th through 99th, in which
senator was a floor generalist)

No. of Congresses	All Senators	Those Who Served 97th–99th	North Dem.	South Dem.	Republicans
0	37	32	12	5	20
1	28	20	9	3	16
2	14	14	5	1	8
3	21	21	11	1	9

modal style of senators of the 1980s, so too does broad involvement across a range of issues. Amendment and bill sponsorship data yield measures of the extent to which senators concentrate on a narrow range of issues or conversely involve themselves across a broad range of issues.

If senators who offered amendments to bills from four or more committees are considered generalists, then in the 99th Congress twenty-nine senators were generalists. An alternative measure defining as generalists those who offered amendments in half or more of the six issue areas yields thirty-seven generalists. These measures probably underestimate the number of senators inclined to be generalists in the 1980s. The Senate's preoccupation with budget and foreign and defense policy issues during the 1980s has resulted in most of the action being concentrated in a relatively small number of issue areas. During the 99th Congress, for example, 75.6 percent of all floor amendments fell into either the government management of the economy area or the international involvement area. During that congress, half of all senators offered floor amendments in both the international involvement area and in a domestic policy issue area.

Like a high level of activity, broad involvement over a range of issues can be a stable element of a senator's style or a response to a particular set of circumstances. A measure that counts the number of congresses from the 97th through the 99th in which a senator was a generalist according to either the number of committees or the number of issues measure makes it possible to distinguish the two behavior patterns. Thirty-five of eighty-seven senators who served in all three congresses behaved as generalists in two or all three of the congresses; for these members, being a generalist appears to be a stable element of their style (see table 9.3). For another twenty senators who behaved as generalists in one congress, it is an option.

A senator may be a specialist or a generalist in his pattern of bill sponsorship as well. In fact, senators tend to sponsor nonsymbolic bills in a broad range of issue areas. In 1985, the typical senator sponsored legislation in 3.8 of a possible six issue areas. Only eighteen senators offered bills in two or fewer of the six areas; forty-nine sponsored bills in three or four areas; and thirty-three in five or all six. These figures suggest that most senators are generalists in terms of their patterns of bill sponsorship. Yet a senator might concentrate most of his effort on one issue area but, by sponsoring a sprinkling of bills in other areas—in response to constituency interests perhaps—score high on this measure. To take this possibility into account, a measure of bill sponsorship specialization was defined as follows: If a senator sponsored bills in half or fewer of the six issue areas and if two-thirds or more of his bills were in one of those areas, he is classified as a specialist. At the other end of the spectrum, if a senator sponsored bills in four or more issue areas and if less than half of his bills were in any one of those areas, he is considered generalist. The remaining senators constitute an inter- mediate category. This is a fairly demanding definition of a generalist, especially for the 1980s. In the 99th Congress, half of all nonsymbolic bills fell into the government management of the economy area.

According to this measure, thirty-three senators were generalists, twenty-four were specialists, and the remaining forty-three fell between the extremes. Senators who are generalists in terms of their bill spon- sorship are not necessarily generalists in their offering of amendments on the floor. The two measures are related, but only moderately so (tau c = .28; gamma = .40).

What characteristics if any distinguish the generalist from other senators? Once freshmen and sophomores who cannot score high on the measure are excluded from the analysis, there is no relationship between seniority and the amendment generalist measure. Those who score high on that generalist measure are on the average more liberal than those who score lower, but the relationship is weak. Northern Democrats are more likely than the average senator to fall into the highest category; 30 percent do. Southern Democrats are most likely to fall toward the specialist end of the spectrum; 50 percent fall into the lowest category and another 30 percent into the next to lowest. Southern Democrats as a group appear less inclined than other members to become broadly involved across many issues, at least in terms of the amendments they offer on the floor. This appears to represent the remnant of a true cultural difference.

That southern Democrats also tend to fall toward the specialist end of the spectrum on the bill sponsorship measure lends credence to this explanation. More generally, the patterns of relationship on the bill generalist measure are similar to those on the amendment generalist measure. In terms of the breadth of the bills they sponsor, northern Democrats are more likely to be generalists than the typical member; so too are liberals, but the relationship is weak. Freshmen are unlikely to be bill sponsor generalists; as we saw earlier, most sponsor a relatively small number of bills during their first year in the Senate. Among more senior members, however, seniority is unrelated to specialization.

Committee chairmen are not significantly different from other members on either measure of specialization. The number of subcommittee leadership positions held is, however, related to both measures. For Republicans, there is a weak to moderate relationship between number of subcommittees chaired and behaving as an amendment generalist (tau b = .28, gamma = .39). Among Democrats that relationship is considerably stronger (tau b = .43, gamma = .62). The tendency for those senators with many subcommittee leadership positions to be bill sponsor generalists, while not as strong, is nevertheless significant (for Republicans, gamma = .30; for Democrats, gamma = .38). Holding a large number of subcommittee leadership positions may entail generalist behavior, but it also seems likely that those senators most inclined to act as generalists are most assiduous about amassing large numbers of subcommittee leadership positions. If the relationship was purely the result of the positions dictating their occupants' behavior, we would expect the bill generalist measure to be more strongly related to the number of subcommittee leadership positions held than the amendment generalist measure. Sponsoring bills in the subcommittees' jurisdiction is more clearly a duty of subcommittee leaders than is sponsoring floor amendments. It is also more clearly a duty of the committee chairman than of the ranking minority member. If the dictates of the office were the primary determinant, the number of subcommittee leadership positions held should be a better predictor of whether the senator sponsored bills in a broad range of issue areas for Republicans (who were in the majority and held the chairmanships) than for Democrats. Yet the relationship is stronger for Democrats than for Republicans.

Combining these two measures into a summary index in a fashion similar to that employed for the measure of legislative activism, one finds that just over half the senators who served in the 99th Congress fell into the generalist category. These fifty-two members were generalists according to one or both of the component measures. Thirty-one senators did not qualify as generalists according to either the bill sponsorship or the floor amendment measure and thus can be considered specialists. A number of these were senators first elected in 1984 or later who, because of the construction of the amendment measure, cannot score high. When these senators are excluded, there remain twenty-six senators for whom specialization as defined here is a relatively stable style.

The tendency to be legislatively active and the tendency to act as a generalist are strongly related (tau b = .53, gamma = .72). Twenty senators—eight Republicans and twelve Democrats—scored low on both measures. This group included retiring senators Russell Long and Paul Laxalt; John Stennis, who was very old and not well; behind-the-scenes players Wendell Ford and J. Bennett Johnston; Jay Rockefeller and Mitch McConnell, freshmen without previous House experience; and such low visibility senators as Chic Hecht, Spark Matsunaga, and Quentin Burdick. On the other end of the spectrum were thirty-eight senators—twenty Republicans and eighteen Democrats—who scored high on both measures. Most of the best-known senators were found in this group, including party leaders Robert Dole and Robert Byrd, Edward Kennedy, Howard Metzenbaum, Daniel Patrick Moynihan, Gary Hart, John Glenn, Bill Bradley, William Proxmire, Lowell Weicker, Jesse Helms, Orrin Hatch, and William Armstrong. These senators employed a style characterized by high levels of legislative activism on a broad range of issues.

Intermittent legislative activism over a moderate to broad range of issues characterizes the final sizable group of members. Eleven of these fell into the middle category on both measures while ten belonged in the middle category on legislative activism and the high category on the generalist measure. Included in this group of twenty-one senators were Thad Cochran, Bill Cohen, Warren Rudman, George Mitchell, Patrick Leahy, and Lloyd Bentsen, one of the two most senior members of the group. The group also included six senators who were freshmen or sophomores; senators such as Phil Gramm, Tom Harkin, and John Kerry are likely to join the consistently highly active generalist group.

Although few in number, the specialist who is highly active legislatively does exist. The seven senators who fit that description were primarily senior committee leaders; Robert Stafford, Richard Lugar, John Chafee, and Daniel Inouye may have found that their committee duties precluded involvement across a broad range of issues, although many committee leaders did not. The senator that Washington insiders most often mention as a specialist did not, in fact, fall into the specialist category by our measures. Sam Nunn scored high on legislative activism and fell into the intermediate category on the specialization measure. As Nunn involved himself in a number of issue areas, his expertise in the defense area clearly was not bought at the expense of narrow specialization.

Legislative Activism on a Hot Issue: A Case Study of Antidrug Legislation

The character of legislative activism in the Senate and some of its consequences for the legislative process can be illustrated by an examination of the response of the Senate and its members to the hottest issue of 1986.

Until mid-June, 1986, drug abuse and drug trafficking had been issues of moderate saliency. Nancy Reagan had made drug abuse her special concern. The killing in Mexico of a United States drug control agent received considerable media coverage. The cocaine-related death of college basketball star Len Bias on June 19, followed a week later by the similar death of footall player Don Rogers, ignited the issue. Media coverage was heavy and sustained. Using the number of pages listed in the Vanderbilt University Archive Index to the nightly network television news programs as the indicator, one finds that from January through June 18 entries under the heading "Drug Abuse, Traffic" averaged 18.3 per month. For the remaining days of June the rate jumped to twenty-four, and there were also twenty mentions of Bias. In July, the indicator increased to fifty-nine; in August to 117; the September figure was ninety.

When they went home for the July 4 recess, members of Congress found their constituents highly concerned about drugs. Opinion polls confirmed members' experiences. In the summer of 1986, the American public considered drugs the most serious problem facing the country.

On July 23, Speaker Tip O'Neill announced a major, bipartisan antidrug initiative to be coordinated by Majority Leader Jim Wright. On August 4, President Reagan delivered a nationally televised speech on the issue.

Individual senators had already begun to react to the issue. Alphonse D'Amato, for whom drugs had been a central issue for several years although he did not serve on any of the relevant committees, was undoubtedly more active than the typical senator. His response illustrates how hot issues can be exploited to advance a senator's goals. On June 20, presumably fortuitously, he and Mack Mattingly introduced a bill to increase penalties for cocaine traffickers. In July, he testified at hearings of the Senate's Permanent Subcommittee on Investigations on the drug Crack. His keynote address before the annual conference of the New York State Sheriffs' Association focused on the drug crisis.

In late July, he offered an amendment to the debt ceiling bill increasing penalties for and stiffening rules regarding money laundering. It passed on a 98–0 vote. In early August, he and Senators DeConcini, Stevens, and Cohen sponsored amendments to the Defense Authorization bill. The amendments providing $512 million for a major interdiction initiative passed unanimously.

Throughout this period his office churned out daily press releases reporting his activities. D'Amato's efforts resulted in attention from the media. He made the evening network news three times on the subject of drugs during July and August, and four New York *Times* stories on his antidrug activities appeared.

D'Amato was only one of a number of senators who became involved in the issue. On August 5, a group of Senate Democrats announced the formation of the Democratic Working Group on Substance and Narcotics Abuse. The nine-member group, led by Lawton Chiles and Joseph Biden, introduced two bills that would increase penalties for users of Crack, authorize funds for drug abuse awareness in schools, and establish a Cabinet-level "drug czar" to oversee the federal drug enforcement and prevention effort. The drug czar bill was cosponsored by thirty-five Democrats.

Individual senators and small groups introduced a number of bills in late July and early August, and in September after the recess. Both the exploitation of a hot issue for reelection purposes and the use of a hot issue to further a preexisting agenda are evident in these bills. Paula Hawkins, in a difficult and ultimately unsuccessful reelection battle, sponsored a large number of antidrug bills that took almost every imaginable approach to the problem. She proposed increasing penalties for selling drugs to pregnant women, eliminating the statute of limitations for drug trafficking, using funds from the Department of Justice Assets Forfeiture Fund for drug education programs, increasing funding for activities to interdict and control drug trafficking, and authorizing the Secretary of Agriculture to expand drug and other law enforcement programs in the National Forest system. At the same time her campaign advertising heavily emphasized her antidrug activities and portrayed her as a leader in the congressional antidrug effort.

The drug issue also lent itself to being used as a vehicle for the pursuit of long-standing policy goals. Thus, to a considerable extent, the bills sponsored by Republicans focused upon increasing criminal penalties. Hoping to use this hot issue to further a policy proposal blocked in the past, Mack Mattingly introduced a bill specifying the death penalty for certain drug traffickers. Democrats, in contrast, saw the drug issue as an opportunity to further social welfare goals stymied during the Reagan era. Their bills tended to focus upon education and treatment programs. Clearly, in these cases, exploiting the drug issue to further policy goals did not conflict with, and in fact contributed to, the goal of reelection.

On September 9, the day after Congress returned from its recess, Senate Democrats at a news conference introduced their omnibus bill to establish a comprehensive policy to combat drug abuse. Every Democrat in the chamber was a cosponsor. The House passed its drug bill on September 11. A number of controversial amendments were added on the floor. Offered by Republicans but passed by bipartisan majorities, these amendments authorized the death penalty for certain drug traffickers, gave military personnel the authority to pursue and arrest drug smugglers in United States territory, and permitted the introduction in court of evidence obtained in a warrantless search if the search was undertaken "in a reasonable, good faith belief that it was in conformity with the Fourth Amendment to the Constitution." On September 14, President and Mrs. Reagan appeared together on national television, calling on the nation to "mobilize for a national crusade against drugs." The next day, the president's legislative proposals were sent to Capitol Hill. On September 19, Majority Leader Dole unveiled the Republican antidrug package, which incorporated many of the president's proposals. A series of meetings produced a bipartisan compromise bill that Dole and Minority Leader Byrd introduced late on September 25. Twenth-three senators, including most of those who had been especially active on the issue in the period since June 19, were cosponsors. Altogether seventy-five senators cosponsored one or more of the antidrug bills introduced after the death of Len Bias.

The antidrug bill that came to the Senate floor on September 26, then, had never been considered by a Senate committee. Proposals for dealing with the problem fell into the jurisdiction of a number of different committees. To speed the process in the House, the majority leader coordinated the activities of the various committees. In the Senate, by contrast, the committees were bypassed altogether; an informal process of negotiation involving the senators most active on the issue produced the compromise bill.

In the Senate, broad-based support for a measure does not necessarily translate into willingness to pass it unamended. Sixty senators offered a total of forty-six amendments to the antidrug bill; of these, forty-two were adopted, one was rejected, and three were withdrawn. A number of senators saw the drug bill as a good vehicle for pursuing their own policy interests. Jeff Bingaman, long a proponent of health promotion programs, offered and had accepted an amendment to establish a community drug and alcohol prevention and health promotion demonstration program. Jesse Helms offered an amendment that would eliminate sugar import quotas for countries involved in the drug trade that fail to cooperate with the antidrug efforts of the United States and would bar sugar quotas for countries that import sugar from Cuba. Mack Mattingly proposed an amendment imposing the death penalty on drug traffickers under certain circumstances.

In a number of instances, senators used the drug bill to further policy preferences not even tangentially related to the topic. The drug bill was one of the few pieces of legislation perceived as sure to pass in the last days of the 99th Congress. Because Senate rules do not require amendments to be germane, a bill seen as certain to achieve final passage and presidential signature offers senators an excellent vehicle for their pet legislative projects. Howard Metzenbaum won adoption of an amendment strengthening federal standards for infant formula, a proposal he had been pushing for several years; Jesse Helms was successful with an amendment prohibiting dial-a-porn operations. Charles Mathias offered as an amendment and had adopted the text of his bill to update federal privacy laws; John Danforth, chairman of the Commerce Committee, secured approval for an amendment establishing national licensing standards for commercial truckers, which was based upon a bill reported from his committee. Pete Domenici offered as an amendment the provisions of two bills extending to the homeless eligibility for federal welfare programs. Alan Simpson had intended to offer immigration reform legislation in amendment form but backed down in the face of a threatened filibuster. In total, about one-quarter of the forty-two amendments accepted were tangentially or not at all related to the subject of the bill.

Thus, the hot issue of drugs offered senators a variety of opportunities to pursue both reelection and policy goals, and many took advantage of those opportunities. Sixty senators sponsored or cosponsored floor amendments; eighty-three took part in the floor debate. Of the senators up for reelection in 1986, all but two took part in the debate.

Thus, the death of a gifted young athlete dramatized an issue already moderately salient and together with heavy media coverage, catapulted drug abuse to the top of the list of problems concerning Americans in the summer before congressional elections. As individuals, parties, and chambers, members responded. When, on September 30, the Senate passed its bipartisan antidrug bill on a 97–2 vote, the bill seemed assured of becoming law.

Nevertheless, differences between the House and Senate versions, combined with individual senators' considerable power to block action, threatened to derail this broadly supported legislation. During consideration of the bill on the Senate floor, Mack Mattingly had offered a death penalty amendment identical to the one adopted by the House. After the Senate refused to table (that is, kill) the amendment on a 60–25 vote, Mattingly withdrew it to avoid a filibuster but claimed the vote should be taken as a signal by the Senate conferees to accept the House's death penalty provision. However, ten moderate Republicans, in a letter to Majority Leader Dole, threatened to filibuster any conference report that contained either the House's death penalty or exclusionary rule provisions. That, they warned, "would make it extremely difficult, if not impossible, to complete action on this vital legislation" (*Congressional Quarterly Weekly Report*, October 4, 1986, 2382). A group of fourteen Democrats conveyed the same message to their leader; they too were prepared to filibuster.

On October 10, Majority Leader Dole filed a cloture petition to cut off the threatened filibuster. Time was getting short; the adjournment target of early October was well past and members were eager to go home to campaign. On October 15, the Senate failed to invoke cloture on a 58–38 vote, two votes short. At a meeting after the vote, Charles Mathias, a leader of the opponents of the death penalty provision, told the sponsor of the House amendment that he was prepared to filibuster until Christmas. Death penalty proponents, including the Republican leadership, were faced with a choice between a bill without the provision and no bill. They chose the former. As Lawton Chiles said, "Neither side wants this bill to die on its doorstep" (*Congressional Quarterly Weekly Report*, October 18, 1986, 2594).

The quantitative analysis and the case study in this chapter portray a Senate of legislative activists and of generalists who involve themselves broadly across issues. Senators use hot issues to further their own agendas, the case study shows, and are willing to hold widely supported legislation hostage to accomplish their individual policy goals.

10 // The Use of Public Arenas and the Changing Bases of Senate Influence

When Ronald Reagan nominated Robert Bork to the Supreme Court in 1987, such politically savvy observers as former Democratic Congresswoman Barbara Jordan and former Ford administration cabinet member William Coleman believed confirmation to be nearly certain (Wermiel, Seib, and Birnbaum 1987). Yet several months later, the Senate rejected the nomination by the largest margin ever. Senators opposed to Bork, together with their civil rights, civil liberties, and labor group allies, persuaded the public that Bork was dangerously outside the mainstream on issues of civil rights and the right to privacy. They did so through the use of public arenas: televised hearings, innumerable television interviews, Op-Ed pieces in major newspapers, speeches, and even television commercials.

Although the Bork battle was, of course, extraordinary, the use of public arenas by senators is not. This chapter examines the availability of various public arenas and the uses senators make of them. It concludes with a consideration of the changing bases of Senate influence.

Public Arenas

The changes in the Washington policy community that have occurred since the 1950s and senators' reactions to them opened up the policy process in the Senate. That process is more permeable than it used to be; it is more responsive to outside influence. Consequently, having an audience outside the chamber can provide a senator with leverage within the chamber. Senators thus have considerable incentive for developing such an audience.

There are, however, not just one but several audiences outside the chamber that can be usefully addressed. There is the general public that can be reached, if at all, through the nightly network news programs and the morning news shows. There are intermediate audiences ranging from the attentive public to political elites that are reached through the major "national" newspapers, the weekend television interview programs, the "MacNeil-Lehrer News Hour," and a number of other interview programs. Finally there are a host of specialized publics reachable through their highly specialized publications and through speeches to their conventions.

A few senators regularly make the nightly network news programs but most receive only modest coverage. During 1985, Majority Leader Robert Dole appeared or was mentioned 125 times by the three network news programs.* Coverage of Dole was of an order of magnitude greater than that of the next most frequently mentioned senator, Edward Kennedy, who received forty-eight mentions. On the other end of the visibility spectrum were seven senators who were never mentioned during 1985. If Dole is excluded, the typical senator made the evening news 8.6 times during 1985, probably enough to yield visibility among the attentive public (especially among those familiar with him from other media) but certainly not enough to have an impact on the general public.

Majority Leader Dole was also the senator most frequently mentioned in stories in the New York *Times*. During 1985, Dole figured in 119 stories. New York's two senators, with eighty-four and sixty-two mentions, were the second and third most prominent senators. The remaining senators were mentioned in 7.7 stories on the average. Because the *Times* is only one of at least three "national" newspapers that are widely read in the Washington political community, the data indicate that a senator is more likely to be covered by the prestige print media than by network news.

Opportunities to appear on the weekend interview programs—"Meet the Press," "Face the Nation," and "This Week with David Brinkley"—are severely limited by the shows' format and periodicity.

---

* The number of page entries in the Vanderbilt Archive index is used as the indicator. The year 1985 is used to avoid contamination by the election coverage in 1986. This was done for the television measure and the New York *Times* measure but not for the Sunday interview show measure, which is much less affected by the elections.

During 1985 and 1986, Richard Lugar, chairman of the Foreign Relations Committee, was the most frequent participant, appearing fourteen times. Dole appeared thirteen times. Excluding Dole, the mean number of appearances was 1.6; forty-seven senators never appeared. There are, however, other interview programs that provide additional opportunities. The "MacNeil/Lehrer News Hour," with its nightly schedule, provides many more slots than the weekend shows do. Through 1985, at least eighty-two of the one hundred senators had appeared on MacNeil/Lehrer at least once, and many had done so on multiple occasions. C-SPAN, Cable News Network, and National Public Radio offer still more opportunities.

Most senators realize that as long as they are neither the majority leader nor a presidential candidate, they cannot expect to make the nightly television news on a regular basis. Certainly remaining continuously visible to the general public nationwide is not a realistic goal for most senators. Favorable visibility in the state is necessary for reelection; but that is much more easily and safely attained through the media of the home state rather than the national media. The press operation in almost all Senate offices is geared to gaining favorable coverage for the senator in the home state media (Hess 1987). Attempting to exploit the national media for purely reelection related purposes is, under most circumstances, an inefficient use of resources.

The national media can, however, be extremely useful in a senator's pursuit of policy and influence. Senators are aware of the value of media exposure, and when an opportunity for mass media exposure arises, most take advantage of it. "If you're asked [to appear on network television], you'd be a fool to turn it down," an aide to a senior senator explained. "The president has shown how much of an opportunity that is. So, if you're offered that kind of audience, that kind of possibility, you've got to use it."

A senator makes the news by being associated with a currently hot issue (see Hess 1986). Such association is not, however, just a function of position or luck; a senator's style makes a difference. Activist senators do get more media attention.

Regression analysis using a variety of position, activity, party, and specialization variables to predict senators' frequency of appearing on the nightly television news reveals that committee chairmen and legislative activists are most heavily covered.* (Dole was excluded from

---

* Dole was excluded from all three media visibility regressional analyses. In the analysis of mentions in the New York *Times,* the actual scores for the New York senators were

the analysis.) Both indicators of legislative activism—number of floor amendments offered and number of substantive bills sponsored—are significant predictors (see table 10.1). The results for the analysis of mentions in the New York *Times* are very similar. Legislative activists and committee chairmen get the most print. Unlike television, with its extreme constraints on the length of stories, the *Times* is also more likely to cover ranking minority members of committees rather than ordinary senators. Committee chairmen and, to a lesser extent, their minority counterparts are perceived by the press as authoritative spokesmen to be consulted as a matter of course when an issue within their committee's jurisdiction becomes newsworthy (see Miller 1977). A senator who is a legislative activist will in the course of pursuing his normal legislative activities become associated with a number of hot issues and consequently receive considerable coverage.

The complex processes and often idiosyncratic circumstances that produce many of the hottest issues result in much of the variation in

Table 10.1 Determinants of Media Visibility

Visibility Measure	Significant Predictors	Beta	R^2
TV News			.266
	Committee Chair	.302	
	Amendment Activism[a]	.294	
	Bill Sponsorship Activism[b]	.213	
NY Times			.285
	Committee Chair	.316	
	Amendment Activism	.296	
	Bill Sponsorship Activism	.238	
	Ranking Minority Member	.215	
Talk Show			.044
	Committee Chair	.210	

Keys to Variables:
TV News—Number of mentions on evening network news shows, 1985
NY Times—Number of mentions, from Index, 1985
Talk Show—Number of appearances on Sunday network interview shows, 1985–86

[a]Number of floor amendments sponsored, 99th Congress.
[b]Number of substantive bills sponsored, 1985.

replaced by the scores predicted by a regression of New York *Times* mentions as a function of television news appearances. That was an attempt to control for the home state newspaper effect.

media visibility not being explainable by stable characteristics of senators. Less than 30 percent of the variance was explained in the analyses of mentions on television news and in the New York *Times*. Idiosyncratic and ephemeral factors are even more important in determining appearance patterns of senators on the Sunday interview programs. To be sure, committee chairs are significantly more likely to appear than other members, but holding a standing committee chairmanship explains less than 5 percent of the variance and no other variables are significant predictors. The big story of the week—and more often than not the producers of the three interview programs agree on what it is— dictates the choice of guests. Committee chairmen, ranking minority members, and others associated with the issue are chosen. However, not all major committees deal with an issue that becomes highly salient during a given congress. Thus, Richard Lugar, chairman of the Foreign Relations Committee, appeared more often than the majority leader; Mark Hatfield, chairman of Appropriations, did not appear once. In some cases, the ranking minority member is in more demand than the chair. Thus, during the 99th Congress, Sam Nunn appeared more frequently than Barry Goldwater, chairman of Armed Services. In addition, prominent involvement with a hot issue, whether or not the senator serves on the committee of jurisdiction, often pays off in an invitation to appear on one of these interview programs. Thus Edward Kennedy appeared on a program focusing on South Africa. He was a prime sponsor of tough sanctions legislation although not a member of Foreign Relations. Kennedy is a legislative activist and gets frequent invitations, but freshman Mitch McConnell's involvement in the South Africa issue also resulted in an appearance. He too sponsored a major sanctions bill although not a committee member. Phil Gramm's role on Gramm-Rudman and James Sasser's on Contra aid are other examples of non-committee based involvements resulting in Sunday interview show appearances. Of course, senators who are committee members (though not necessarily leaders) have an even better chance of becoming recognized as a player on a hot issue within their committee's jurisdiction and thus getting an invitation, as for example, Howard Metzenbaum did for his role as an opponent of confirming William Rehnquist for Chief Justice of the Supreme Court. During the battle over the confirmation of Robert Bork to the Supreme Court, those Judiciary Committee members who remained uncommitted and constituted the swing votes on the panel were in great demand by the Sunday interview shows. So too were the leaders of the pro- and anti-Bork factions.

A senator's media visibility and therefore his access to public arenas is only partly under his own control. The processes that determine issue saliency and particularly those that result in some issues becoming hot can at best be marginally influenced. Whether he chairs or is ranking minority member on a committee is also not under the senator's immediate control. He is, however, not completely at the mercy of events. Sustained legislative activism and prominent involvement in a hot issue does pay off with access to public arenas. Furthermore, there are a variety of public arenas useful for reaching various kinds of audiences. Most senators cannot command the attention of the mass media on a regular basis. Narrower audiences are, however, easier to reach and often at least as useful.

Public arenas can be used to publicize problems, to shape debate on an issue, and to build pressure for action. These three aims are highly interrelated and not easily disentangled; nevertheless, in a given effort, one may predominate.

Publicizing a problem is the earliest stage of agenda setting. Some of these efforts are aimed at the general public. Thus, the campaign by civil rights groups to publicize the evils of apartheid in South Africa was intentionally dramatic, the aim being to make the network news as frequently as possible. The members of Congress who participated by picketing outside the South African Embassy and getting arrested were purposely contributing to the newsworthiness of the story. When Senator Lowell Weicker was arrested in January 1985, his being led away in handcuffs made a dramatic picture. Edward Kennedy's trip to South Africa in the same month focused even more attention on South Africa and produced a stream of stories.

Getting arrrested is, of course, an atypical means of drawing attention to a problem for senators. Foreign trips are a less unusual instrument. Speeches, press conferences, and especially hearings are the common means employed. When the aim of hearings is to publicize a problem, they are put together in such a way as to be as attractive as possible to the audience at which they are aimed. If the purpose is to reach a mass audience, witnesses that appeal to television will be sought. Playing a farm wife in a film may not make an actress an expert on farm problems, but Jane Fonda and her Hollywood colleagues were much better at attracting media attention to hearings on farm problems than an expert could be. A witness with a bag over his head will draw the television cameras.

The more typical effort to publicize a problem is, however, aimed at an audience narrower than the mass public. Jeff Bingaman had come to believe that there are serious problems with aspects of the defense research effort by the United States. In the spring of 1987, he used the newly created subcommittee on Defense Industry and Technology to launch a series of hearings into the state of defense research and technology. This effort at publicizing a problem was aimed at a specialized audience of defense and science and technology experts inside and outside the government. On highly technical subjects, these are the people who need to be convinced.

The various public arenas can be used to shape debate on an issue. How an issue is defined including how the sides are delineated are critical phases in the natural history of an issue. Bork's opponents succeeded in focusing that debate on questions of civil rights and the right to privacy. Had Bork's supporters managed to define the debate in terms of support or opposition to abortion, gay rights, and criminals' rights, the outcome would almost certainly have been different.

Senators may be able to influence the definition of an issue through speeches on the floor or before concerned groups, Op-Ed pieces in major newspapers, and appearances on television interview programs. In mid-March, 1987, Sam Nunn used a series of speeches on the Senate floor to present a comprehensive attack on the Reagan Administration's case for a broad interpretation of the Anti-Ballistic Missile (ABM) Treaty. Nunn's purpose was to shape debate on the ABM Treaty interpretation and on the related issue of Strategic Defense Initiative (SDI) funding. Because his views on defense issues are widely respected and because he chairs the Armed Services Committee, Nunn knew that his detailed presentation would be covered by the press and that the administration and other senators would be highly attentive. "Nunn's studies," the Los Angeles *Times* reported, "are expected to figure prominently in the continuing debate" (March 14, 1987).

The Sunday interview programs are considered an excellent arena for shaping the character of debate on an issue. Because of their focus on timely issues, they deal with matters that are already on the minds of people in the Washington political community. And because of the character of their audience, they are an excellent way of communicating with that community. Furthermore, because Sunday is a slow news day, what is said on the programs often gets reported in the Monday morning newspapers.

The national newspapers are also an important medium of communication among members of the Washington policy community and, in fact, among senators. Senators are increasingly turning to writing Op-Ed articles as another tool for shaping debate and as a means of publicizing problems as well. The national newspapers—New York *Times*, Washington *Post*, and *Wall Street Journal*—publish a substantial number of such pieces during a typical week and many other newspapers also use them. Accordingly, there are more slots than on the Sunday interview shows; pieces on subjects other than the week's hottest story do get accepted; and an audience that includes but may well extend beyond the Washington policy community is reached. Furthermore, print lends itself to somewhat more complex arguments than do oral presentations, especially on television. Bill Bradley used an Op-Ed piece to present his arguments against Gramm-Rudman; Pete Domenici did likewise to argue for a complicated program to deal with the long-term problems of the mentally ill among the homeless. Writing that he hoped to "refocus" debate, Frank Murkowski presented his plan for dealing with Nicaragua in an Op-Ed piece (Los Angeles *Times*, April 6, 1987). In another such piece, William Cohen, Nancy Kassebaum, and Warren Rudman presented their proposal for dealing with the same problem.

Public arenas can also be used to build pressure for action within the Senate. A staffer explained:

> There are inside issues and there are outside issues, issues that are going to move only if there is a lot of outside pressure applied. Obviously, tax reform is the latter sort. Here there are lots of vested interests that are opposed to tax reform. The easy strategy, the strategy that most people will play is a defensive game. You try to make as few strong vested interests mad at you as possible, and that means you don't touch something like tax reform unless you are forced to by outside pressures. So, obviously, on something like tax reform you've got to build that outside pressure.

"It's become more and more obvious that it's necessary to affect public opinion if you want to accomplish something," an aide to another senator said. "It's important that senators perceive that people are concerned, that they see newspaper articles, get letters, etc. Around here not making decisions is the easiest course. There's great competition around here for time and energy. Senators will respond to public pressure."

A full-scale effort to create enough public pressure to move the Senate can be extremely time consuming. As an aide explained:

> This kind of outside campaign takes an extraordinary amount of time and of the senator's time. It is not something that the staff can actually do. The kind of one-on-one lobbying he did on the House side, the kind of being available for media appearances, for giving interviews, that all just takes a lot of time, and you cannot do that on very many things and certainly not on very many things at the same time.

Another staffer talked about a major effort his boss had undertaken: "[He] spent eight months traveling and building support for [his position]. He was giving a speech just about every day. But that takes tremendous effort. That is very time-consuming, very hard on the system, and you can't do that all the time."

In 1985, farm-state Democrats perceived the midwestern states to be faced with a farm crisis worse than that during the Great Depression, yet the federal government, particularly the Reagan Administration, seemed unwilling to respond. The administration and the Republican Senate would have to be pressured into action. Farm groups and members of Congress set out to do just that. Farmers in large numbers descended upon Washington. Media events were staged; Senator Tom Harkin planted 250 white crosses representing farms that had gone under in Lafayette Park across from the White House. State legislators from affected states came to Washington to lobby en masse. Almost the entire South Dakota legislature made a highly televised visit. Press conferences in front of the White House and appearances on television programs like MacNeil/Lehrer were also employed by members of Congress to spread their message.

Because Republicans controlled the Senate and newly elected Majority Leader Dole was determined to uphold the administration's position, getting emergency farm credit aid to the top of the Senate agenda required strong action. Farm-state Democrats staged a filibuster of the nomination of Edwin Meese to be attorney general. Their price for allowing the Meese nomination (or any other Senate business) to go forward was Dole's agreement to prompt floor action on several farm credit measures. This dramatic tactic brought even more media coverage. When the key vote was taken, eight Republicans deserted their party and provided the winning margin for the farm aid measure. All but one of the eight was from a midwestern farm state and half were up for reelection in 1986 (*Congressional Quarterly Weekly Report*, March 2, 1985, 371-74).

Senators use public arenas to put pressure on the president and the administration as well. When Orrin Hatch, conservative chairman of the Labor and Human Resources Committee, sent out a press release announcing a news conference entitled "Why The President Should Sign S. 1744, the Omnibus Health Package," his purpose was to make the costs of a veto clear to the president, and it had the effect of raising the cost. After such a press conference, a veto would be perceived as a slap in the face of Hatch, a loyal ally, and of the participating groups that included the National Alliance for the Mentally Ill, the American Academy of Pediatrics, the Alzheimer's Disease Association, the American Association for Retired Persons, Dissatisfied Parents Together, the American Medical Association, the National Medical Association, and the Group Health Association.

When, during the election crisis in the Philippines, Sam Nunn sent Ronald Reagan a letter accusing Ferdinand Marcos of "massive fraud, intimidation and murder," he made impossible further administration support for Marcos. The administration may have been ready to change its policy in any case, but after Nunn's strong and public letter, the administration could no longer argue that the strategic importance of United States bases in the Philippines dictated coming to terms with Marcos (*Congressional Quarterly Weekly Report* February 15, 1986, 331). Coming as it did from a highly respected conservative, the letter received intensive media coverage. So as not to dilute the media attention focused on the letter, Nunn refused to appear on the Sunday interview programs that weekend, thus letting the letter's strong language speak for itself.

The use of public arenas was integral to Bill Bradley's years-long effort to get tax reform onto the agenda, shape the debate on the issue, and pressure Congress toward action. Bradley's public concern with tax reform dates back to 1978 and his first campaign for the Senate. After several years of work drafting legislation, Bradley introduced his proposal in an April, 1982, speech to the National Press Club. In the next few years, he took his proposal for a "low-rate, broad-based tax system that is fair, simple and efficient" before many diverse audiences. The effort involved "speaking across the country, speaking to business groups, innumerable speeches . . . endless interviews, TV appearances, radio talk shows," an aide reported.

Bradley promoted the plan by writing a book, *The Fair Tax*, and many Op-Ed pieces. In mid-1982, he spoke at the Democratic midterm convention, trying to convince Democratic activists to become supporters. In 1984, he undertook a similar lobbying effort by distributing 5,000 copies of his book to the Democratic national convention. When the Democratic platform did not endorse his proposal, he visited nominee Walter Mondale in Minnesota, hoping to persuade him to make it a campaign issue (*Washington Post National Weekly Edition*, June 2, 1986, 24).

Although Mondale did not adopt the issue, Ronald Reagan did. The president's doing so was, of course, crucial. Because of the wide array of powerful interests opposed to it, major tax reform stood no chance of becoming law without a president's clout behind it. Even with a popular president making it his top priority, passage was by no means assured.

A widely publicized report by Citizens for Tax Justice gave the advocates of tax reform added impetus and may have contributed to Reagan's decision to make tax reform a priority issue. The labor-funded group found that 128 large firms had paid no federal income taxes for at least one of the years between 1981 and 1983 despite combined profits of $56.7 billion (*Washington Post National Weekly Edition*, July 14, 1986, 14–15). The report's findings were picked up by newspapers and television news shows across the country and widely disseminated. Members of Congress began to hear about it from irate constituents. "We'd all go home to town meetings and you'd see some postal clerk get up and say, 'Why is General Dynamics paying no taxes and I'm paying 30 percent of everything I make to the government?'" Senator David Pryor says. "You couldn't answer a question like that except by saying, 'I'm going to go back to Washington and do something about that. I'm going to plug those loopholes'" (ibid).

Bradley continued his efforts in 1985. Despite Reagan's support, political experts gave tax reform little chance of passing. In February, Bradley and his cosponsor, Representative Richard Gephardt, joined Republicans Jack Kemp and Robert Kasten, who were sponsors of another tax reform proposal, in a news conference. There they introduced a number of business executives who supported the concept of tax reform. Bradley continued his heavy speaking schedule in Washington and across the country; he made himself available to the media and continued to write Op-Ed pieces.

As the House began to work on tax legislation, Bradley supplemented his media-based strategy with an insider strategy of attempting to persuade House members directly. In an unusual step for a senator, "he met with House Democrats in groups and individually and did a great deal of one-on-one lobbying," a participant reported. That, his staff reported, was "an extraordinarily time-consuming sort of process"; like his continuing editorial board interviews and television appearances, it was something that only the senator could do.

When the Senate Finance Committee began its work on the bill, the reform process was derailed by an avalanche of special interest provisions. As the committee accepted more and more expensive tax breaks for a variety of industries, Bradley argued for real reform. More importantly, after each session he met with reporters to make sure they understood what was being done (*Congressional Quarterly Weekly Report*, January 3, 1987, 12). The harshly negative press coverage of the committee's actions was instrumental in reversing the process. Finance Committee Chairman Robert Packwood suspended the mark-up, called together a small group of committee members genuinely dedicated to reform, and this group, of which Bradley was a key member, put together a new tax bill. This bill, with few changes, passed the committee unanimously and the Senate on a 97 to 3 vote. At this stage too "Bradley played a key role in bringing along liberal Democrats, arguing the intellectual merits of major sections of the measure and dealing with the press" (ibid.; also see Birnbaum and Murray 1987).

Legislation of lesser import can be promoted via public arenas as well. William Armstrong's sodbuster measure is a case in point. At a town meeting in his home state of Colorado, a rancher told Armstrong of the problem: "people tearing up the soil and the government subsidizing it." After researching the matter, Armstrong, who is not a member of the Agriculture Committee, introduced legislation to prohibit the payment of price supports and other federal farm benefits to farmers who cultivate highly erodible land. That was, however, only the beginning of a long process. "The first year," a staffer said, "was spent persuading people there was a problem. A lot didn't think so." Persuading people that a real problem existed involved "an enormous educational effort," much of which was aimed at organized groups. "We had to go around to lots of organizations to try to persuade them that it was a good idea to get their national meetings to adopt positions agreeing with us," a staffer explained. A second focus was the attentive public. The sodbuster concept was broadly attractive across the ideological spectrum, and Armstrong wrote "innumerable" Op-Ed pieces to publicize it.

The second year involved putting together a coalition of environmentalists and farm groups. After "many, many" meetings with affected groups, Armstrong and his staff forged an agreement that both the farm organizations and the conservation groups could support. By the third year, the bill was "universally popular"—so popular, an Armstrong aide said, that the House kept adding "riders they thought the bill could support" to Senate-passed versions. The fourth time the Senate passed the sodbuster provision, it became law.

The problems that Armstrong and Bradley faced were quite different, but both found public arenas useful for accomplishing their goals. Armstrong had a broadly appealing idea to which he needed to draw attention. He could concentrate on organized groups and the attentive public; no powerful entrenched interests needed to be overcome. The need was to create enough interest in the proposal to get it onto the Senate agenda; once there, its intrinsic appeal assured passage. In the early years, Bradley also faced the problem of drawing attention to his proposal, of getting people to listen long enough to understand what he was suggesting. After the president's endorsement of tax reform, the problem shifted to pressuring the Congress into passing a tax bill that represented true reform as Bradley defined it. Of course by then Bradley was only one of a number of central players. To counter the vast array of powerful special interests opposed to reform, Bradley sought to use all the available public arenas but especially those through which a broad audience could be reached. In fact, no ground swell for tax reform among the general public ever developed. Yet the media strategy was successful. Given the extremely heavy coverage of the tax bill, members of Congress did not want to appear to be catering to special interests at the expense of the general public. Constituents might not be paying a lot of attention at the moment, but prospective opponents certainly were.

Skillful use of public arenas can pay off beyond the immediate policy battle. If a senator's activities result in his becoming identified as a major player on the issue, groups interested in the issue are likely to look to him for continuing leadership. Experts will bring him their ideas. The next time the issue becomes prominent, members of the press are likely to seek him out. By becoming publicly identified with the issue, the senator has established a claim to continued participation in decision making on the issue and has increased the resources he will bring to his future activity regarding it.

The development of a reputation as a player on an issue usually depends upon the senator's activities having some impact on the Senate. Groups and the national media can recognize pure grandstanding for what it is; they can distinguish between a real player and a play actor. Thus, a senator may choose to get involved in a given issue because it lends itself to being pursued in the broader public arenas and therefore is likely to pay off in national recognition. For that payoff actually to materialize, however, the senator's activities have to have some impact in terms of agenda setting, shaping debate, or pressuring the Senate toward action.

Although senators vary in the effort they make to use public arenas and in their success in doing so, the old distinction between work horses and show horses is not useful for describing or explaining such differences. In the contemporary Washington policy community, inside and outside reputations tend to interact and reinforce each other. Said an aide to a committee leader often mentioned as highly influential in the Senate:

> He just gets lots and lots of invitations and it's almost always to speak on defense issues. And, then, of course, he's asked to make a lot of television appearances and to give a lot of newspaper interviews. There's a kind of snowball effect there. He's known as a defense expert within the Senate and so, on that basis, he is asked to speak on defense issues on television, for example, and he's identified then as being a defense expert, which increases his reputation as a defense expert which results in more requests for TV appearances.

Although this senator does not accept all the invitations to appear on television that he receives, he does appear frequently. "If there's a key issue to be discussed, he will accept because he thinks he should contribute to public debate," the aide reported. "Also if he has an issue he wants to promote." As this senator is aware, debate in the public arena may define the issue in such a way that, by the time it comes to his committee for decision, members' choices are severely constrained. Thus even committee leaders have strong incentives for attempting to shape the debate in the public arena.

Senate Influence

If influence is defined as having a share in the making of Senate decisions, then the bases of Senate influence have changed. To simplify only a little, active participation has replaced institutional position as the most important basis of Senate influence.

In the 1950s, institutional position—especially in the committee system—was the primary determinant of who had how much share in the making of which decisions. The resulting distribution of influence was relatively unequal; committee leaders had much bigger shares than rank-and-file members. In addition, influence was specific to a senator's committee; consequently, decision making was highly segmented. The Senate norms of apprenticeship, specialization, and reciprocity served to protect and maintain this distribution of influence, as did the relatively unequal distribution of resources.

In the contemporary Senate, no special standing due, for example, to institutional position is deemed necessary to entitle a senator to participate in an issue. Junior committee members now have a greater share in the making of committee decisions. Furthermore, it is now much easier for a senator to involve himself in issues within the jurisdiction of committees on which he does not serve. The Senate floor has always been formally available as an arena for such involvement. The ample staffs and the decline of restrictive norms have made it much more possible for many senators to thus use the floor. And, given that the floor is available for these purposes, committee members often find it in their interests to bargain with interested nonmembers before the matter at issue reaches the floor. Not only can nonmembers often influence the shape of legislation, they can often influence committee agendas. Through skillful use of public arenas, a nonmember may be able to pressure committee members to take up an issue they would rather ignore. The very fact that a senator can force floor consideration of any issue by the use of non-germane amendments exerts pressure on the committee.

Thus if a senator and his staff are skillful, it will be difficult for anyone to prevent him from participating in the making of decisions on almost any issue before the Senate. A reasonably skillful senator can become a significant player on almost any issue. Consequently, influence is less dependent upon institutional position and more dependent upon a senator's decision to become involved in a range of significant issues.

The major limitation a senator faces is time. Staff can do a great deal, but a senator cannot be a major player on an issue without an understanding of the issue and without some commitment of personal time. A senator has to know what he is talking about, and he has to understand the issue both substantively and politically if he is to be effective, the staffers interviewed agreed. Despite the widespread admiration that is expressed for Sam Nunn, true in-depth expertise obtainable only from several years of study is not considered necessary. The aide to a freshman on a highly technical committee talked about the importance of expertise and then told of how his boss had gotten a number of amendments accepted in committee during his first months of service. Of course, if true expertise were considered necessary, senators could not become involved as broadly as they do. Even so, the involvement in a myriad of issues that is typical of many senators requires long hours and very hard work. In this sense, influence in the Senate is dependent upon hard work. "The lazy senator," according to a senior staffer, "is always behind the power curve."

Asked their prescription for effectiveness in the Senate, these senior staffers often mentioned efficient time allocation. "Making an intelligent use of time and building an effective office organization" that allows the senator to concentrate on legislative tasks "are most important," said the aide to a committee chairman. "Most important is figuring out how to use your time right," a freshman senator's aide echoed. The senator's own time is the scarcest resource; efficient management is critical so as to make possible the involvement in many issues that maximizes a senator's influence.

Committee positions are still significant bases of influence because, as discussed earlier, committee membership reduces the time costs of involvement. The more committee assignments and the more subcommittee chairmanships a senator has, the more likely he will be able to become involved in a hot issue or have available an appropriate forum for raising an issue in which he is interested. Senators, thus, have an incentive to stockpile assignments. Finance, Appropriations, Armed Services, and Foreign Relations are still the most attractive committees. These committees tend to have the largest contested workloads, and membership in them gives the senator a share in the making of a large number of consequential decisions. Contested workload appears to be an important determinant of the attractiveness of a committee or subcommittee. One senior aide related a subcommittee's power directly to its workload. Power "depends especially on how much legislation is referred to the subcommittee. . . . If the subcommittee deals with more issues, this elevates it in the eyes of your colleagues and of outsiders. Then more people pay attention to the subcommittee."

Committee leadership positions, especially committee chairman-ships, are still much prized, but they do not carry quite the influence they once did. A chairman must share the making of decisions in the area of his committee's jurisdiction much more widely than in the past. The chairman formally controls the committee's budget and staff and must authorize hearings; to what extent he actually controls these resources depends upon committee traditions and his bargaining position.

Agenda control is potentially one of the greatest powers a chair can possess. In the 1950s, committee chairmen possessed nearly absolute negative agenda control; that is, they could block committee consider-ation of almost any measure they opposed. Now the chairman's control over the agenda is primarily a positive power. A chair can put those matters that interest him most on the committee agenda and make them top priority. There is no question about either the power or the legiti-macy of a chair doing so. It is much more difficult and less acceptable for a chair to keep something off the agenda if other members feel strongly that it should be taken up. "Now there are rules that make it possible for members to get things on the agenda over the chairman's objections if the member has the votes," a chairman's aide explained. Members also can bring outside pressure to bear on the chairman if he attempts to block consideration of an issue with considerable public support. A chairman can refuse to authorize a hearing, an aide to a chairman ex-plained. "Then what they do is hold ad hoc hearings; get a room, invite witnesses, call the press. Of course this has no effect on the legislative process, but it's very effective in attracting the press and it does put pres-sure on the chairman."

In the contemporary Senate, there are various, not necessarily mutu-ally exclusive, ways for a senator to establish a claim to a share in the making of decisions on a given issue. Becoming publicly identified with the issue is a major way. Usually this is an interactive process. Visible participation produces an identification with the issue, which, in turn, makes future participation easier and more likely to be effective. Once a senator is identified with an issue, "then those outside experts will come to you with their ideas. You get to be a focus for the experts and you get the ideas in that way." Concerned groups who share the senator's views come to him for leadership on the issue, and other participants recog-nize the senator as speaking for these groups. The media recognize the senator as a player and come to him for his views, thus providing him with a public forum, which makes him a more valuable ally and a more formidable player.

Although it is easier for a senator to become identified with an issue that falls within the jurisdiction of a committee on which he serves, having a committee base is not essential. Also, because it is visible participation, not in-depth expertise, that produces identification with an issue, a senator can become identified with a number of issues.

Another strategy for establishing a claim to a share in the making of decisions on a given issue is to make full use of the immense powers vested in individual members by the chamber's rules. A senior staffer to another senator said of Howard Metzenbaum:

> Although he's not on the committee, he's made himself a major player on tax legislation and on other legislation as well. He's geared up and he has a staff that's geared up to acting on the floor. He's willing to filibuster and to take the abuse that entails. And he has an impact.

The story goes that senators approaching recent chairmen of the Finance Committee with floor amendments have been told to "clear it with Howard." Toward the end of the session, the Democratic floor staff clear all legislation with Metzenbaum's staff before they agree to have it scheduled. Of course, Metzenbaum is not the only senator who uses this strategy; many others employ it at least occasionally.

Asked their prescription for being an effective senator, several staffers (not attached to senators particularly known for pushing their powers to the limit) responded that the senator who does not care if he is liked can be very effective. There is perhaps no better indicator of how much the Senate has changed.

11 // The Contemporary Senate: An Assessment

"Colleagues Tell of Chiles 'Martyrdom' on Bill," the Washington *Post* headline read (Auerbach July 18, 1987). The story recounted events surrounding the Senate leadership's attempt to work out an agreement to schedule final action on the trade bill, one of the Democratic congressional leaders' top legislative priorities. Lawton Chiles intended to offer an amendment that would have banned ships from United States ports for six months after visiting Cuba, a proposal attractive to the large anti-Castro Cuban population in Florida, where he faced reelection in less than two years. However, Lowell Weicker threatened to filibuster the bill if the amendment was offered. After much "anguish" and a promise from the Democratic and Republican leaderships to bring up his proposal as a freestanding resolution as soon as possible, Chiles agreed to withdraw his amendment and let the trade bill proceed. "This action on the part of Mr. Chiles is a demonstration of reasonableness that we too often fail to see here," said Majority Leader Robert Byrd. Without it, "this trade bill would be around here a long, long time," he added. "It was not entirely fair" to ask him to give up his amendment, Republican Leader Robert Dole conceded. No other senator had been asked to do likewise. "It is one of those unfortunate circumstances where—if you are reasonable and want to see the Senate do its work—then you are at a disadvantage," Dole continued.

A body in which individual senators are willing and able to disrupt the legislative schedule of the joint leadership and possibly block enactment of high priority legislation, one in which a senator's act of self-restraint is labeled a martyrdom by his peers and considered worthy of news cov-

erage, is a very different institution from the clubby, restrained Senate of
the 1950s. This chapter summarizes what this study has revealed about
how and why the Senate has changed. It then assesses the impact of that
change on the Senate's role in the political process.

The Senate and Institutional Change

The Senate will change, it was hypothesized, when old arrangements
become a barrier to the achievement of their goals for a significant number of its members. Given the Senate's small size and the Constitutionally stipulated equality of its members, a structure that thwarts the goal-
advancing efforts of large numbers of senators is unstable. The norms,
informal arrangements, and rules that structure behavior within the
institution will be altered if the behavior they dictate hampers, rather
than facilitates, the advancement of senators' goals.

If the costs of conforming with existing norms increases significantly, individual senators can simply choose not to conform. To be sure, a
lack of conformity may be sanctioned. However, leaders' stock of sanctions is severely limited, and the most effective sanction—exclusion
from the mutual favor exchange network—will not work if the group of
defectors is large. Consequently, if behavior proscribed by the norms
gains greatly in its value for the advancement of senators' goals, the
norms will give way.

Rules, whether written or just firmly established practices, differ
significantly from norms in character. Norms specify what form individual members' behavior should take; if conformity is too expensive,
the individual can simply act differently. By contrast, if the individual
finds the seniority rule for awarding committee chairmanships or the
rule limiting the number of committees on which a senator may serve
not to his liking, he cannot refuse to comply. Such rules can be changed,
but only by a collective decision, not by an individual.

For most senators most of the time, the best strategy for achieving
their goals is to work within the existing structure. Even if it is fairly far
from optimal for the advancement of a senator's goals, attempting to
change that structure would be costly and probably futile. Thus, given
that collective action is needed for change, the Senate may sustain a
structure that hinders the goal advancement of an appreciable proportion of its members for some period of time. It cannot, however, do
so indefinitely, because the problems of collective action are less severe
in the Senate than in many institutions.

For senators who find current Senate structure a barrier to the
achievement of their goals, rules changes are a collective good. As such,

a given senator's decision whether to join a coalition attempting to institute change can be characterized by the prisoner's dilemma and its attendant problems of cooperation. All the affected senators would be better off if they all cooperated to change the rules, but each would gain even more if the others brought about the rules change without his investing his own time and effort. Each has an incentive to be a free rider, because if the rules are changed, all the affected senators would reap the benefits whether or not they had paid any of the costs. If the membership of the affected group was large, one would expect no action unless special circumstances prevailed (for example, if selective benefits were available). However, the affected senators constitute at most an intermediate group and possibly, in some cases, a small group in Olson's terms (1965, 43-55). Certainly, the group is small enough that any individual's participation or nonparticipation is clearly perceptible. The group's small size and the frequent prior interactions among the members result in small initial organizing costs. Thus the costs of providing the collective good—the rules change—consist of time commitment and any sanctions that opponents may be able to apply. Even if, as is often the case, the opponents are Senate leaders, their stock of resources usable as sanctions is not likely to be so great that a large group of senators will find them a severe deterrent. A successful revolt can reduce leaders' resources and further constrain their use. Consequently, the costs of providing the collective good are not great, as long as there are enough affected senators to actually be able to institute the change. At one extreme, two-thirds of the full chamber membership was required to alter certain Senate rules—specifically Rule 22, the cloture rule. At the other, a majority of one party contingent can alter party rules. In addition, pressure from smaller contingents can lead to changes in well-established practices, such as those regarding committee assignments.

Both the theoretical framework and the examination of Senate change suggest a rough sequence in the processes of institutional change. Because no collective action is required, norms change first. A sharp increase in the cost of conformity results in increasing violations that are less and less frequently sanctioned. Individuals and small ad hoc groups importune those with control over resources—party and committee leaders—for a greater share. The problems of collective action are, at worst, minor for such attempts. Relatively modest formal rules changes may also be attempted. If such efforts are successful and the resulting new arrangements are better suited to the advancement of members' goals, the next stage may never be reached. Broadly supported attempts to institute comprehensive structural change will occur only if less costly routes to the desired end have failed.

If one contrasts the processes that resulted in institutional change in the House and Senate, the impact of size becomes apparent. Much more organization, in the form primarily of the Democratic Study Group, was required to bring about change in the larger House, and much more of the change was accomplished through formal rule changes. Because of the Senate's small size and the great power conferred upon the individual by the Senate rules (which is possible only because of that small size), informal accommodation played a greater role in Senate change. Some of the expansion in the number of subcommittees, for example, was the result of individual members successfully importuning their committee chairmen. In addition, those formal rules changes the Senate did make were, by and large, more modest than those instituted in the House and frequently just codified existing practices.

Yet the cumulative effect of the various changes on how the institution functions was even greater in the Senate than in the House. In a body with rules as permissive as those of the Senate, norms are a critical determinant of how the institution actually functions. In the House, although norms are important, rules and rule-derived institutional structures constrain behavior more than norms do. Norms may no longer restrain participation on the floor in the House, but House rules severely limiting debate and requiring that amendments be germane still do. In contrast, once Senate norms specifying restraint lost their hold, Senate rules allowed unrestrained floor activity by any senator so inclined.

The ultimate equality of the Senate's members—derived from the Constitution and bolstered by the party and electoral systems—when combined with the body's small size makes the Senate a very unusual institution. Some of the major impediments to institutional change are much weaker in the Senate than in other institutions.

Between the 1950s and 1980s, major institutional change did occur. The norms of the 1950s lost their hold. The Senate greatly increased the supply of valued committee positions; both the number of slots on attractive committees and the number of subcommittee chairmanships grew substantially. The distribution of valued positions was significantly broadened; by the 1980s, four of five senators held a position on one of the four most desirable committees and almost all majority party members chaired a subcommittee. Even freshman members did very well. Committee and personal staff were greatly increased and distributed more broadly across members. The powers of committee chairmen were circumscribed, giving rank-and-file committee members a considerably greater share in the making of committee decisions. Finally, during this period most committee mark-ups and conference committee hearings became open to the public.

The change in membership that occurred between 1958 and 1965 and the major change in the external environment that transpired during the late 1960s and 1970s provide the best explanation for institutional change. The new northern Democrats who entered the chamber between 1959 and 1965 found some of the norms and current structures to be a barrier to the advancement of their goals. Pressure from them did lead to some change. The apprenticeship norm died a quick death. Informal accommodation and modest rules changes resulted in a broadening of the distribution of resources. By the end of the 1960s, the Senate was a more participatory and less committee-centered institution than it had been in the 1950s. Pressure from the large cohort of liberal Democrats that entered the chamber between 1959 and 1965 produced a number of small changes that culminated in institutional change.

The 1970s, however, saw a greater transformation. Senators' behavior changed and the norms of specialization, legislative work, reciprocity, and institutional patriotism became defunct or drastically changed their form. Most of the increase in the supply and the broadening of the distribution of valued committee assignments occurred in the 1970s, as did the broadening of the distribution of staff resources. That change can best be explained as a response by senators to the altered Washington policy community. Senators changed institutional arrangements so that they would better advance their goals under the conditions of the new environment. The new environment rewards senators for broad involvement across a number of issues. Considerable staff are a prerequisite to such involvement, and holding multiple committee positions facilitates it. The more committee assignments and the more subcommittee chairmanships a senator has, the more likely he will be able to become involved in a hot issue or have available an appropriate forum for raising an issue in which he is interested. Within the new system, committee membership is not a prerequisite to involvement in an issue, but it does reduce the time costs of involvement considerably.

The Impact of Change on the Senate's Role in the Political Process

What sort of institution have senators produced? And what is the impact upon the Senate's ability to perform the functions expected of it?

Although terminology and nuance differ, there is wide agreement about the functions that Congress is expected to perform within the political system. We expect Congress to provide a forum in which the demands, interests, needs, and opinions of citizens find articulation. We also expect Congress to be a reasonably efficient decision-making body, responding effectively to pressing national problems and translating majority sentiments into law (see Cooper 1977; Vogler 1983; Rieselbach 1986).

That there is a certain intrinsic conflict beteen these two functions must be taken into account in one's evaluation of how well the Senate performs them. A process that allows for the articulation of a wide variety of interests will perforce be slow; efficiency and dispatch in decision making require limiting the number of interests heard, the duration of predecision consultations, and the size of the decision-making group. Given that there is a tradeoff between the two functions, not perfection in both but some reasonable balance between the two can realistically be expected.

The contemporary Senate, compared to the Senate of the 1950s, is an institution in which influence is much more equally distributed and members are accorded very wide latitude; it is an open, staff-dependent, outward-looking institution in which decision making takes place in multiple arenas. These characteristics, many analysts claim, have made the Senate a considerably less efficient decision making body. Given the large number of actors who can and usually do get involved in the making of any significant decision and the power each actor has to delay and obstruct, the Senate, it is said, has found it increasingly difficult to come to decisions at all (see, for example, Ehrenhalt 1982).

If the Senate does, in fact, have great difficulty in coming to decisions, the institution would seem to be failing in the performance of a central function. Certainly, a Senate that over the long term cannot arrive at decisions that respond reasonably effectively to pressing national problems will lose power to other institutions in the political system. Because each senator's probability of attaining his goals—be they getting reelected, promoting policy, or gaining influence—depends ultimately upon the Senate's power in the system, each has an interest in maintaining that power. Again we have the problem of collective action to provide a public good. In this case, however, each individual senator's behavior has little to no perceptible impact upon the provision of the collective good. The preservation or erosion of the power of the institution is the cumulative result of senators' behavior over the long or at least the medium term. If there is any cost in acting in such a way as to contribute to the preservation of the institution's powers, senators will not do so on their own.

This is a problem many institutions face, and a standard response is to place in the hands of leaders selective incentives that can be used to induce institution-regarding behavior. The Congress has done that. Because their reputation is partly a function thereof, leaders do have a direct incentive to maintain the power of the institution. The Senate membership has been willing to coerce itself by giving leaders resources usable for inducing institution-regarding behavior, but only a little. Because most senators cannot attain their goals if the Senate is completely unable to arrive at decisions, senators have been willing to give their leaders powers sufficient to prevent total breakdown, but often not much more. During most of the Senate's history, senators have been particularly unwilling to confer any but the most meager resources upon central leaders. The Senate's small size has made it possible for the institution to function with weak central leadership. Furthermore, however great leaders' resources are at any given time, the members collectively can always severely reduce them if leaders are perceived to be abusing them. Leaders use of their resources to induce senators to behave in a way that is costly in terms of their individual goal advancement is likely to be perceived as abuse. In addition, although leaders do have a direct incentive to maintain the institution's power, they are subject to a number of other imperatives as well (partisan success for party leaders, for example) and these also call upon the leaders' often meager stock of resources. Thus, at the best of times, leaders' ability to elicit institution-regarding behavior via the use of selective incentives is likely to be marginal. If the costs of such behavior rise for a significant number of members, the leaders' resources are unlikely to be sufficient to prevent widespread behavior that is damaging to the institution.

Because the Senate's falling below a minimum level of task performance has an immediate impact upon senators' chances of achieving their goals, and because senators are aware of the longer range result of eroded institutional power, the Senate membership has periodically responded to severe problems in how the body functions with reforms. For a majority of senators, whatever their goals, legislation is their most important currency for the achievement of their goals; consequently, if the Senate cannot legislate, they cannot achieve their goals. Thus members have been willing on occasion to pass rules that dictate institution-regarding behavior, even at the expense of individual goal-directed behavior. The 1946 and 1970 Legislative Reorganization Acts, the 1977 committee reorganization, other lesser rules changes limiting the number of committee positions a senator may hold, and the filibuster reforms of the 1970s were, in part, attempts to improve institutional functioning. Majorities concerned about the failure of the Senate to perform its functions effectively have voted to coerce themselves to behave in more institution-regarding ways. Most of these rules changes did, however, include provisions conducive to the advancement of the goals of individual members, and these undoubtedly contributed to passage.

Furthermore, those provisions that contributed to more efficient institutional functioning but were inimical to the advancement of members' goals tended to erode quickly. Limits upon the number of committee assignments a senator may hold are a good example. During the 1970s and 1980s, various Senate select committees repeatedly concluded that senators being spread so thin had a deleterious effect on the effectiveness of the institution. In response, Senate majorities passed rules changes limiting the number of positions an individual could hold, although never as severely as initially proposed. After each such rules change, the Senate quickly began to approve individual exemptions, and within a few years, the rule had become meaningless. Multiple committee positions have simply become too valuable for the advancement of senators' goals.

To a very considerable extent, how well or ill the Senate performs the functions expected of it is a byproduct of individual goal-directed behavior. Because each senator's behavior will have only an imperceptible impact upon the performance of the Senate, a senator will direct his behavior at realizing his own goals, whatever the ultimate impact upon institutional functioning. Leaders have a more direct interest in and impact upon institutional effectiveness, but their resources for inducing institution-regarding behavior from other senators are meager.

Given that the quality of institutional functioning is a byproduct, how do the Senates of the 1950s and of the 1980s compare? The system of the 1950s allowed a small membership with little staff to process a substantial workload. Committee-centered decision making reinforced by norms of specialization, legislative work, reciprocity, and apprenticeship fostered the development of expertise and a strict division of labor. This decision-making structure, when combined with the quite unequal distribution of influence by seniority, ensured that the number of significant actors involved in making any given decision was small. The fewer the significant decision makers, the faster decisions could be made, as long as those decision makers were willing to act.

This was a system that had the potential to produce decisions with relative speed, and in some areas it did so. However, the system's "efficiency" derived from restricting decision making to a small number of directly interested senators whose work received little or no review. Such a highly segmented decision-making process produced decisions more responsive to the desires of well-organized, well-connected clientele groups than to the needs of the citizens as a whole.

In such a system, it is possible for pressing national problems or majority sentiments to be ignored. The seniority system will not necessarily produce a committee leadership cadre that is representative of the Senate membership, much less one representative of the sentiments of the

American public. The system gave senior leaders great powers to prevent as well as to expedite action. The conservative chairmen of the 1950s often used that power to stymie liberal policy initiatives. Before the 1958 election, the committee leaders collectively were reasonably representative of the Senate membership as a whole. Of course, because each state has two senators regardless of its population, the Senate membership may not be representative of the nation even by fairly crude criteria. Thus, during the 1950s, urban interests were clearly underrepresented in the Senate. When the composition of the Democratic Senate membership changed drastically during the period from 1959 to 1965, the inevitable lag built in by the seniority system resulted in a wildly unrepresentative committee leadership group, a group that within this structure wielded a great deal of power.

The Senate of the 1950s cannot be rated as particularly successful at providing a forum in which the demands, interests, needs, and opinions of citizens found articulation. It was an inward-looking institution, which was reinforced by the institutional patriotism norm. It was relatively closed to public scrutiny: rules closed most committee decision-making sessions, and norms militated against using the floor, a public forum, for decision making. The relatively unequal distribution of influence and the constraining norms made it difficult and somewhat costly for rank-and-file members to engage in agenda setting and policy promotion. Some of the liberals of the 1950s nevertheless did so, but they were considered mavericks and paid a price.

In contrast, the Senate of the 1980s is superbly structured for the articulation of interests, agenda setting, and the promotion of policy. The extremely broad distribution of relevant resources—specifically highly valued committee positions and staff—and the very wide latitude accorded to individual members make it possible for any senator to engage in these activities. Groups that are not rich and powerful have a much better chance now than in the 1950s of finding a senator willing and able to take on their cause.

Agenda setting broadly defined is a more important part of the policy process than it used to be. Given the huge number of groups and individuals actively attempting to focus attention on an issue and get it onto institutional agendas, the selection process has become critical. In the 1950s, most political actors seem to have regarded the political agenda as primarily determined by exogenous forces, not as something they could manipulate. Now most actors realize that getting agenda status for one's issue is often the most important step. Senators, well equipped by their access to institutional arenas and to the media, are central participants in the process. They thereby ensure that the president will not dominate the process and that the Congress will also play a significant role. Furthermore, by multiplying the number of governmental actors who are centrally involved, they make the process more open and contribute to its being perceived as fair. With increased recognition of the centrality of agenda setting, the perception that the process is reasonably fair is important to the legitimacy of the system.

The shaping of debate on issues is a second aspect of agenda setting that has become increasingly important. There is growing recognition that the framer of the debate is fighting the battle on the field of his own choosing. Because of the multitude of issues and the velocity with which hot issues change, relatively unfamiliar issues on which lines of debate are not firmly set come to the fore more frequently. Senators have become important participants in the struggle to shape the terms of debate on such issues, thereby making the policy process richer and more diverse, and preventing the president from being the dominant governmental actor.

The changes that have made the Senate a more effective forum for the articulation of interests and agenda setting have created problems of decision making. An institution that gives its members extremely wide latitude even if it is used to obstruct the majority, one that allows any member to take a significant part in the making of any decision in which he is interested, will not be an efficient decision-making entity and will sometimes have trouble arriving at decisions at all.

Yet the significance of the Senate's performance of the interest articulation and agenda setting functions should not be underestimated. If Congress were to allow the president to dominate agenda setting and the shaping of debate as those functions become increasingly central aspects of the policy process, it would lose power vis-a-vis the executive just as surely as it would if the decision-making problems of the body became intractable. Ronald Reagan has shown the extent to which an adept president can constrain the legislature's discretion by using the media to shape agendas and the terms of the debate.

Is it, in fact, essential that the Senate be an efficient decision-making entity? Do we need two Houses of Representatives? The House was intended to be an efficient decision-making body, expeditiously translating majority sentiments into law. Despite some contrary effects, the reforms of the 1970s have on balance contributed to making the House in fact a majority-rule institution. That is not to say that the House arrives at decisions with ease. Conflicts with the president and the constraints imposed by huge budget deficits have made legislating difficult for both houses in the 1980s. However, given the majority-rule thrust of House rules, the weakening of the power of committee chairmen, and the strengthening of the party leadership, a policy majority in the House can work its will. Furthermore, leaders are much better equipped with resources for forging majorities (see Sinclair 1983). In addition, the structure of the House still encourages its members to specialize and develop expertise. In sum, the House, by the intention of the Framers and by its current structure, is much better suited than the Senate to perform the traditional legislative decision-making function we expect of the Congress. Members of the House also engage in agenda-setting activities, but unless they are leaders, they cannot do so as effectively as senators. They do not have the same sort of access to institutional agendas or to the media.

Thus, rather than bemoaning the fact that the Senate is not the House, we should recognize that a de facto division of functions exists (see Polsby 1968) and that, by playing a central role in agenda setting, the Senate performs a crucial function in the policy process.

Nevertheless, a Senate completely unable to arrive at decisions cannot be tolerated, and one in which, by virtue of the power given to individuals, minorities regularly thwart the will of majorities cannot be considered acceptable. The Senate may not yet have reached either state, but the events of 1987 make the danger clear. When Democrats retook the Senate in the 1986 elections, Republicans responded with a filibuster strategy that blocked most of the majority's priority legislation into the summer and some of it into the following year. The price of movement was often major concessions on policy (see Calmes 1987). These party-based filibusters were added to individual senators' use of the rules to block legislation and nominations they opposed.

As a result, calls for reform became louder and more insistent. The eleven-member Democratic class of 1986 has been especially critical. "We are legislators. Like baseball players who like to play nine innings, like farmers who like to plant all their fields, we like to pass laws," said Tom Daschle, a former House member. "In an era of fast moving, globalized issues, the possibility that the world could pass the Senate by increases immeasurably" (Hook 1988, 124). Criticism is by no means restricted to this group; senior senators are also dissatisfied (see, for example, Kassebaum 1988).

Are significant reforms likely to result, and if so, what form will they take? Reforms that go beyond a modest tightening of procedures to save time are likely only if a majority of senators concludes that the costs of current arrangements are greater than their benefits in advancing the senators' individual goals. Are the multiple opportunities to participate outweighed by the legislation foregone? Does the chamber's difficulty in legislating and the power minorities sometimes wield in the decision-making process cost senators enough in the pursuit of their goals that they would be willing to curtail their power as individuals to alleviate those problems? As a former aide to Majority Leader Robert Byrd said of the freshmen, "A couple of them already have found out all the sandbags and delays are pretty handy in an emergency. As long as it was someone else's emergency, they did not want to have much to do with it" (Hook 1988, 125). Certainly, any reforms instituted are likely to be lasting only if they contribute to the ability of individual senators to advance their goals.

Some change may come and certainly a little better balance between the requisites of interest articulation and agenda setting on one hand and legislative decision making narrowly defined on the other would be welcome. Yet the Senate is never likely to become a truly efficient decision-making body and, if it were, something more valuable would be lost as a result. Because of their central involvement in agenda setting and the shaping of debate, activities furthered by the current structure of the Senate, senators perform a key function in the political process. In the complex modern world, this function must be performed if Congress is to have any hope of coming to decisions that respond effectively to pressing national problems and translate majority sentiments into law.

Finally, an assessment of the contemporary Senate should consider that, although decision making has become more difficult, to the extent that this results from broader participation, decisions may have become more reflective of the preferences of the entire membership and more responsive to public opinion. On balance, the committee system is more representative of the membership as a whole than it was in the 1950s and 1960s. With committees more internally democratic and more open to influence from nonmembers, and with the floor a more active and significant decision-making arena, participation in Senate decision making is broader and less segmented than it used to be. Although the process of reaching a decision in the glare of press scrutiny may be more time consuming, the result will almost certainly have to take more account of public opinion—potential as well as actual. In addition, more and more diverse interests can have an impact on Senate decisions. Interests that in the 1950s were outside the system are more likely to be able to find a senator to champion their causes, and the more open decision-making processes make it much easier for such interests—both directly and through their Senate champion—to have an impact upon the decision. Certainly one of the reasons that Senate decision making has become more difficult is that more interests are involved in the typical legislative battle. Although decision making is less efficient, outcomes may be more responsive to the desires of citizens as a whole.

References

Asbell, Bernard. 1978. *The Senate Nobody Knows*. Baltimore: Johns Hopkins University Press.

Auerbach, Stuart. 1987. "Colleagues Tell of Chiles 'Martyrdom' on Bill," Washington *Post*, July 18.

Axelrod, Robert. 1984. *The Evolution of Cooperation*. New York: Basic Books.

Baker, Ross. 1980. *Friend and Foe in the U .S. Senate*. New York: Free Press.

Berry, Jeffrey. 1984. *The Interest Group Society*. Boston: Little, Brown.

Beth, Richard S. 1983. "Senate Changes in the 97th Congress: Issue Brief Number IB81043." Congressional Research Service, Library of Congress.

Birnbaum, Jeffrey H., and Alan S. Murray. 1987. *Showdown at Gucci Gulch*. New York: Random House.

Broder, David. 1986. "Who Took the Fun Out of Congress?" *Washington Post National Weekly Edition*, February 17.

Bullock, Charles S. 1985. "U.S. Senate Committee Assignments: Preferences, Motivations, and Successes," *American Journal of Political Science* 29:789–808.

Calmes, Jacqueline. 1987. "'Trivialized' Filibuster Is Still a Potent Tool," *Congressional Quarterly Weekly Report*, September 5, pp. 2115–20.

Clark, Joseph S. 1963. *The Senate Establishment*. New York: Hill and Wang.

Clausen, Aage. 1973. *How Congressmen Decide*. New York: St. Martin's Press.

Cobb, Roger W., and Charles D. Elder. 1972. *Participation in American Politics: The Dynamics of Agenda-Building*. Boston: Allyn and Bacon.

Cohen, William S. 1981. *Roll Call: One Year in the United States Senate*. New York: Simon and Schuster.

Congress and the Nation. 1965. Washington D.C.: Congressional Quarterly.

Congress and the Nation. Vol 3. 1973. Washington, D.C.: Congressional Quarterly.

Congress and the Nation. Vol. 5. 1981. Washington, D.C. Congressional Quarterly.

Congressional Quarterly Almanac. 1953–1986. Washington, D.C.: Congressional Quarterly.

Congressional Quarterly Weekly Report. 1971–1988. Washington, D.C.: Congressional Quarterly.

Congressional Record. 1975–1986. Washington, D.C.: U.S. Government Printing Office.

Cooper, Joseph. 1977. "Congress in Organizational Perspective." In Lawrence C. Dodd and Bruce I. Oppenheimer, eds., *Congress Reconsidered.* New York: Praeger.

Davidson, Roger H. 1981. "Two Avenues of Change: House and Senate Committee Reorganization." In Lawrence C. Dodd and Bruce I. Oppenheimer, eds., *Congress Reconsidered,* 2nd ed. Washington, D.C.: Congressional Quarterly Press.

———. 1985. "Senate Leaders: Janitors for an Untidy Chamber?" In Lawrence C. Dodd and Bruce I. Oppenheimer, ed., *Congress Reconsidered,* 3rd ed. Washington, D.C.: Congressional Quarterly Press.

Davidson, Roger H., and Thomas Kephart. 1985. "Indicators of Senate Activity and Workload." Congressional Research Service Report No. 85-133S.

Deckard, Barbara Sinclair. 1983. *The Women's Movement,* 3rd ed. New York: Harper and Row.

Dewar, Helen. 1984. "Is 'the World's Greatest Deliberative Body' over the Hill?" *Washington Post National Weekly Edition,* December 10, p. 12.

———. 1985. "What Do Senators Do All Day?" *Washington Post National Weekly Edition,* November 18, p. 14.

Dodd, Lawrence C., and Bruce I. Oppenheimer, eds. 1981. *Congress Reconsidered,* 2nd ed. Washington, D.C.: Congressional Quarterly Press.

Ehrenhalt, Alan. 1982. "In the Senate of the '80s, Team Spirit Has Given Way to the Rule of Individuals," *Congressional Quarterly Weekly Report,* September 4, pp. 2175–82.

Evans, C. Lawrence. 1986. "Influence in Senate Committees: The Role of Formal Leadership." Paper delivered at the annual meeting of the American Political Science Association, Washington, D.C.

Evans, Rowland, and Robert Novak. 1966. *Lyndon B. Johnson: The Exercise of Power.* New York: New American Library.

Fenno, Richard. 1973. *Congress in Committees.* Boston: Little, Brown.

———. 1978. *Home Style.* Boston: Little, Brown.

———. 1982. *The United States Senate: A Bicameral Perspective.* Washington, D.C.: American Enterprise Institute.

———. 1986. "Adjusting to the U.S. Senate." In Gerald Wright, Leroy Rieselbach, and Lawrence Dodd, eds., *Congress and Policy Change.* New York: Agathon Press.

Foley, Michael. 1980. *The New Senate.* New Haven, Conn.: Yale University Press.

Fox, Harrison, and Susan Webb Hammond. 1977. *Congressional Staffs.* New York: Free Press.

Gais, Thomas L., Mark A. Peterson, and Jack L. Walker. 1984. "Interest Groups, Iron Triangles and Representative Institutions in American National Government," *British Journal of Political Science* 14:161–85.

Gallup, George. June 1965– . *Gallup Opinion Index.* Princeton, N.J.: Gallup International.

Gold, Martin. 1981. *Senate Procedure and Practice.*

Grabowski, Gene. 1987. "'Greatest deliverative body' greatly vexes many senators," Washington *Times,* November 17.

Granat, Diane. 1985. "Senators Seeking to Improve 'Quality of Life'," *Congressional Quarterly Weekly Report,* December 7, p. 2569.

Green, Nancy. 1985. "Freshman McConnell: Making a Mark on Policy," *Congressional Quarterly Weekly Report,* June 8, p. 1085.

Hall, Richard L. 1987a. "Participation and Purpose in Committee Decision Making," *American Political Science Review* 81:105–27.

———. 1987b. "Measuring Legislative Influence." Paper delivered at the annual meeting of the American Political Science Association, Chicago, Ill.

Harris, Louis. 1970, 1971, 1975, 1976. *The Harris Survey Yearbook of Public Opinion.* 4 vols. New York: Louis Harris Associates.

Heclo, Hugh. 1978. "Issue Networks and the Executive Establishment." In Anthony King, ed., *The New American Political System.* Washington, D.C.: American Enterprise Institution.

Hess, Stephen. 1981. *The Washington Reporters.* Washington, D.C.: Brookings Institution.

———. 1986 *The Ultimate Insiders: U.S. Senators in the National Media.* Washington, D.C.: Brookings Institution.

———. 1987. "A Note on Senate Press Secretaries and Media Strategies." Brookings Institution Discussion Paper.

Hook, Janet. 1988. "Freshmen Challenge Reagan and the Senate," *Congressional Quarterly Weekly Report,* January 16, pp. 122–25.

Huitt, Ralph K. 1961. "The Outsider in the Senate: An Alternative Role," *American Political Science Review* 55:566–75.

———. 1965. "The Internal Distribution of Influence: The Senate." In David Truman, ed., *The Congress and America's Future.* Englewood Cliffs, N.J.: Prentice-Hall.

Jones, Rochelle, and Peter Woll. 1979. *The Private World of Congress.* New York: Free Press.

Kassebaum, Nancy Landon. 1988. "The Senate Is Not In Order," Washington *Post,* January 27.

King, Anthony. 1978. "The American Polity in the Late 1970s: Building Coalitions in the Sand." In King, ed., *The New American Political System.* Washington, D.C.: American Enterprise Institute.

Kingdon, John W. 1984. *Agendas, Alternatives and Public Policies.* Boston: Little, Brown.

Ladd, Everett. 1985. *The American Polity*. New York: W. W. Norton.

Linsky, Martin. 1986. *Impact: How The Press Affects Federal Policy Making*. New York: W. W. Norton.

MacNeil, Neil. 1970. *Dirksen: Portrait of a Public Man*. New York: World Publishing Co.,

Malbin, Michael. 1980 *Unelected Representatives*. New York: Basic Books.

McFarland, Andrew S. 1984. *Common Cause: Lobbying in the Public Interest*. Chatham, N.J.: Chatham House Publishers, Inc.

Matthews, Donald E. 1960. *U.S. Senators and Their World*. New York: Vintage Books.

Miller, James A. 1986. *Running in Place: Inside the Senate*. New York: Simon and Schuster.

Miller, Susan H. 1977. "News Coverage of Congress: The Search for the Ultimate Spokesman." *Journalism Quarterly* 54:459–65.

Miller, Warren, Arthur Miller, and Edward Schneider. 1981. *American National Election Studies Data Sourcebook, 1952–1978*. Cambridge, Mass.: Harvard University Press.

Nie, Norman, Sidney Verba, and John Petrocik. 1976. *The Changing American Voter*. Cambridge, Mass.: Harvard University Press.

Olson, Mancur. 1965. *The Logic of Collective Action*. Cambridge, Mass.: Harvard University Press.

Oppenheimer, Bruce. 1985. "Changing Time Constraints on Congress: Historical Perspectives on the Use of Cloture." In Lawrence C. Dodd and Bruce Oppenheimer, eds., *Congress Reconsidered*, 3rd ed. Washington, D.C.: Congressional Quarterly Press.

Ornstein, Norman J., Robert L. Peabody, and David W. Rohde. 1977. "The Changing Senate: From the 1950s to the 1970s." In Lawrence Dodd and Bruce Oppenheimer, eds., *Congress Reconsidered*. New York: Praeger.

———. 1985. "The Senate Through the 1980s: Cycles of Change." In Lawrence C. Dodd and Bruce Oppenheimer, eds., *Congress Reconsidered*, 3rd ed. Washington, D.C.: Congressional Quarterly Press.

Ornstein, Norman J., Thomas E. Mann, Michael J. Malbin, Allen Schick, and John F. Bibby. 1984. *Vital Statistics on Congress 1984–85*. Washington, D.C.: American Enterprise Institute.

Peabody, Robert L. 1976. *Leadership in Congress: Stability, Succession and Change*. Boston: Little, Brown.

———. 1981. "Senate Party Leadership: From the 1950s to the 1980s." In Frank H. Mackaman, ed. *Understanding Congressional Leadership*. Washington, D.C.: Congressional Quarterly Press.

Peabody, Robert L., Norman J. Ornstein, and David W. Rohde. 1976. "The United States Senate as a Presidential Incubator: Many are Called but Few are Chosen," *Political Science Quarterly* 91:237–58.

Pertschuk, Michael. 1982. *Revolt Against Regulation*. Berkeley, Calif.: University of California Press.

Plattner, Andy. 1985. "The Lure of the Senate: Influence and Prestige," *Congressional Quarterly Weekly Report,* May 25, pp. 991–98.

Polsby, Nelson W. 1968. "The Institutionalization of the U.S. House of Representatives," *American Political Science Review* 62:144–68.

———. 1975. "Goodbye to the Senate's Inner Club." In Norman J. Ornstein, ed., *Congress in Change.* New York: Praeger.

———. 1981. "Transformation of the American Political System 1950–1980." Paper delivered at the annual meeting of the American Political Science Association.

———. 1984. "What Hubert Humphrey Wrought," *Commentary,* November: 47–50.

Price, David E. 1972. *Who Makes The Laws? Creativity and Power in Senate Committees.* Cambridge, Mass.: Schenkman.

———. 1985. "Congressional Committees in the Policy Process." In Lawrence C. Dodd and Bruce Oppenheimer, eds., *Congress Reconsidered,* 3rd ed. Washington, D.C.: Congressional Quarterly Press.

Ranney, Austin. 1983. *Channels of Power.* New York: Basic Books.

Rieselbach, Leroy. 1986. *Congressional Reform.* Washington, D.C.: Congressional Quarterly Press.

Ripley, Randall B. 1969. *Power in the Senate.* New York: St. Martin's Press.

Roberts, Steven V. 1984. "Senate's New Breed Shuns Novice Role," New York *Times,* November 28.

Robinson, Michael J. 1981. "Three Faces of Congressional Media." In Thomas Mann and Norman Ornstein, eds., *The New Congress.* Washington, D.C.: American Enterprise Institute.

Rohde, David, Norman Ornstein, and Robert Peabody. 1985. "Political Change and Legislative Norms in the U.S. Senate, 1957–1974." In Glenn Parker, ed., *Studies of Congress.* Washington, D.C.: Congressional Quarterly Press.

Rubin, Richard L. 1981. *Press, Party and Presidency.* New York: W. W. Norton.

Salisbury, Robert H. 1984. "Interest Representation: The Dominance of Institutions," *American Political Science Review* 77:64–76.

Scholzman, Kay Lehman, and John T. Tierney. 1983. "More of the Same: Washington Pressure Group Activity in a Decade of Change," *Journal of Politics* 45:351–75.

———. 1986. *Organized Interests and American Democracy.* New York: Harper and Row.

Schneider, Judy. 1982. "Senate Rules and Practices on Committee, Subcommittee and Chairmanship Assignment Limitations, as of April 30, 1982." Congressional Research Service, Library of Congress.

Sinclair, Barbara. 1982. *Congressional Realignment.* Austin: University of Texas Press.

———. 1983. *Majority Leadership in the U.S. House.* Baltimore: Johns Hopkins University Press.

Smith, Steven S., and Christopher J. Deering. 1984. *Committees in Congress.* Washington, D.C.: Congressional Quarterly Press.

Sundquist, James L. 1968. *Politics and Policy: The Eisenhower, Kennedy and Johnson Years.* Washington, D.C.: Brookings Institution.

Swanson, Wayne R. 1969. "Committee Assignments and the Nonconformist Legislator: Democrats in the U.S. Senate." *Midwest Journal of Political Science* 13:84–94.

Tumulty, Karen. 1986. "Sasser: New Approach on Contras," Los Angeles *Times,* April 7.

U.S. Congress, House. 1980. *Final Report of the Select Committee on Committees, Appendix 1: Congressional Staffing: 1947–1978.* Washington, D.C.: U.S. Government Printing Office.

U.S. Congress, Senate. 1976. *The Senate Committee System: First Staff Report to the Temporary Select Committee to Study the Senate Committee System.* Washington, D.C.: U.S. Government Printing Office.

———. 1979. Committee on Rules and Administration. *Senate Cloture Rules.* Committee Print. Washington, D.C.: U.S. Government Printing Office.

———. 1984. *Hearings of the Temporary Select Committee to Study the Senate Committee System, Part I.* Washington, D.C.: U.S. Government Printing Office.

———. 1984. *Report of the Temporary Select Committee to Study the Senate Committee System.* Washington, D.C.: U.S. Government Printing Office.

———. 1986. *Congress and Pressure Groups: Lobbying in a Modern Democracy.* Report prepared for the Subcommittee on Intergovernmental Relations of the Committee on Governmental Affairs. Washington, D.C.: U.S. Government Printing Office.

Vogler, David. 1983. *The Politics of Congress,* 4th ed. Boston: Allyn and Bacon.

Walker, Jack L. 1983. "The Origin and Maintenance of Interest Groups in America," *American Political Science Review* 77:390–406.

Wermiel, Stephen, Gerald F. Seib, and Jeffrey H. Birnbaum. 1987. "How Reagan's Forces Botched the Campaign for Approval of Bork," *Wall Street Journal,* October 7.

White, William. 1956. *Citadel: The Story of the United States Senate.* New York: Harper and Brothers.

Williams, Robin M. 1968. "The Concept of Norms." In David L. Sills, ed., *International Encyclopedia of the Social Sciences,* Vol. 10. New York: Macmillan.

Wilson, Graham. 1981. *Interest Groups in the United States.* Oxford: Clarendon Press.

Index

Abortion, 5; filibusters against, 135; as
  item on Senate agenda, 160;
  legalization of, 55; New Right
  opposition to, 61; roll call vote on,
  166; Weicker and, 172
Abourezk, James, 128, 172
Affirmative action, 55
Agendas, political, 51–57, 59–60, 117–20,
  123, 124; effect of media on, 67;
  senators' impact on, 69–70
Aging, Special Committee on, 157, 159.
  See also Bingaman, Jeff
Agriculture: environmentalism and, 56;
  federal aid to, 117, 118; and
  immigrants in U.S., 164; as item on
  Senate agenda, 56–57. *See also*
  Farmers
Agricultural Committee, Senate, 11, 17;
  conservative nature of, 27, 109; floor
  challenges to bills of, 119, 120; Helms
  and, 99; 1960s complexion of, 40
AIDS, 160
Alcoholism, 160–61, 162
Allen, James, 81, 128; filibustering of, 137
Alzheimer's Disease Association, 196
Amendments, floor, 16, 18–20, 22, 23, 91,
  115–17, 119–26, 163–82; from freshman
  senators, 83–85, 93–94; increase in
  number of, 42, 79–88; to 1986 drug
  bill, 185–87; as personal ploys, 90; and

seniority, 83–85; success of, 120–25;
  threat of as bargaining chip, 169–70.
  See also Filibuster(s); Roll call votes;
  Senate, U.S., floor activity of
American Academy of Pediatrics, 196
American Association of Retired
  Persons, 196
American Bankers Association, 142, 145
American Enterprise Institute, 62
American Hospital Association, 60
American Medical Association, 196
Andrews, Mark, 99
Anti-Ballistic Missile (ABM) Treaty, 165,
  194
Antitrust laws, 95, 173
Apartheid. *See* South Africa
Appointments, presidential, 3
Appropriations Committee, Senate:
  change in makeup of, 73;
  conservative character of, 27, 110;
  floor challenges to bills of, 87, 120,
  122; during 1950s, 11; 1958 freshman
  appointees to, 34; 1960s conservatism
  of, 41; perquisites of members, 158;
  Weicker and, 161–62
Armed services. *See* Military, the
Armed Services Committee, Senate, 11;
  conservative character of, 27, 40–41,
  109; floor challenges to bills of, 87,
  120, 122; 1958 freshman appointees

to, 34; and 1985 Department of
Defense budget, 163–64, 165; Nunn
and, 156
Arms control, 149, 165, 194. *See also*
International involvement
Armstrong, William, 134, 140, 145, 148,
182, 198–99
Arts, federal aid to, 55
Aspartame, 160
Associations, professional, lobbying of,
62
Automobiles, federal standards for, 56

Baker, Howard, 85, 94, 130, 131, 132, 134,
167; and Grove City decision, 171
Banking Committee, Senate, 40, 109
Bankruptcy, changes in laws of, 173. *See
also* Metzenbaum, Howard
Banks, regulation of, 95. *See also* Finance
Committee, Senate; Financial sector
Barkley, Alben, 13
Battleships, as Senate floor topic, 164
Baucus, Max, 172
Bayh, Birch, 32
Beer industry, antitrust immunity for,
173
Bentsen, Lloyd, 163, 182
Bias, Len, 183, 185
Biden, Joseph, 98, 99, 184
Bills, Senate: floor challenges of, 111–17,
119–40 (*see also* Filibuster(s); Roll
call votes; Senate, U.S., debate in);
holds against, 130–31, 137, 169, 170,
172, 173; "must," 119, 129, 169; repeal
of provisions in, 168; riders to, 167;
sponsorship of, 175, 177–78, 180–82
Bingaman, Jeff, 149–50, 159, 163, 165; and
defense research, 193–94; and
Government Affairs Committee, 161;
and 1968 drug bill, 185; and Special
Committee on Aging, 162
BIZNET, 63
Bonner, Yelena, 146
Boren, David, 133, 164
Bork, Robert, 188, 192, 194
Bradley, Bill, 71, 81, 158, 182, 197, 198; and
aid to education, 149; against
Gramm-Rudman, 195; and tax
reform, 199
Breaux, John, 142, 145

Brinkley, David, 189
Brooke, Ed, 150
Brookings Institution, 62
Buckley, James, 81, 85
Budget, federal: balancing of, 145, 169;
Gramm and, 168–69. *See also*
Gramm-Rudman legislation
Budget Committee, Senate, 110, 120
Bumpers, Dale, 165
Burdick, Quentin, 182
Business Roundtable, 61
Busing, 54, 55; filibusters against, 129,
136–37; Hatch and, 171; New Right
opposition to, 61; roll call vote focus
on, 166; Weicker and, 172
Byrd, Harry, Jr., 73
Byrd, Robert, 99, 129, 131, 132, 133, 164,
182, 205, 216; and drug legislation,
185; and Gramm-Rudman, 169; and
Grove City decision, 171; against
Hatch, 170
Byrd amendment, 135–36

Cable News Network, 190
Campaign financing: legislation on, 117;
Senate debate on, 94
Carter, Jimmy, 128, 172
Case, Clifford, 13
Castro, Fidel, 205
Central America, human rights in, 149
Chafee, John, 182
Chamber of Commerce, U.S., 61, 63
Chase Manhattan Bank, 95
Chicanos, civil rights of, 59
Children: civil rights of, 54;
handicapped, 161–62; missing, 160;
runaway, 160
Children, Family, Drugs, and
Alcoholism, Subcommittee on,
160–61, 162
Child welfare, Dodd and, 162
Chiles, Lawton, 2, 105, 130, 187; against
drug abuse, 184; and trade bill, 205
Citicorp, 95
Cities, U.S., Washington-based interest
groups representing, 59
Citizens for Tax Justice, 197
Citizens' lobbies. *See* Interest groups,
citizens'
Civil disobedience, 54

Civil liberties, 53, 54–55, 117, 118. *See also* Abortion; Civil rights

Civil rights, 49, 54, 60, 61, 67; and by-passing of Senate Judiciary Committee, 82; filibusters and, 20, 44, 53, 67, 94, 95, 127; as item on political agenda, 59, 117; marches in name of, 65, 67; as 1950s issue, 53–54; in 1960s/1970s, 54–55; pressure for, 43; Washington-based interest groups promoting, 58. *See also* Civil liberties; Civil Rights Bill of 1964; Grove City decision; Human rights

Civil Rights Bill of 1964, 43–44, 115, 116, 120n

Clark, Joseph, 42, 46

Clean Air Act, 56, 137

Cloture, 127–30, 134–36, 171; alteration of rules of, 127, 128, 207; difficulty of invoking, 126; liberal assault on, 45

Cochran, Thad, 154, 182

Cohen, William, 182, 184, 195

Cold War, 52

Coleman, William, 188

Collective bargaining, federal regulation of, 56

Commerce Committee, Senate, 103

Committees, Senate, 10–14, 17; chairmanship of, 11, 12–14, 23–24, 158–59; changes in, 102–11, 208–9; closed mark-up sessions of, 24, 25; and effect of Legislative Reorganization Act of 1970, 47–49; establishment control of, 42; hearings of, as personal forums, 159–60; ideological makeup of, 108–11; increased activity of, 89, 102–4; influence and, 25–28; perquisites of membership in, 92, 157–63; power of, 49–50, 202–3, 204; power of chairmen of, 23–24, 158–59; "prestige" (*see* Appropriations Committee, Senate; Armed Services Committee, Senate; Finance Committee, Senate; Foreign Relations Committee, Senate); reform of, 211–12; service on, 74; shifting regional/philosophical makeup of, 34–41, 44–45, 72–73, 74–79; and staff, 24, 25, 45, 93, 103 (*see also* Senators, U.S., staffs of); strength of 1950s, 23–25; and

sunshine rules, 106. *See also* Johnson rule; Subcommittees, Senate; *and names of individual committees*

Commodity Credit Corporation (CCC), 154

Common Cause, 62, 63, 106; and Senate reform, 105

Comprehensive Employment and Training Act (CETA), 55

Congress: duties of, 2, 3, 209–10; and lobbying of interest groups, 64; and reform, 11, 45–49, 211. *See also* House of Representatives, U.S.; Senate, U.S.

Conrail, Senate debate on, 95

Constitution, Subcommittee on, 161

Consumerism, 56, 59, 60; filibusters against, 127, 135. *See also* Antitrust laws; Interest groups, citizens'; Product liability

Consumer Product Safety Act, 56

Consumer Product Safety Commission, 56

Consumer Subcommittee, Senate Commerce Committee, 162

Containment, of Soviet expansion, 52

Contras, aid to, 133, 149, 150, 192

Corporations: Washington-based representatives of, 58, 60–61; zero-tax status of, 197–98

Crack, 183, 184

Cranston, Alan, 141, 149

Crime, 54, 55, 117. *See also* Drugs, abuse of

Criminals, rights of, 54

C-SPAN, 66, 190

Cubans, anti-Castro, 205

Curtis, Carl, 13

D'Amato, Alphonse, 158, 183–84

Dams, legislation on, 173

Danforth, John, 186

Daschle, Tom, 215

Davis-Bacon Act, 164

Day-care centers, liability insurance for, 151

Death penalty, for drug traffickers, 184, 185, 186, 187

Debt, national. *See* Budget, federal; Economy, national; Gramm-Rudman legislation

DeConcini, Dennis, 184
Defense. *See* National defense
Defense, Department of: controversial
    budget of, 163–64; and waste, 6
Defense industry, 161
Defense Industry and Technology,
    Subcommittee on, 161, 193
Deficit, federal. *See* Budget, federal;
    Economy, national; Gramm-Rudman
    legislation
Democratic Study Group, 208
Democratic Working Group on
    Substance and Narcotics Abuse, 184
Democrats, 107; dichotomy among 1950s,
    10, 27; and freshman senators, 78;
    1958 electoral gains of, 30–31
Denton, Jeremiah, 161
Dependents, care of, 160
Desegregation, school, 53. *See also*
    Busing
Dial-a-porn, 186
Dirksen, Everett, 34
Disabled. *See* Handicapped
Discrimination. *See* Civil rights
Dissatisfied Parents Together, 196
District of Columbia Committee, Senate,
    12, 28, 122
Dividends, 167–68
Dixon, Alan, 136
Dodd, Christopher, 99, 131, 162
Dole, Robert, 99, 130–33, 136, 166, 177, 178,
    182, 187, 205; and drug legislation, 185;
    and Gramm-Rudman, 169; and
    interest/dividend income
    withholding levy, 167–68; and New
    York *Times,* 189; and 1985 farm crisis,
    196; on television, 189, 190
Domenici, Pete, 100; and Gramm-
    Rudman, 169; and homeless, 186, 195
Douglas, Paul, 22
Draft, military, Senate debate on, 94
Drug czar, cabinet-level, 184
Drug Enforcement Administration, 151
Drug industry, 173
Drugs; 54, 160–61, 162; abuse of, 160,
    183–87

East, John, 97, 160, 171
Economic Opportunity Act of 1964, 55
Economy, national: as item on political
    agenda, 56; as dominant Senate floor
    topic, 117, 118; Eisenhower and
    Truman administrations and, 52. *See
    also* Appropriations Committee,
    Senate; Banking Committee, Senate;
    Banks; Budget, federal; Finance
    Committee, Senate
Education, 149; drug, 160; federal aid to,
    53, 55, 59; of handicapped children,
    161–62; sex discrimination in, 135, 171;
    tax credits for private, 171; of
    teachers, 165. *See also* Schools
Eisenhower, Dwight, 52
Elderly, 55, 60; civil rights of, 54
Electoral college, proposed abolition of,
    127–28
Employment: federal government and,
    55; racial discrimination in, 54. *See
    also* Unemployment
Energy: as issue, 5, 56, 118, 152, 160;
    Carter bill on, 128–29, 172. *See also*
    Gas tax; Natural gas; Oil
Energy Committee, Senate, 160
Engle, Clair, 34
Environment and Public Works
    Committee, Senate, 156
Environmentalism, 5, 56, 59, 60;
    Washington-based interest groups
    promoting, 58. *See also* Clean Air
    Act; Sierra Club
Equal Rights Amendment, 54, 61
Ervin, Sam, 70
Evans, Dan, 2
Exon, James, 164

"Face the Nation," 189
Fair housing. *See* Open housing
Fair Tax, The (Bradley), 197
Falwell, Jerry, 61
Farmers: during Eisenhower
    administration, 53; federal subsidies
    to, 56–57; 1985 crisis among
    midwestern, 196; Washington-based
    interest groups representing, 58. *See
    also* Agriculture
Filibuster(s), 94–97, 134, 135–36, 169, 170,
    215; against antiabortion legislation,
    172; against Carter energy bill, 172;
    against civil rights, 20, 44, 53, 67, 94,
    95, 127; effectiveness of, 126, 136, 137;

against gas tax, 171; increase in use
of, 88, 126–30; against labor law reform, 170; liberal assault on, 45;
against Meese appointment, 196; in
1950s Senate, 19, 20; against 1986 drug
bill, 187; against open housing laws,
170; post-cloture, 128–29, 135 (see also
Allen, James); range of targets of,
94–95; reform of, 211; against school
prayer, 172; time limits on, 129 (see
also Cloture); Weicker's use of, 171–
72. See also Cloture; Helms, Jesse;
Metzenbaum, Howard; Weicker, Lowell
Finance Committee, Senate, 11; conservative character of, 27, 41, 110; floor
challenges to bills of, 87, 120, 122;
1958 freshman appointees to, 34; and
tax reform, 106, 157–58, 162, 198
Financial sector, 95, 142; interest groups
representing, 63
Financial Services Competitive Equity
Act, 95, 127
Fonda, Jane, 193
Ford, Wendell, 148, 156–57, 182
Foreign aid, 52; to repressive regimes,
57. See also Contras, aid to
Foreign policy, 52. See also International
involvement
Foreign Relations Committee, Senate,
11, 149; floor challenges to bills of,
120, 122; character of, 27, 28, 41,
109–10.. See also Lugar, Richard
Foreign trade, 149, 205
Formula, infant, federal standards for,
186

Game theory, 14–15
Gardner, John, 62, 68. See also Common
Cause
Garn, Jake, 137
Gas, nerve, 165. See also Natural gas
Gas tax, Senate fight over, 97, 129, 133,
171
General Dynamics, 198
General Motors, 61
Genocide treaty, Senate debate on, 94,
127
George, Walter, 12
Gephardt, Richard, 198

Glenn, John, 163, 182
Glickman, Dan, 93
Goldwater, Barry, 35, 99, 192
Gore, Albert, 164
Government Affairs Committee, Senate,
161. See also Bingaman, Jeff
Gramm, Phil, 129, 168–69, 182, 192; as
budget critic, 149, 150, 152 (see also
Gramm-Rudman legislation); as
freshman activist, 94
Gramm-Latta I (II), 168
Gramm-Rudman legislation, 94, 149, 150,
168–69, 192; Bradley against, 195
Grandfather clauses, 48
Grassley, Charles, 93, 165
Great Society, 44, 49, 50, 55, 118
Griffin, Robert, 85
Group Health Association, 196
Grove City decision, 135, 171
Gun control, 166, 171, 173

Handicapped, the: civil rights of, 54, 59;
federal aid to, 158, 161–62 (see also
Weicker, Lowell)
Handicapped, the, Subcommittee on,
161–62
Harkin, Tom, 85, 99, 142, 144, 152, 182;
and farm crisis of 1985, 196; as fresh-
man activist, 94; to Nicaragua, 149
Hart, Gary, 169, 182
Hart, Phillip, 31, 84
Hatch, Orrin, 135, 145, 151, 182; as Consti-
tution Subcommittee chairman, 161;
and Grove City decision, 171; and gun
control legislation, 166; as master ob-
structionist, 170–71; and Omnibus
Health Package, 196
Hatfield, Mark, 108, 158, 192
Hawkins, Paula, 160–61, 162, 184
Hayden, Carl, 26, 71
Health. See AIDS; Handicapped, the;
Hospitals; Illness; Medicaid; Medi-
care; Omnibus Health Package
Hecht, Chic, 182
Heinz, John, 99
Helms, Jesse, 81, 99, 140, 166, 182; and
drug bill of 1986, filibustering of, 95,
97, 170, 171, 186; and gas tax filibuster,

Helms, Jesse, *(cont'd)*
171; against labor law reform, 170;
against pornography, 186; and Senate
Agriculture Committee, 99
Heritage Foundation, 62
Higher Education Act, 156
Hildenbrand, William, 132
Hill, Lister, 26
Holds, 130–31, 137, 169, 170; Metzenbaum
use of, 172, 173
Hollings, Ernest, 85, 136, 148, 158; and
Gramm-Rudman, 169
Homeless: federal aid to, 186; mental
illness among, 195
Homosexuals: civil rights of, 55, 59; New
Right antipathy for, 61
Hospitals, Washington representation
of interests of, 60
House of Representatives, U.S., 214–15;
changes in, 208; Congress-bashing
by, 101; constrictedness of, 93; drug
legislation of, 185, 187; floor activity
of, 163
Housing, public, 53. *See also* Open
housing
Humanities, federal encouragement of,
55
Human rights, as item on Senate
agenda, 149
Humphrey, Hubert, 22

Illness: catastrophic, 160; mental, 195
Immigration, legislation affecting, 129,
148, 155, 164, 186
Imports, textile, 148
Indians. *See* Native Americans
Inflation, 56
Inouye, Daniel, 182
Institute for Policy Studies, 62
Interest, bank, withholding of income
from as agenda item, 167–68
Interest groups, 24, 57–64; citizens', 58,
66, 105–6 (*see also* Common Cause);
explosive growth of, 57–64;
individual, 62–63; intergovernmental,
58–59; and PACs, 62
Interior Committee, Senate, 17
International involvement, 52, 57, 117.
See also Arms control; Contras, aid
to; Foreign trade

International Telephone and Telegraph
(ITT), 60
"Iron triangle," 24

Javits, Jacob, 81
Johnson, Lyndon, 18; antipoverty
program of, 55; and cloture, 134; as
Senate Majority Leader, 34, 45. *See
also* Great Society
Johnson rule, 13, 34
Johnston, J. Bennett, 169, 182
Joint Committee on the Organization of
Congress, 46, 48. *See also* Legislative
Reorganization Act of 1970
Joint Economic Committee, and
unemployment, 52
Jordan, Barbara, 188
Judiciary Committee, Senate: and Civil
Rights Bill of 1964, 43, 82; extreme
conservatism of 1950s, 27; floor
challenges to bills of, 120; increased
activity of in 1980s, 103; under
Thurmond chairmanship, 161

Kansas City Board of Public Utilities, 59
Kassebaum, Nancy, 195
Kasten, Robert, 132, 158, 198; and
interest/dividend income with-
holding levy, 167–68; and product
liability legislation, 151, 162
Kefauver, Estes, 18
Kemp, Jack, 198
Kennedy, Edward, 32, 81, 182; against
apartheid, 192, 193; and gun control
legislation, 166; as Labor and Human
Resources Committee chairman, 160;
against 1985 Pentagon budget, 164; as
television regular, 189, 192
Kennedy, John, 18, 42; assassination of,
65; 1960 victory of, 43. *See also* Great
Society; New Frontier
Kennedy, Robert, 32; assassination of, 65
Kerry, John, 85, 182; committee
assignments of, 92; to Nicaragua, 149
Korean War, 52

Labor and Human Resources
Committee (formerly Labor
Committee; Labor and Public
Welfare Committee), Senate, 27, 40,
151, 160; Arts and Humanities,

Subcommittee of, 156; increased
activity of in 1980s, 103; character of,
28, 109
Labor, Health and Human Services, and
Education, Subcommittee on, 161–62
Labor unions: federal regulation/reform
of, 53, 56, 94–95, 127, 129, 135, 170;
Washington-based interest groups
representing, 58
Latinos, civil rights of, 54
Laxalt, Paul, 182
Leahy, Patrick, 165, 182
Legal Services Corporation, 54
Legislative Reorganization Act of 1946,
11, 211
Legislation Reorganization Act of 1970,
45–49, 211; and committee
assignments, 73
Lewis, John, 67
Liberals: attempt by, to change Senate
rules, 45–49; in 1950s Senate, 22; 1958
ascension of, 30–33, 35; 1960s growth
in power, 49–50
Lobbies. *See* Interest groups; PACs
Long, Russell, 125, 182
Lugar, Richard, 71, 134, 182; against labor
law reform, 170; as TV interviewee,
190, 192

McCarthy, Eugene, 31, 34, 84
McCarthy, Joseph, 53
McCarthyism, 53
McClure, James, 148, 160, 165; and gun
control legislation, 166, 173; as Soviet
critic, 149
McConnell, Mitch, 149, 150, 151, 182;
against apartheid, 192
McGee, Gale, 34
McGovern, George, 32, 84
"MacNeil/Lehrer Report," 66, 68, 69,
189, 190, 196
Mansfield, Mike, 45, 133
Marcos, Ferdinand, 196–97
Marijuana, legalization of, 54
Mark-ups, 24, 25, 104; floor, 122; open,
66, 105, 139, 208
Mass transit, federal aid to, 55
Mathias, Charles, 108, 161, 186;
opposition of, to death penalty for
drug traffickers, 187

Matsunaga, Spark, 99, 182
Mattingly, Mack, 132, 183; against drug
traffickers, 184, 186, 187
Mavericks, 16, 21–22, 81, 213. *See also*
Obstructionism
Media, 64–68; coverage of Congress by,
5, 6, 64–65, 66–67, 69–70; as
mobilizers of public sentiment, 63,
67; and open mark-ups, 105; and
product liability crisis, 151; Reagan
manipulation of, 190, 214; senators'
home state, 190; as senators' means
of reaching publics, 189–92, 194–95,
197. *See also* Newspapers; Television
Medicaid, 55, 60
Medicare, 55, 60
Meese, Edwin, 126n, 130, 196
"Meet the Press," 189
Melcher, John, 81
Mental illness, 195
Metropolitan Washington Airports
Transfer Act, 95, 127
Metzenbaum, Howard, 81, 128, 134, 140,
182, 186, 204; and aspartame, 160;
against Carter energy bill, 172; com-
mittee assignments of, 92, 157; as
filibusterer, 95, 97, 137; and gun
control legislation, 166; obstruction-
ism of, 172–73; against Rehnquist
confirmation, 192; as tax-equity
watchdog, 149
Military, the: budget of, 57; drug abuse
in, 160
Mines, safety in, 160
Minimum wage, 53, 56
Missiles, MX, 164. *See also* Anti-Ballistic
Missile (ABM) Treaty
Mitchell, George, 182
Moffett, Toby, 141
Mondale, Walter, 32, 197
Money, laundering of, 184
Monroney, A. S. Mike, 46–47
Moral Majority, 61
Morse, Wayne, 9, 22
Moynihan, Daniel Patrick, 81, 182
Murkowski, Frank, 195
Muskie, Edmund, 1, 30, 100
MX missiles, 164

Nader, Ralph, 68

Narcotics. *See* Drugs
National Alliance for the Mentally Ill, 196
National Association for the Advancement of Colored People (NAACP), 53
National Association of Manufacturers, 61
National Association of Student Financial Aid Administrators, 60
National Competitive Strategy of the Government Affairs Committee, 150
National Conservative Political Action Committee (NCPAC), 62, 166
National defense, 160, 161, 164, 165; on political agenda, 52; procurement for, 5; research into, 193–94; Senate debate on spending for, 130. *See also* Arms control; Bingaman, Jeff; Defense, Department of
National Football League, 173
National League of Cities, 59
National Medical Association, 196
National Public Radio, 190
Native Americans, civil rights of, 54
Natural gas, floor debate over price of, 127
Nelson, Gaylord, 32, 84
New Christian Right, 61
New Deal, 52, 53, 60
New Frontier, 118
New Hampshire, disputed Senate seat from, 95, 127, 129
New Right, 61; and use of roll call vote, 166; Weicker against, 150, 172. *See also* Hatch, Orrin; Helms, Jesse
Newspapers, as medium of reaching senators' publics, 189, 191, 192, 194–95, 196. *See also* Op-Ed essays; Press conferences
New York *Times*, 68, 189, 191, 194
Nicaragua, 131, 133, 195; drug trafficking in, 160; Harkin/Kerry trip to, 149. *See also* Contras, aid to
Norms, 14–22, 206. *See also* Senate, norms of
Northern Democrats, 10, 107
Nunn, Sam, 71, 156, 182–83, 202; against Ferdinand Marcos, 196–97; against MX missile, 164; national security

concerns of, 160; speechmaking of, 194; on television, 192

Obstructionism, on Senate floor, 125–40. *See also* Hatch, Orrin; Mavericks; Metzenbaum, Howard; Weicker, Lowell
Oil, 1973 Arab embargo on, 56
Oil shale lands, leasing of, 173
Older Americans Act, 60
Omnibus Health Package, 196
O'Neill, Thomas (Tip), 183
Op-Ed essays, 68, 70, 194, 195; Armstrong's use of, 199; Bradley's use of, 197, 198; Gramm's use of, 168
Open housing, 54; filibusters against, 135, 170
Oregon Hearing Institute, 158

Packwood, Robert, 81, 98, 108, 157, 198; against anti-abortion legislation, 172; and Grove City decision, 171; against school prayer, 172
Peak associations, 61
Pentagon. *See* Defense, Department of
Percy, Charles, 85, 108, 136
Pesticides, federal control of, 56
Policy, Washington as focus of national, 51–70
Political action committees (PACs), 62
Pollution, environmental, 56
Poor: civil rights of, 54; federal programs for, 55 (*see also* Medicaid); Washington-based interest groups representing, 58. *See also* Homeless
Pornography, 166, 186
Post Office and Civil Service Committee, Senate, 12, 28
Press conferences, 193, 196, 198
Press releases, 196
Prisoner's dilemma, 14–15, 21, 207
Privacy, federal laws protecting, 186
Product liability, 136, 150–51, 162. *See also* Kasten, Robert
Proxies, 153
Proxmire, William, 22, 182
Pryor, David, 165, 198
Public accommodations, racial discrimination in, 54
Public works, and priming the economic pump, 52–53

Quayle, Dan, 75, 103
Quorum calls, 103, 134

Race, as national issue. *See* Civil rights
Radio Marti, 136
Reagan, Nancy, 183, 185
Reagan, Ronald, 132, 133, 160; and ABM
   agreement, 165; and aid to handicapped, 162; and Bork nomination,
   188; and destruction of CETA, 55;
   against drugs, 183, 185; and education
   funding, 149; and farm crisis of 1985,
   196; and Gramm-Rudman, 169; and
   interest/dividend income withholding levy, 167; manipulation of media
   by, 190, 214; and MX missile, 164;
   and Omnibus Health Package, 196;
   and Philippine elections, 196–97;
   radio talks of, 149; and SALT II
   agreement, 165; and tax reform, 197,
   198, 199
Reciprocity, 19–20, 28, 90, 94, 96, 97–98.
   See also Senators, U.S., bargaining
   among
Rehnquist, William, 192
Religion, interest groups promoting, 61.
   See also School prayer
Republicans: and committee
   chairmanships, 107–8; and freshman
   senators, 77–78
Resolution 60, Senate, 78–79, 127
Retraining, job, 53, 55
Ribicoff, Abraham, 32, 84
Rice Production Act, 95, 127
Riders, to bills, 167
Riots, ghetto, 54, 55; TV coverage of, 65
Robert A. Taft Institute for
   Government, 158
Rockefeller, Jay, 182
Rogers, Don, 183
Roll call votes, 111–16, 119–20, 132–33, 163,
   165, 168, 174; in 1950s Senate, 23; 1960s
   increase in number of, 43; as ploy to
   create campaign issues, 166
Roth, William, 105, 149
Rudman, Warren, 169, 182, 195
Rules, 206–8
Rules and Administration Committee,
   Senate, 12, 28, 46, 132
Rule 22. *See* Cloture

Russell, Richard, 18, 46
Russia. *See* USSR

SALT II, 165
Sarbanes, Paul, 96, 127
Sasser, Jim, 150, 192
Savings and loan associations, 142
School prayer, 61, 127, 135, 172
Schools, desegregation of, 53, 54. *See also*
   Busing
Security. *See* National defense
Security and Terrorism, Subcommittee
   on, 161
Selma (Ala.), civil rights march on, 67
Senate, U.S.: activism in, 174–87, 190;
   bargaining in (*see* Reciprocity;
   Senators, U.S., bargaining among);
   Bork rejected by, 188; changes in,
   102–40, 205–16; committee system of
   (*see* Committees, Senate; Subcommittees, Senate); as conservative
   establishment, 41, 42–43; debate in,
   20, 88, 94–97, 125–40, 165–73, 214 (*see
   also* Cloture; Filibuster(s); Roll call
   votes); decision making in 1950s, 23;
   duties of, 3, 10; floor activity of, 79–
   89, 91, 94–97, 111–40, 163–73, 201 (*see
   also* Amendments, floor; Cloture;
   Filibuster(s); Roll call votes);
   functioning of, 102–40, 210–16; as
   gateway to presidency, 3–4, 6, 18, 70,
   89–90, 100; and impact of changes in
   Washington policy system, 51–70;
   and impact of television, 5, 18;
   influence within, 201–4; inherent
   resistance to change of, 4; and "iron
   triangle," 24; majority leader of, 11;
   newsworthiness of hearings, 193–94;
   in 1950s, 8–29; 1950s and 1980s memberships of compared, 2, 212–14; and
   1950s interest groups, 214; and 1960s
   shift from conservative domination,
   49–50; 1986 anti–drug abuse activity
   in, 183–87; norms of, 89–101, 207–9;
   and obstructionism, 19, 125–40 (*see
   also* Mavericks); reform within, 105,
   211–12; rules of, 11; and scheduling,
   131–32; self-criticism of, 101; style of,
   71–101, 141–216; today, 210, 213–16. *See
   also* Committees, Senate; Congress;

Senate, U.S.: *(cont'd)*
    Senators, U.S.; Subcommittees,
    Senate
Senators, U.S.: as activists, 174–87, 190;
    bargaining among, 97–98, 123, 124
    (*see also* Reciprocity); and centrality
    of reelection, 17, 144, 145, 146, 156, 196;
    choice of issues by, 143–87; and com-
    mittee assignments, 147–49, 155–63;
    contemporary, 141–54; courtesy
    among, 20–21, 98–100; freshman,
    13–14, 18–19, 77–78, 83, 88, 93–94;
    generalist, 87–88, 179–82, 187;
    heterogeneous publics of, 189; home-
    state pressures on, 142, 144–45, 146,
    148; "hyperactive," 81, 85; influence-
    oriented, 18; integrity of, 98; and
    issues, 143–87; and media, 5, 6, 64–70,
    100, 189–95; obstructionist, 125–40
    (*see also* Hatch, Orrin; Mavericks;
    Metzenbaum, Howard; Weicker,
    Lowell); outside pressures on, 142–
    43; policy-oriented, 18; power of, 6;
    and public arenas, 188–201; sanctions
    against nonconformists within, 22,
    89; as specialists, 179–82, 187; staffs
    of, 14, 78–79, 93, 94, 146–47, 153–54
    (*see also* Committees, Senate, and
    staff); time as enemy of, 202; variety
    of orientations among, 6
Seniority, 13, 14, 28, 36–37, 41, 42, 76–77,
    212–13
Service Committees, Senate, 103
Services, armed. *See* Military, the
Shipping industry, 173
Sierra Club, 63
Simpson, Alan, 97, 129, 164, 186
Sit-ins, 67
Small Business Committee, Senate, 74n,
    157, 162; perquisites of membership
    in, 159
Social Security, 168, 169
Social welfare, 117, 118; during
    Eisenhower administration, 53;
    legislation promoting, 49; and 1960s
    political agenda, 55; in 1970s, 55–56;
    during Truman administration, 53;
    Washington-based interest groups
    promoting, 58. *See also* Great Society;
    New Deal

Sodbuster bill, 145, 198–99
South, the: anti-black outbursts in, 54,
    67; defined, 10
South Africa, 193; sanctions against, 127,
    133, 135, 149, 192
Southern Democrats: against civil rights
    legislation, 20, 43–44, 94, 95, 127;
    representation of, on committee
    chairs, 107; power of, 10, 26, 32, 38–39
Soviet Union. *See* USSR
Speechmaking, 189, 193–95, 197
Stafford, Robert, 108, 156, 182
"Star Wars," 165–66, 194
States, interest groups representing
    individual, 59
Steering Committee, Democratic, 34, 42,
    45
Stennis, John, 73, 182
Stevens, Ted, 184
Strategic Defense Initiative (SDI),
    165–66, 194
Subcommittees, Senate: chairmanship
    of, 12–14, 23; increase in number of
    meetings of, 89; limits imposed on
    assignments to, 103; 1970s
    proliferation of, 74–75; as personal
    forums of chairmen, 104–5, 158–59,
    160–63, 173; power of, 104–5, 202–3;
    shifting regional/philosophical
    makeup of, 36–37, 39, 44–45; special,
    48n; usefulness of, 73–74
Subsidies, agricultural, 56–57
Subversion, as item on floor agenda, 117
Sugar, 1986 drug bill and, 186
Sunshine rules, 106, 139
Supreme Court: and aid to handicapped,
    161; Bork nomination to, 188, 192, 194;
    and Grove City decision, 135, 171;
    legalization of abortion by, 55, 61;
    proscription of school segregation
    by, 53
Surface Transportation and Uniform
    Relocation Assistance Act, 95, 127
Supersonic Transport, Senate debate on,
    94
Symms, Steven, 165

Taft, Robert, Jr., 85
Tariffs, Metzenbaum and bills affecting,
    173

Task forces, minority party, 163
Taxes: bills on, 116, 167; gas (see Gas
   tax); progressive, 52
Tax reform, 157–58; Bradley efforts for,
   197, 198; Reagan and, 197, 198, 199
Television: impact on politics of, 5, 18;
   Congress and, 64–66, 69, 189–90, 192,
   194, 196, 197, 200; and news, 64–66;
   rallying power of, 63
Temporary Select Committee to Study
   the Senate Committee System, 134
Terrorism, 161
Textiles, importation of, 148
Think tanks, 61–62
Third World, 57
"This Week with David Brinkley," 189
Thurmond, Strom, 134, 148; as Judiciary
   Committee chairman, 161
Timber industry, 173
Tobacco, legislation concerning, 148
Trade associations, 58
Traffic Safety Act of 1966, 56
Transportation. See Mass transit
Treaties, Senate and, 3
Trucking industry, legislation affecting,
   186
Truman, Harry S., 52
Tsongas, Paul, 131

Unemployment, 52–53, 56, 160; federal
   aid to, 55
Unions. See Labor unions
United States, role of in Third World, 57
Universities, as interest groups, 61
USSR: and arms control, 149, 165; U.S.
   containment policy toward, 52

Veterans Affairs Committee, Senate, 12,
   103, 157
Veto, line-item, 135
Vietnam: protests against U.S.
   involvement in, 54, 55, 57, 59; TV
   coverage of, 65
Violence, domestic, 160. See also Riots,
   ghetto
Voting rights, civil rights legislation
   concerning, 54

Wallop, Malcolm, 165
Wall Street Journal, 68, 194
Washington, D.C.: civil rights march on,
   67; farmers' march on, 196; 1960s
   changes in, 5; policy system of, 51–70
Washington Post, 68, 194
Watergate, TV coverage of, 65
Weicker, Lowell, 99, 136–37, 182, 205; and
   aid to handicapped, 158, 161–62;
   against anti-abortion legislation, 172;
   against apartheid, 193; arrest of, 193;
   Committee and Subcommittee
   assignments of, 92, 157; and Gramm-
   Rudman, 169; against New Right,
   150, 172; obstructionism of, 171–72
Welfare. See Social welfare
Weyrich, Paul, 166
Whitten, Jamie, 154
Wilderness, legislation designating,
   148–49
Wilson, Pete, 92, 148, 164
Women: civil rights of, 54, 59 (see also
   Equal Rights Amendment); research
   centers relative to, 62
Wright, Jim, 183

Lightning Source UK Ltd.
Milton Keynes UK
UKHW012015140222
398663UK00001B/24